LIVING JUSTICE and PEACE

saint mary's press

Nihil Obstat: Rev. Krzysztof K. Maslowski, STD
Censor Librorum
August 19, 2022

Imprimatur: Cardinal Joseph W. Tobin, CSsR
Archbishop of Newark
August 24, 2022

The nihil obstat and imprimatur are official declarations that a book or pamphlet is free of doctrinal or moral error. No implication is contained therein that those who have granted the nihil obstat or imprimatur agree with the contents, opinions, or statements expressed, nor do they assume any legal responsibility associated with publication.

Contributing Authors:
Steven Ellair
Kathleen Crawford Hodapp
Lorraine Kilmartin
Christine Schmertz Navarro
Ivy Wick
Michael Wilt
Jerry Windley-Daoust

This course was developed and designed by the expert teams at Saint Mary's Press.
Cover image: © KateChe / Shutterstock.com

Copyright © 2023 by Saint Mary's Press, Christian Brothers Publications, 702 Terrace Heights, Winona, MN 55987-1320, www.smp.org. All rights reserved. No part of this book may be reproduced by any means without the written permission of the publisher.

Printed in the United States of America

1172 (PO7107)

ISBN 978-1-64121-181-9

CONTENTS

**1 The Call to Justice:
Learning to Act with Compassion** 5
Responding to Suffering 6
The Way God Created the World to Be 13
Justice: The Reign of God's Goodness 19
The Compassionate Way of Jesus 25

**2 Catholic Social Teaching:
Envisioning a World of Justice and Peace** 35
The Development of Catholic Social Teaching 36
Catholic Social Teaching Documents 41
Themes of Catholic Social Teaching, 1–3 48
Themes of Catholic Social Teaching, 4–7 60

**3 Living Justice:
Faith in Action** 70
A Call to Action 71
Awareness: Friendship with the World 75
Analysis: Asking Why 88
Action: Bringing Life to the World 99

**4 Choosing Life:
Compassion for All** 107
All Human Life Is Sacred 108
A Culture of Life versus a Culture of Death 114
Standing for Life 119

**5 Building Community:
Celebrating Unity and Diversity** 133
Mixing It Up 134
What Makes a Community? 137
The Anatomy of Exclusion 142
Building Inclusive Communities 151

6 Working with Dignity:
Our Effort toward Positive Change 163
Inspired to Make a Difference 164
Two Views of Work 169
Creating Human-Centered Work 178
Restoring Work's Promise 186

7 Choosing the Option for the Poor and Vulnerable:
Breaking the Cycle of Poverty 197
Seeing the Face of Christ in Others 198
Poverty in One of the World's Wealthiest Nations 205
Poverty in the World's Poorest Nations 218

8 The Gift of Simple Living:
Focusing on the Essentials 232
The Wealth of Joy 233
A Poverty of Riches 237
A Eucharistic Response to Poverty 245
Living Simply So Others Can Simply Live 254

9 Respect for the Earth:
Caring for God's Creation 261
Our Common Home 262
Creation as Gift 270
Our Environmental Responsibility 275
Make a Difference 282

10 Working toward Peace:
The Christian Path of Peacemaking 288
Solidarity in the Face of Violence 289
Violence, Nonviolence, and Peace 292
Following Jesus to Peace 298
The Christian Response to War 305
Peace through Love 312

Glossary of Key Words 318
Index 327
Acknowledgements 344

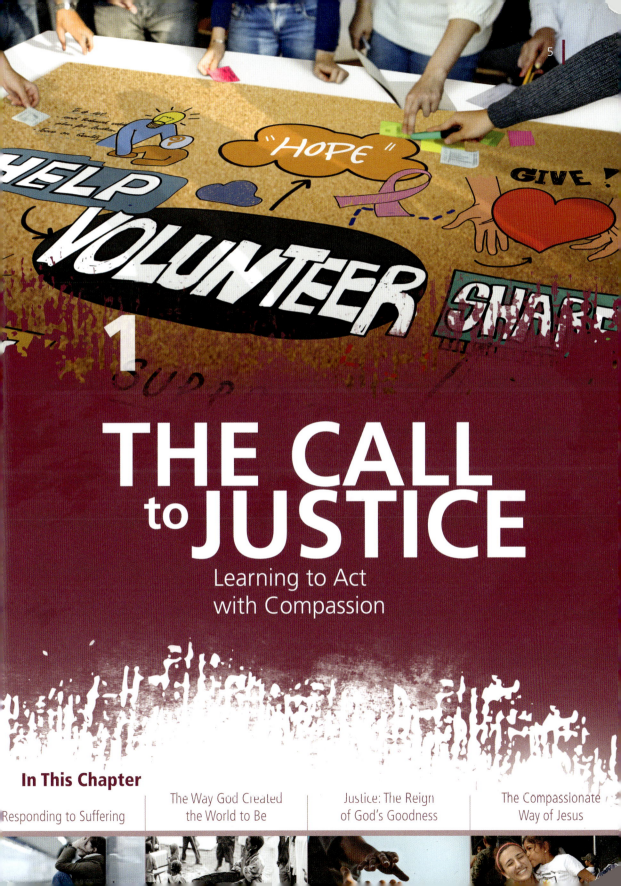

THE CALL to JUSTICE

Learning to Act with Compassion

In This Chapter

Responding to Suffering | The Way God Created the World to Be | Justice: The Reign of God's Goodness | The Compassionate Way of Jesus

Responding to Suffering

What is the world as you know it like? What do you feel is good about it? What do you feel is bad about it? Imagine you have the power to change the world. What would this new world look like?

Many people find the world to be full of goodness and joy: a first kiss, music and lyrics that speak to you, the jeweled beauty of new snow, the vastness of the ocean, basketball played so hard your body aches, friends who make you laugh, extra-cheese pizza, a loving family . . . the list could go on and on.

But, for many people, this world is not only one of goodness and light but also one of shadows and suffering. Perhaps you have already encountered the shadow side of the world, as the following young people have.

Twelve-year-old Craig Kielburger was looking for the comics in the *Toronto Star* one morning when he saw this front-page headline: "Battled Child Labour, Boy, 12, Murdered." The story told of Iqbal Masih, a twelve-year-old Pakistani boy who had been sold to a carpet factory owner when he was four, and forced to weave carpets, chained to a loom, along with other boys. When human rights activists bought his freedom, he traveled the world, speaking out against the widespread practice of child labor—until he was shot dead, presumably by the carpet manufacturers.

The story deeply troubled Craig. But what could he do for kids halfway around the world?

The world is a place of beauty, wonder, and joy. But for many, there is also pain and suffering.

© Patryk Kosmider / Shutterstock.com

"You aren't sick; you're pregnant," the nurse said. "You can have an abortion, but if you do, it will need to be soon."

Abortion? Mary was still trying to wrap her mind around the word *pregnant!* She opposed all forms of killing, including abortion, but she was scared.

Mary knew that the school didn't really offer any assistance for pregnant students or single moms. She wasn't sure how to tell her parents, and she knew they would be disappointed. Would she have to sacrifice a decent education to choose life for her child?

When Elliot started high school, it wasn't the fun, social, engaging environment he had been hoping for. As a gay student, he often found himself the target of bullying. It was exhausting trying to plan where to sit, who to have lunch with, and which people to avoid in the hallways. He tried to stick with his small group of friends who accepted him for who he was, but that wasn't always possible. And the people who bullied him were bold and aggressive. Walking into the cafeteria was open season for mockery.

Over the course of the year, he had been pushed and shoved in the hallways, openly made fun of in the cafeteria and commons, had his gym clothes stolen twice, and had his books knocked out of his arms. Elliot felt he would make the situation worse if he went to his parents or administrators. He often wondered, Why am I trying so hard to stay where people hate me?

Exploitation of children, desperation, discrimination, and violence—the world is far from perfect, as the young people in these scenarios discovered. Confronted with the harsh reality of such suffering and darkness, each of them had to decide how to respond.

In different ways, we each face the same decision. We will return to the true stories of these people later in the course. First, let's look at some possible responses to the suffering we encounter in the world.

How Do We Respond to Suffering?

When we confront suffering in the world around us, we have two choices: we can do something about the situation, or we can do nothing. People choose one option or the other for many different reasons. For the sake of simplicity, however, we will consider only four reasons: hopelessness, individualism, enlightened self-interest, and compassion.

Hopelessness

Sometimes it feels as if we hear too much about suffering in the world. Many people deal with the overwhelming nature of all the suffering in the world by choosing to ignore it. Others see or hear news of people suffering but choose not to act. They might offer several reasons for not responding, such as the following:

- "There are so many problems, and I'm just one person. Even if I make a small contribution, *what difference will it make* in the big picture?"

More than half of young people in the US experience feeling down, depressed, or hopeless. When you feel that you cannot change your situation or alleviate the suffering in the world today, those feelings are magnified.

- "The problems in our community are beyond my control. . . . *I have no power* to change the situation."

- "I'm *afraid* that if I speak up, people might get mad at me. My personal safety might even be at risk. I'd rather stay silent than rock the boat."

These responses to the world's suffering, though understandable, reflect a lack of hope on the part of the people who offer them. To hope is to believe in the possibility that what one wants can actually happen. If people do not believe they can make a difference—if they have no hope—they are not likely to act to change things.

Individualism

The independence of individuals to pursue their own destiny is an important value that has led to such good things as democracy, the promotion of equal opportunities for all people, and the notion that people can achieve anything if they try hard enough.

Too much emphasis on individual independence, however, can break the ties that connect people with God and one another as a community. Have you ever heard comments similar to the following?

- *"That problem doesn't affect me personally,* so why should I care?"
- "If homeless people want shelter, they should get a job and work for it like everyone else. *They should help themselves* instead of expecting everyone else to help them."
- "The trouble she has now is the result of her own decisions—*she's just getting what she deserves.*"
- "The pollution our paper mill puts into the water is a necessary *trade-off.* Cleaning it up would cost so much that we would probably lose our jobs."

Such responses to suffering might be called individualistic. Someone who is motivated by **individualism** believes that each person should take responsibility for their own life, and that when people fail to take responsibility for themselves, others should not be expected to help them. An overemphasis on individualism can lead to a me-first attitude in which individuals seek good things only for themselves—even if others must suffer as a result.

Enlightened Self-Interest

Hopelessness and individualism lead many people to respond to suffering by doing nothing. However, many other people respond to suffering in the world by attempting to relieve it.

> **Many people respond to suffering in the world by attempting to relieve it.**

---

individualism A belief that each person should take responsibility for their own life, and that others should not be expected to help them if they fail to take responsibility for themselves.

In some cases, such responses are primarily motivated by **enlightened self-interest**—the realization that by helping others we are really helping ourselves in the end. People who act out of enlightened self-interest understand that every person needs other people to live a satisfying life. People acting out of enlightened self-interest might make the following comments:

- "The government should spend more money educating people about how to avoid health problems because it costs less to prevent health problems than to treat them later. *It may take more resources now, but the benefits will be greater in the long run.*"

- "If we continue to allow toxins to pollute our drinking water, people in our community will face an increased risk of cancer. *We must act now, or we'll face the consequences later.*"

- "I help my elderly neighbor keep his yard and sidewalk neat because someday I may be in his shoes, unable to do yard work. *If I don't help others, I can't expect them to help me.*"

As these examples illustrate, one reason people choose to help others is that they might receive benefits in return. Sometimes, helping others does not result in direct benefits though. The person in the third example might never receive help in return from their neighbor. But they know that in a society in which people value helping one another, they are more likely to get help for themselves if they need it someday. By helping their neighbor, they are contributing to the importance their community places on that value.

Compassion

The realization that everyone in a society benefits when people help one another is one reason people respond to suffering with action. But what about people who help others well beyond any benefit they might receive in return?

Consider the young men in the Notre Dame chapter of the Knights of Columbus who support the Women's Care Center in South Bend, Indiana. Pregnant teens and young adult college students come to the Women's Care Center desperate for the services provided. Many of these women do not have health insurance, and even if they do, they still can't afford the high costs of prenatal care and childbirth. Finding solutions for health care, baby items, and childcare while trying to finish school or find a livable-wage job are just some of the issues that can lead to more than just monetary problems. These young mothers face high levels of stress that can lead to mental-health concerns including depression, suicidal ideation, and posttraumatic stress disorder (PTSD). Scared, often alone, and in high-risk situations, women who seek help at the Women's Care Center don't have anywhere else to turn.

enlightened self-interest The realization that by helping others we are, in the end, really helping ourselves.

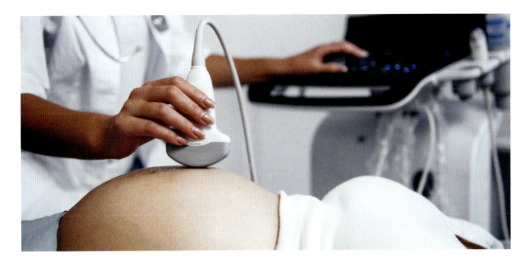

The young men of the Notre Dame chapter of the Knights of Columbus raise money for local charities by grilling and selling steak sandwiches at the home football games. Their concerted effort to alleviate the suffering of the clients of the Women's Care Center has allowed them to purchase an ultrasound machine every year since 2011.

A more precious gift than money is that of time. Meeting the clients of the care center and spending time with them helps the young men understand what these women are experiencing. Twice a week, a group from this chapter heads over to the Women's Care Center to help with childcare and packaging diapers. They experience how satisfying it is to see the fruits of their labor in the grateful faces of the mothers and babies they are serving. Clients at the center are treated with compassion and dignity by these young men, who are eager to rock and feed babies, and package diapers and clothes. There is no substitute for understanding the struggle and suffering these women experience than by serving them in person.

Pope
Francis
on Charity

Charity is born of the call of a God who continues to knock on our door, the door of all people, to invite us to love, to compassion, to service of one another. Jesus keeps knocking on our doors, the doors of our lives. He doesn't do this by magic, with special effects, with flashing lights and fireworks. Jesus keeps knocking on our door in the faces of our brothers and sisters, in the faces of our neighbors, in the faces of those at our side. (Pope Francis, "Greeting of the Holy Father," September 24, 2015)

> Which of the four responses to encounters with suffering in the world most closely matches your own? Why?

These young men are motivated by **compassion**, a word from the Hebrew plural of the word *womb*. The biblical sense of compassion is similar to the feeling a mother has for the child in her womb—a feeling of life-giving closeness and protective care. People who have compassion understand, both in their mind and heart, others' experiences of struggle or suffering. When compassion is accompanied by hope, it moves people to commit themselves to easing suffering. In other words, it moves them to love.

Called to Respond with Compassion

Although we cannot avoid the shadows of suffering in this world, we can choose how we respond to that suffering. Fortunately, we have many models who have demonstrated in words and actions how we might respond. For Christians, and for many non-Christians as well, Jesus is such a model. Jesus shows us that we can respond to the world's suffering as he did, with compassion—even to the point of giving oneself for the good of the world.

> Read your local newspaper or watch a local TV news program. Clip, copy, or write down examples you find that illustrate hopelessness, individualism, enlightened self-interest, and compassion.

Such a response might seem unreasonable and even extreme to some. Are people who are willing to give of themselves in service to others naive fools? If not, what would bring them to sacrifice themselves to help alleviate the suffering of others? How can we find hope amid ongoing suffering in the world? Understanding something about how God created the world to be will help clarify the Christian response to these questions.

compassion Concern for the suffering of others and the desire to relieve it.

For Review

1. When confronted with suffering in the world, what are two basic ways we can choose to respond?
2. Name four reasons for our responses to suffering, and provide a definition for each.
3. When accompanied by hope, what does compassion lead to?
4. Provide your own example of each of the four types of responses to suffering.

The Way God Created the World to Be

Why is there suffering? It is an important and challenging question, especially for anyone who believes in a good and all-powerful God. Why doesn't God just stop the suffering of the world with the snap of a finger? To answer that question, Catholics turn to the Tradition of the Church and to Scripture, which they believe contain the truth God has revealed to humanity. Two main themes found in this revelation provide some insight into the question of suffering:

- **God is love.** Love has many meanings in our culture, but in the way Christian faith means it, to love is to will the good for another. God is love because he is the source of all goodness, bringing everything into being and bringing everything into harmony with itself and the rest of creation.

> God is love because he is the source of all goodness, bringing everything into being and bringing everything into harmony with itself and the rest of creation.

Selfishness on an individual or governmental level can cause the suffering of others.

- **When humans fail to love as God does, the result is disorder, destruction, and suffering.** The opposite of love is selfishness—seeking things for oneself in a way that ignores the good of others and causes suffering. According to Scripture, God did not create a world of suffering. The original state of the world was one of harmony and abundant goodness. You have heard the Creation story many times by now. Still, it contains religious truths that so significantly influence the Christian response to suffering that it is worth examining the story again on a deeper level.

As we revisit the Creation story (you can begin by reading Genesis, chapters 1 to 3), it is important to know that Catholics focus on the religious, rather than the scientific, truth of the story. After all, Genesis was not written for the purpose of recording a scientifically accurate account of Creation; rather, the purpose of the Genesis Creation story is to reveal the more important truths about the nature of God, humanity, and creation (see *Catechism of the Catholic Church,* 282–289).

[Handwritten notes: "If God did not create a world of suffering how did the devil get on earth" and "I wonder how God thought how to create earth so beautiful"]

Creation: God Saw It Was Good

The Genesis Creation story begins by describing the universe as a deep darkness that would be completely empty except for the Spirit of God, which moves through it like a wind (see 1:1–2). God could let the universe remain that way, full of nothing but God. Instead, out of love, God creates something else. And so the darkness is dispelled with the words, "Let there be light" (1:3).

God continues to speak new things into being: water, land, plants, stars, animals, and so on. He is depicted working much like an artist does, stepping back occasionally to judge what is being made. God judges it to be *good*. As if to emphasize the point, the phrase "And God saw it was good" is repeated five times in the Creation account. Creation is good because it unfolds from God's own goodness.

Humans are capable of imitating God's creative giving. Childbirth is the most obvious example: a pregnant woman gives up part of her physical self for the sake of bringing a new person into being. And both parents inevitably give up part of their lives to help their child grow into the best person they can be.

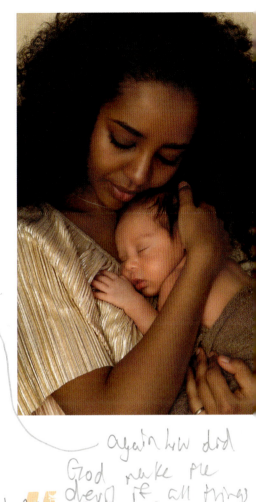

Humans: Made in the Image of God

Genesis tells us that the similarity of human love to God's love is no accident. In fact, God intentionally made humans in the image of God:

> God created humankind in his image,
> in the image of God he created them;
> male and female he created them.
> (1:27)

What does it mean to be made "in the image of God"? Think of your reflection in a pool of still water: your reflection, or image, is not you, but it resembles you. Similarly, as images of God, humans are reflections of God. Because God is a mystery, what it means to be an image of God is also something of a mystery. But we can be certain of at least three truths: we were made good, we were made to be in relationship with God and others, and we were made free.

> **Creation is good because it unfolds from God's own goodness.**

Can you think of three other examples in which people sacrifice something for a good cause?

Human Dignity

The first attribute of human beings is that they are made good. God says "very good," in fact (Genesis 1:31). The only reason anything or anyone in creation exists is because God wills it to exist because he loves it.

The basic goodness of human beings that comes from always being loved by God is called **human dignity**. Only humans were created to share in God's own life by knowledge and love; this special destiny is the reason for their dignity. Nothing can take away the love of God, so nothing a person does can take away their inherent dignity.

Made to Love and Be Loved

God made creation in order to love it by sharing his goodness with it. God desires to be loved in return. Because we are made in God's image, people also desire to love and be loved. In other words, human beings are made not to be alone but to be in relationship.

With other people. In the Genesis story, God makes humans to be "partners" or "helpers" to one another because "it is not good for the man to be alone" (2:18). God brought Adam and Eve together to form a family—the most basic unit of society.

The very nature of God is three persons (Father, Son, and Holy Spirit) united as one through their shared love. As images of God, each of us is also made to be united with all other people through love.

With creation. Human beings are meant to have a loving relationship with creation too. Genesis depicts God giving humans "dominion" over everything on the earth (1:28). Some people have interpreted this to mean that humans "own" creation and can do whatever they want to with it, but Genesis makes it clear that creation is a gift from God.

Humans are placed in the Garden of Eden, which represents all creation, "to cultivate and care for it" (2:15). Like God, then, humans are creative. God calls

> Draw a portrait of someone you know, or use a mirror to draw a portrait of yourself. The quality of your drawing is unimportant for this activity. Instead, as you form an image of your subject on the paper, reflect on Genesis 2:7, "Then the LORD God formed the man out of the dust of the ground and blew into his nostrils the breath of life, and the man became a living being." When you are finished, record at the bottom of the portrait a few words from your reflections.

human dignity The basic goodness and equal worth of human beings that comes from being created in God's image and being loved by God.

them to share in his work of creation—work that is carried on today whenever people help make the world the good place God intended it to be.

With God. Finally, humans are made to have an intimate friendship with God. That is the very reason God made us. Humans have a deep longing to complete themselves by connecting with the loving power of God. It has been said that all people have a "God-shaped hole" inside themselves. We may try to fill that inner sense of emptiness with many things, but nothing really makes us feel complete until we enter an intimate friendship with God that begins in this life and reaches its fulfillment when we are united with God. The state of perfect communion with the Holy Trinity is called heaven. Although heaven is something we hope to experience after we die, the *Catechism of the Catholic Church (CCC)* tells us that heaven is not so much a place as it is a way of being (2794). As such, we get a little taste of heaven whenever God lives in us.

> **As images of God, each of us is also made to be united with all other people through love.**

[handwritten note: I can say life is better with God when you have nothing]

[handwritten note: I'm lost on this, so we are still dead in the coffins but also in heaven]

God's love is present in all creation.

The Call to Justice

Respond to each of the following reflection questions in a few sentences:
- In what ways do others see your human dignity?
- What kind of relationship do you have with other people, with creation, and with God?
- What is the most important way you have used free will, and why is it important?

Free Will

Another attribute humans have because they are created in God's image is **free will**, the ability to choose what to do. Without free will, people would not be able to love, because love is always a freely given gift—it cannot be forced or taken, bought or sold.

That is why God does not stop people from doing things that cause suffering for themselves or others. If, for instance, you could be forced by God to be nice to others, you would not have free will, and so you would not truly love others. You would be just a puppet in God's hand, not the reflection of his goodness that you were made to be.

Of course, if humans are free to choose love, it also means they are free not to love. The first humans (represented in Genesis by Adam and Eve) chose to turn away from God's goodness, a choice that disrupted the harmony that existed at the beginning of creation.

free will The ability of a person to choose among options and to make decisions with freedom. Free will or self-determination is the grounds for an authentic relationship with God.

We are all created with free will—the ability to choose what to do for ourselves.

For Review

1. What are three truths about human beings that result from their being made in the image of God?
2. What is human dignity? Can anyone lose their human dignity? Why or why not?
3. What is the difference between wanting what is good for oneself and being selfish?

Justice: The Reign of God's Goodness

How did the devil play a role in this?

God did not bring suffering into the world. People did. The Original Sin of Adam and Eve disrupted the order of creation. God does not take away the freedom that allows people to bring suffering into the world, because that same freedom is what enables us to love. Although God allows people to bring suffering into the world, he does not want people to suffer. In fact, the whole history of God's relationship with humanity is the story of how he has acted to lead us out of a world of suffering into a world of goodness.

I don't think earth is suffering but heaven is def better

God does not want us to suffer. Throughout human history, God has acted to lead us out of a world of suffering and into a world of goodness. We need only to reach out.

> **God shows compassion for the poor, the oppressed, the weak, and the outcasts from society . . . because they are more in need of his attention by virtue of their suffering.**

I Have Heard My People's Cry

Throughout the Scriptures, God shows compassion for the poor, the **oppressed**, the weak, and the outcasts from society—not because God loves them more than others, but because they are more in need of his attention by virtue of their suffering.

In the Old Testament, the best-known story of God's concern for oppressed people is in the Book of Exodus, about how God frees the Israelites from slavery in Egypt. As slaves, the Israelites work hard building cities and farming the land—yet all the benefit of their work goes to the Egyptians. To ensure that the Israelites do not become powerful enough to revolt against their oppressors, Pharaoh decrees that all newborn Israelite boys be drowned in the Nile River, which the Egyptians regard as a god.

When the people of Israel cry out to God for help, he responds through a revelation to Moses. The words of God that follow are directed to the Israelites specifically, but they are also an expression of compassion for suffering people everywhere:

> But the LORD said: I have witnessed the afflictions of my people in Egypt and have heard their cry against their taskmasters, so I know well what they are suffering. Therefore I have come down to rescue them from the power of the Egyptians and lead them up from that land into a good and spacious land, flowing with milk and honey. . . . Now, go! I am sending you to Pharaoh to bring my people, the Israelites, out of Egypt." (Exodus 3:7–10)

Note that although God promises to take the people from a place of suffering (Egypt) to a place of goodness (the Promised Land), he will not accomplish that transition with a snap of a finger; rather, God recruits Moses, who at the time is a shepherd and a fugitive from the Egyptians, to help win freedom for the Israelites.

God sent Moses to free the Israelites from suffering and oppression in Egypt and lead them to freedom in the Promised Land.

[handwritten: I wish God still did this to save ppl]

[handwritten: Why did God choose Moses]

---

oppressed Those who are subjected to another's abuse of power or authority.

Justice: The Reign of God's Goodness

Moses balks at God's invitation to leadership. As it turns out, he has good reason to be hesitant. The road to freedom is not quick and easy, but takes years of struggle and hardship. Moses himself never lives to enter the Promised Land. Yet, in the end, the Lord and his people are victorious.

A Source of Hope for People Everywhere

The Exodus story is the central story of the Jewish people. But it also has long been a source of hope for oppressed peoples everywhere, one that has motivated them to take courageous action for the sake of goodness. Slaves in the United States often referred to the Exodus story in their songs, and it inspired the leaders of the twentieth-century civil rights movement as well. The Exodus story has also influenced movements in support of the poor and oppressed in South America and around the globe.

Life in the Promised Land

Before the people enter the Promised Land, Moses gives them a law to live by. The requirements of the Law seek to promote goodness and harmony among the people. Moses tells the people they must live in a way that promotes goodness and peace among them "so that you may live and possess the land the Lord, your God, is giving you" (Deuteronomy 16:20).

Moses was referring to the land of Israel, but anyplace where people live in God's goodness is the Promised Land. Like the Garden of Eden, the harmony and abundant goodness of the Promised Land is a rich symbol of God's life-giving love.

The Law Moses gave the people included not only the Ten Commandments but also hundreds of specific rules about the way people were to live. At the heart of all these laws was the **Shema**, which Jews still recite daily. Here is the beginning of that prayer:

> Recall a time when you were called on to take leadership or responsibility—in a job, on a sports team, or in a social situation. Describe your experience: Were you hesitant? How did it turn out? How did it affect your willingness to take on leadership roles in the future?

> Make a collage depicting a modern Exodus by pasting or taping pictures from old magazines and newspapers onto poster board. Here are some images you might include in the collage: people who are oppressed or suffering, landscapes symbolizing Egypt or the Promised Land, leaders working for change ("Moses"), barriers to freedom, people living in goodness. Use newspaper headlines to serve as captions.

[Handwritten notes: "Why didn't God do the same with African Americas with the Israelites" and "Is heaven different for everyone?"]

Shema A Jewish confession of faith, which Jews recite daily.

> **The Law also emphasized that true worship is expressed in the way people live with one another.**

Hear, O Israel! The Lord is our God, the Lord alone! Therefore you shall love the Lord, your God, with your whole heart, and with your whole being, and with your whole strength. (Deuteronomy 6:4–5)

The Israelites lived out the Shema in part by following the many rules about worship and holiness. They saw keeping their worship pure and perfect as a way of loving God with everything they had.

Love Your Neighbor as Yourself

The Law also emphasized that true worship is expressed in the way people live with one another. The Law commanding the Israelites to "love your neighbor as yourself" (Matthew 19:19) was expressed in many specific regulations that reflected God's compassion for poor and oppressed people. For example, Israel was given the following regulations:

- Leave some of the harvest for gleaning by those who are poor.
- Do not set dishonest prices.
- Welcome the stranger; treat foreigners as you would your own people.
- Every seven years, cancel all debts.
- Give God thanks for your harvest by giving the first part of it to foreigners, orphans, and widows, "that they may eat and be satisfied" (Deuteronomy 26:12).

Sprinkled in among these laws are constant reminders of how much God has given the people by bringing them from slavery into the Promised Land. The implication is that these are not just rules the people are to follow but a way to give thanks to God by sharing what they have been given.

The Prophets: Voicing God's Call

Despite the Law, the people of Israel were often unfaithful in their relationship with God. Fortunately for the Israelites, God did not turn away from them but instead chose prophets to call the people back to

---

Sidebar: Make an inventory, or detailed list, of all the things you own, listing how many types of clothes, sports equipment, games, electronic devices, or cars you have, and how many movies, video games, shoes, shampoos, jewelry, money, and so on, that you have. Now imagine that you live in ancient Israel. The Law asks you to give part of your "harvest" away for the benefit of others. Would you do it? If so, why? What would you give? If not, why not?

Justice: The Reign of God's Goodness

divine friendship. But often the prophets had as little self-confidence about their mission as Moses did; it is a habit of God to choose the lowly or the most unlikely people for the most important roles.

A common theme of the prophets' call was the important connection between love of God and love of neighbor. Often, the people would focus on the laws pertaining to proper worship and sacrifice but would neglect the laws about loving their neighbors. The prophets made it clear that following all the rules about worship was pointless—even offensive to God— if that worship was not accompanied by compassion for others.

> **A common theme of the prophets' call was the important connection between love of God and love of neighbor.**

This is why we need God

Key Passages Highlighting the Social Justice Messages of the Prophets

Passage	Summary of Prophet's Message
Isaiah 1:11–16, 21–23; 2:13–15	God condemns the kingdoms of Israel and Judah. Their religious observances are empty of meaning because they have failed to act justly, and they mistreat people who are poor and vulnerable.
Isaiah 58:5–11	God declares that the fasting he desires is the freedom of oppressed people and the care of those in need.
Jeremiah 22:1–17	God warns the kings of Judah that he will bring their kingdoms to ruin if they do not act justly, care for the vulnerable, respect human life, and give workers fair wages.
Amos 2:6–8, 3:9–10, 4:1–3, 5:7–15, 6:4–7, 8:4–7	In a series of prophecies spoken by Amos, God condemns the mistreatment of people who are poor and vulnerable, material greed, bribery, corruption, and the arrogance of wealthy people who ignore human needs around them.
Micah 2:1–3, 3:1–4	God condemns those who develop schemes to take other people's lands, and leaders who do evil to their people.
Micah 4:1–7	In this optimistic prophecy from Micah, God promises a future in which he will bring justice and peace to the world's people.
Micah 6:8	In this inspirational quotation, Micah proclaims: "You have been told, O mortal, what is good, / and what the Lord requires of you: / Only to do justice and to love goodness, / and to walk humbly with your God."

There is a lot of evil leaders right now

Do you find echoes of the prophets in the music you listen to? Write down the lyrics of songs you think might be prophetic for people today, and explain why you think so.

Why did an apple lead us down this path, one mistake shouldn't do this from the rest

The Call to Justice

In both Isaiah and Micah, **justice** is the first thing God names when the people ask what he wants of them. And what happens when justice rules the land? Isaiah says that "your light shall rise in the darkness" (58:10)—the shadows of suffering are dispelled.

God created the world good, but the Fall of our "first parents" disrupts the harmony and goodness of relationships in creation. Justice actively seeks to reestablish the original goodness and order. We might say justice is the establishment of loving relationships among human beings, God, and creation so life can flourish in the way God intends. **Injustice**, on the other hand, is a condition in which people have put obstacles in the way of loving relationships, thus preventing life from flourishing as God intends.

An Impossible Dream?

People are called by God to respond compassionately to suffering with justice so that the world becomes the good place it was always meant to be. That call might seem unrealistic, even impossible, and it would be if people were expected to change the world by themselves. But believers hear the voice of God reply: "Don't be afraid! I am with you."

Christians believe that God's compassion for humanity is so great that the Son of God became human in the person of Jesus Christ. Through Jesus, God dives deep into human suffering and uses that suffering to break open a way through death into goodness and eternal life. When we follow the way opened by Jesus, we too can pass through a world of suffering to a world of hope.

life is just a way to see if we are worthy of God?

---

justice The establishment of loving relationships among human beings, God, and creation so life can flourish in the way God intends.

injustice A condition in which people have put obstacles in the way of loving relationships, thus preventing life from flourishing as God intends.

For Review

1. Name at least three ways God asked the Israelites to live out the Law "Love your neighbor as yourself" (Matthew 19:19).
2. According to the prophets, what kind of worship does God want from humans?
3. Define *justice* and *injustice*.
4. Why is worship of God pointless if people do not love one another?

The Compassionate Way of Jesus

Who is Jesus? Christians believe Jesus is the second person of the Holy Trinity, Son of the Father, and the one God sent to save the world from sin and death. They believe that those who follow Jesus will live a new life, both on earth and in heaven.

But what does justice have to do with following Jesus? Justice is a central part of the Christian faith. In other words, a full response to Jesus involves more than just believing in him, praying to him, and going to church—although those are essential parts of the Christian faith. Truly following Jesus means more than just saying yes to God with our lips; it means actually *living* that yes as Jesus did. A closer look at the life and teaching of Jesus reveals the meaning of justice.

Living a life of justice means more than believing in Jesus. We must put our intentions into action by finding ways to ease the suffering of others.

> **The compassion that moved God to enter humanity is imitated whenever Christians have compassion for those who suffer, by being with them.**

God Is with Us

The Gospel of Matthew calls Jesus Emmanuel, a name that means "God is with us." Jesus' followers eventually came to recognize that in him, God was quite literally with them, for Jesus Christ is "true God and true man," to use the language of the Church—that is, fully the divine Son of God and fully a human being at the same time.

That must have been a stunning realization: God the Father loved humankind so much and thought humankind was so good that he sent his Son to be "coming in human likeness; and found human in appearance" (Philippians 2:7) in the person of Christ. The **Incarnation**—the Son of God becoming human in the person of Jesus Christ—was the result of God's choice to be with humanity to lead us out of suffering and death, just as Moses led the Israelites from Egypt to the Promised Land. The compassion that moved God to enter humanity is imitated whenever Christians have compassion for those who suffer, by being with them.

Jesus' Mission of Justice

In the Gospel of Luke, Jesus begins his public ministry by going to the synagogue in his hometown and reading from the scroll of the prophet Isaiah, whose vision of a just and peaceful world was described earlier. The passage Jesus reads is about one who was sent by God

> to bring glad tidings to the poor, . . .
> to proclaim liberty to captives
> and recovery of sight to the blind,
> to let the oppressed go free,
> and to proclaim a year acceptable to the Lord.
>
> (Luke 4:18–21)

> Scripture tells us that God is like a mother comforting her child (see Isaiah 66:13). Think of a time you were suffering from sickness, disappointment, or rejection. How did the presence of a friend or parent make you feel better? Are there times when you would rather be alone when you suffer? Why or why not?

Incarnation The central Christian belief that the Son of God assumed human nature and became flesh and lived among us.

What is one example of a loving relationship in the world today?

In choosing to read that passage, Jesus identifies himself with the one who would bring about the just world imagined by Isaiah. In fact, Jesus' ministry is characterized by the same outpouring of God's love that made the world such a good place to begin with. Through his words, actions, and miracles, Jesus works to restore a world of loving relationships.

The Kingdom of God

For Jesus, the **Kingdom of God** was not an earthly kingdom held together by armies and soldiers. Nor was it a specific place at all. Because God's rule is love, we can say the Kingdom of God is the way things are when love is more important than anything else in people's lives.

We know from our experiences, though, that people's actions in the world are characterized not only by love but also by cruel indifference. Clearly, the

> **Through his words, actions, and miracles, Jesus works to restore a world of loving relationships.**

Kingdom of God The center of the preaching of Jesus and the way things are when love is more important than anything else in people's lives. It is both initiated and fulfilled in Jesus Christ.

What does it mean to you to "love your neighbor"?

Kingdom is not yet completely here, or the world would be a different place. But Jesus' call is that we continue to strive for the Kingdom of God here on earth. How do we do that? We must love not only God but also one another. Jesus teaches that love of God (a commandment from the Shema) is impossible without love of neighbor (a commandment from the Book of Deuteronomy):

> One of the scribes . . . asked [Jesus], "Which is the first of all the commandments?" Jesus replied, "The first is this: 'Hear, O Israel! The Lord our God is Lord alone! You shall love the Lord your God with all your heart, with all your soul, with all your mind, and with all your strength.' The second is this: 'You shall love your neighbor as yourself.' There is no other commandment greater than these." The scribe said to him, "Well said, teacher. You are right in saying, 'He is One, and there is no other than he.' And 'to love him with all your heart, with all your understanding, with all your strength, and to love your neighbor as yourself' is worth more than all burnt offerings and sacrifices." And when Jesus saw that [he] answered with understanding, he said to him, "You are not far from the kingdom of God." (Mark 12:28–34)

Jesus does not answer with just one commandment but with two. The scribe sees that Jesus is teaching that love of neighbor is essential to loving God. Jesus says that those who understand this important lesson "are not far from the kingdom of God."

Love God by Loving One Another

Jesus takes his point even further in the story of how the Kingdom of God will be fulfilled through Jesus, the king, in the final judgment at the end of time. Jesus shows how his Kingdom is based on love:

> Then the king will say to those on his right, "Come, you who are blessed by my Father. Inherit the

kingdom prepared for you from the foundation of the world. For I was hungry and you gave me food, I was thirsty and you gave me drink, a stranger and you welcomed me, naked and you clothed me, ill and you cared for me, in prison and you visited me." Then the righteous will answer him and say, "Lord, when did we see you hungry and feed you, or thirsty and give you drink? When did we see you a stranger and welcome you, or naked and clothe you? When did we see you ill or in prison, and visit you?" And the king will say to them in reply, "Amen, I say to you, whatever you did for one of these least brothers of mine, you did for me." (Matthew 25:34–40)

Jesus and the prophets agree that *true love of God is best shown by loving one another.* Genuine worship comes from a sincere heart, one that recognizes God in the needs of others.

Love Turns the World Upside Down

As strange as it may sound, Jesus' "kingdom of love" frightened the political leaders of the time. If love reigned, they would lose their power.

We hear the word *love* so much that it may be difficult to imagine how it could be so threatening. But, in fact, when love, willing the good for one another, is the most important law in a society, everything changes. By making love the law of the land, Jesus was turning the world of first-century Palestine upside down.

He's Got the Whole World in His Hands

It is not uncommon to feel discouraged or overwhelmed as you learn about all the suffering and injustice in the world. That's okay. Some of the greatest figures in the Bible and in Christian history have had similar feelings.

At the same time, Christians find reason to hope when they remember that God has a plan for peace and justice to reign. For Christians, all work for justice and peace flows out of God's plan of salvation, which can be summarized as follows:

- God is love.
- God made the world good.
- Sin is the root of injustice.
- Jesus Christ is the source of all justice and peace.
- Christ continues to transform the world through his church.
- We are called to continue Christ's saving mission in the world, to bring about the Kingdom of God.

Understanding God's plan helps us realize that it is ultimately God who saves the world, not us. God invites us to fulfill our human dignity by participating in his ongoing work of creation. Pursuing justice and peace is part of that work. Moreover, Scripture makes it clear that we cannot really love God while ignoring the suffering of others.

As we work for justice and peace, knowing that we are not responsible for saving the whole world can be a source of hope. As the old Christian hymn says, God's "got the whole world in his hands": he is doing justice for us, alongside us—and, if we let him, through us.

The Social World of First-Century Palestine

By knowing the social situation of Jewish society at the time of Jesus, we can more fully appreciate the impact of Jesus' mission. Jesus did not challenge only Jewish society but all societies not ruled by love—and his challenge is as valid today as it was then.

Imagine the Jewish society of Jesus' time as a pyramid, with those at the top of the pyramid closest to God (and therefore "most holy"), and those at the bottom farthest from God ("least holy"). Below is how the "pyramid of society" might have looked at the time of Jesus.

Of course, this quick sketch of ancient Jewish society does not reflect its complexities. But the point is clear: Jewish society was one of division, as ours is today.

High Priest
The only man who could go into the holiest part of the Temple.

Religious authorities
Followed the Law exactly, viewed as closer to God than others.

Rich, healthy men
Followed the Law, and their prosperity was supposedly a sign of God's favor.

Women
Treated as property, only had worth in relation to the males in their lives.

Foreigners
Anyone who was not Jewish was considered outside of God's covenant.

Sinners
Poverty and sickness were seen as evidence of sin. People who worked in unclean professions, such as shepherds or tax collectors, were considered sinners as well.

Prostitutes and murderers
Those at the top of the pyramid did not associate with those at the bottom. If they entered a sinner's house, ate with sinners, or touched a leper, they would become unclean and have to perform elaborate rituals to purify themselves.

The Last Come First

In the Kingdom of God, that pyramid is turned on its head. Jesus taught that, far from being unloved by God, the well-being of people who are poor, suffering, and oppressed should be given special preference. In the **Beatitudes**, Jesus calls them "blessed." They are blessed not because poverty, suffering, and oppression are good, but because their experience teaches them the importance of love and justice—a lesson that rich and comfortable people may have more difficulty understanding.

On the other hand, anyone who wants to be "first" must not be selfish but must bring goodness to others:

> Let the greatest among you be as the youngest, and the leader as the servant. For who is greater: the one seated at table or the one who serves? Is it not the one seated at table? I am among you as the one who serves. (Luke 22:26–27)

Can you imagine what society would look like if instead of trying to get ahead, everyone tried to serve everyone else? Cofounder of the *Catholic Worker* and social activist, Peter Maurin, put it this way:

> Everybody would be rich
> if nobody tried to become richer.
>
> And nobody would be poor
> if everybody tried to be the poorest.
>
> And everybody would be what he ought to be
> if everybody tried to be
> what he wants the other fellow to be.
>
> (*Easy Essays*)

> Consider what would happen if people suddenly started living out Peter Maurin's vision. Draw an image that represents what this would be like, or write or create a skit with others.

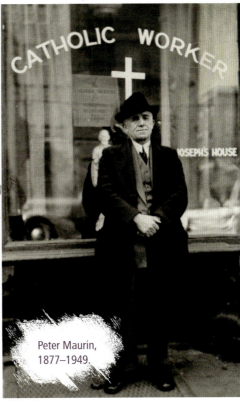

Peter Maurin, 1877–1949.

Beatitudes Blessings spoken by Jesus as part of the Sermon on the Mount and the sermon on the plain that reveal the path to happiness and holiness. The Beatitudes are often considered to represent the heart of the preaching of Jesus.

> **In the Kingdom of God, love is more valuable than gold.**

Everyone is made in the image of God

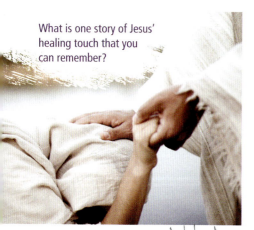

What is one story of Jesus' healing touch that you can remember?

Nobody can be holier than another person

A New Family

In Jesus' Kingdom, *all* people are related to one another when they love one another: "[For] whoever does the will of God is my brother and sister and mother" (Mark 3:35). Throughout the Gospels, Jesus constantly breaks through society's divisions to bring everyone into his family, including the following:

Women. Jesus talked to women in public all the time—his disciples "were amazed that he was talking with a woman" at the Samaritan well (John 4:27). Jesus touched women to heal them, and he was touched by them in return. Jesus taught women and had them among his disciples. And women, who were not thought to be reliable witnesses, were the first witnesses of the **Resurrection**.

Sick people. Jesus challenged the notion that all sickness was the result of sin. He touched the sick and healed them. Over and over, the religious leaders charged Jesus with breaking the command not to work on the **Sabbath** because Jesus healed people on that day. Jesus said that having compassion for the suffering "keeps the Sabbath holy," but ignoring them to honor God does not.

Sinners. Jesus frequently associated with sinners and even ate at their homes, an act that would have made him ritually unclean. Likewise, he forgave sins—an act punishable by death. On the other hand, Jesus said that the ones who think they are holier than everyone else are also sinners because they sin by scorning others.

Rich and powerful people. Jesus must have known that the top of the pyramid can be a lonely place. He challenged rich and powerful people to give up their wealth and power—not just to benefit poor and oppressed people, but because doing so would allow those who are rich and powerful to love. In the Kingdom of God, love is more valuable than gold.

Resurrection The bodily rising of Jesus from the dead on the third day after his death on the cross and his burial in the tomb.

Sabbath The weekly day of rest to remember God's work through private prayer and communal worship.

The Compassionate Way of Jesus

Enemies. Jesus even wanted to bring our *enemies* into the Kingdom of God. He said people should respond to violence not with retaliation but with love: "You have heard that it was said, 'You shall love your neighbor and hate your enemy.' But I say to you, love your enemies, and pray for those who persecute you" (Matthew 5:43–44). This is a hard saying for people to accept even today because it seems to be the way of weakness. In fact, the power of love is stronger than the power of violence.

Love's Surprise: The Cross and the Resurrection

As we have seen, the mission of Jesus was to take a world built in large measure on selfishness and turn it upside down to make it a world built on love. But the people in power feared Jesus' new Kingdom based on love. They were afraid of a man who questioned everything about how the world works, everything that made sense to them. In a world based on Jesus' teaching, how would they fare? In fact, love multiplies God's goodness for everyone—but their deep fear kept them from understanding that truth, so they sought to kill Jesus.

Jesus could have avoided suffering and death by giving up the mission God had given him. After all, he was afraid of pain, suffering, and death just like any other human being. But Jesus was totally committed to following the will of his Father, which is for people to love one another as God has loved them. Jesus loved God and humanity completely, even though this meant that some people would cause him to suffer and die. On the cross, Jesus gave up everything he had for the sake of love. He lived out the will of his Father through his loving sacrifice for us, and, in doing so, restored the relationship of all humans with God.

That was not at all what the political leaders expected to happen; the Resurrection was a complete surprise to them. But to those who believed, it was a sign that God, through his Son, had succeeded in turning the world upside down. Unselfish love, not selfishness, led to goodness, joy, and life.

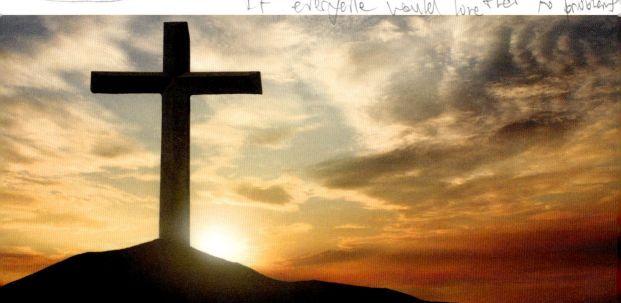

> Recall a time when you were surprised by love. If you cannot think of a personal experience, think about a way you or someone you know might like to be surprised by love.

It is through the loving sacrifice of Jesus Christ that people receive the grace to follow him by loving God and neighbor, even through suffering. In loving God and neighbor, they live in Christ and become more fully images of God, whose love never runs out, even though it is constantly given away.

The Story Continues

Christians believe that the source of compassion is the Holy Spirit alive and moving within us. God gave himself to humanity in Jesus, and Jesus continues to give all of himself—his Body and Blood—to his followers in the Eucharist. Just as the bread and wine are changed into the Body and Blood of Jesus, those who receive the Eucharist with open hearts are changed as well. They are called to become like Jesus, giving themselves in love for the goodness of the whole world. Responding to the call of grace unites us more closely with God, who makes it possible for us to work for God's justice in the world.

Of course, it is easy to talk about the *idea* of justice; responding to God's grace by *doing* justice is a messier matter, one that requires good supplies of imagination, creativity, endurance, courage, and hope. Yet we seek it anyway, because, in doing so, we find the true joy that comes only from being united in love with God and one another.

> Read the following statements:
> - God alone can bring justice to the world.
> - Humans can bring justice to the world on their own.
>
> Do you agree or disagree with each statement? Why?

For Review

1. Why did the Son of God become a human being in the person of Jesus Christ?
2. What is the Kingdom of God?
3. According to Jesus and the prophets, how is true love for God best shown?
4. Briefly explain how Jesus invited each of the following groups of people into the Kingdom of God: women, sick people, sinners, rich and powerful people, enemies.

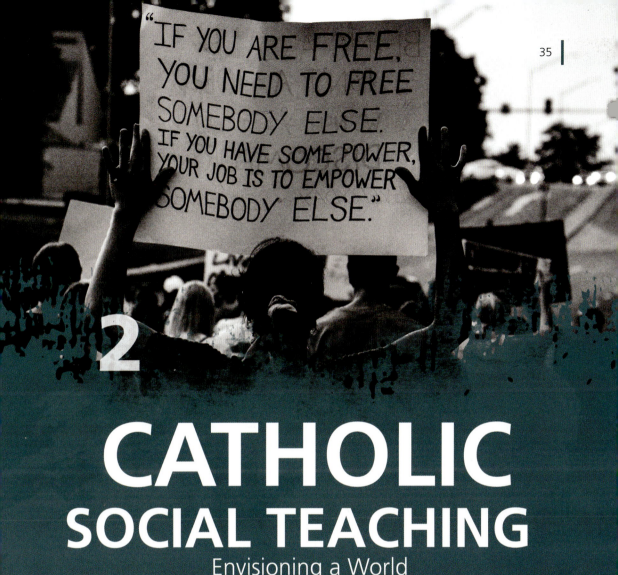

2

CATHOLIC SOCIAL TEACHING

Envisioning a World of Justice and Peace

In This Chapter

The Development of Catholic Social Teaching

Catholic Social Teaching Documents

Themes of Catholic Social Teaching, 1–3

Themes of Catholic Social Teaching, 4–7

The Development of Catholic Social Teaching

The Church in the World

In 1933, the Great Depression was well underway, leaving millions without work, food, or shelter. The previous winter, thousands of farmers and unemployed workers had come together for a hunger march on Washington, DC, as a dramatic appeal for help from politicians, only to be rebuffed by armed police and soldiers. To many of the hungry and unemployed, the Communist Party seemed to be the only group that cared about their plight.

To counter the appeal of communism, Dorothy Day distributed a new newspaper, the *Catholic Worker*. Many of those who were frustrated with poverty, hunger, and the lack of government response recognized Dorothy, a journalist and social activist who had frequently run in communist and socialist circles prior to her conversion to Catholicism four years earlier.

Not all reacted in a positive way to Dorothy and the supporters of the *Catholic Worker*. In fact, many of those marching for workers' rights often reacted with hostility, claiming that religion was the enemy of the poor.

However, the *Catholic Worker*'s message was exactly the opposite. It attempted to make others aware that the Church was on their side and that the Church had a history of social justice teachings. Eventually, with the plight of the worker as their focus, the Catholic Worker movement grew in popularity.

What Is Catholic Social Teaching?

From its humble beginnings, the *Catholic Worker* was soon read by more than one hundred thousand people who wanted to hear about the ideas for **social justice** described in Church documents that are collectively known as **Catholic social teaching**. Those ideas can change the world—so much so that in some countries, Church people who voice them are risking their lives. Catholic social teaching calls for society to be transformed in ways that will make it easier for all people to experience the goodness God wills for them, but that transformation requires changes that make some people uncomfortable.

> **social justice** The defense of human dignity by ensuring that essential human needs are met and that essential human rights are protected for all people.
>
> **Catholic social teaching** The teaching of the Church that examines human society in light of the Gospel and Church Tradition for the purpose of guiding Christians as they carry on the mission of Jesus in the world.

The Development of Catholic Social Teaching

What is Catholic social teaching? Simply put, it is the call of the popes and bishops for people to let the reign of God's love shape their world, a call that is rooted in the mission of Jesus Christ.

Jesus' mission did not end with his Ascension into heaven. Rather, he handed it on to the Apostles, so that it continues even today through the Church. That mission is nothing less than to save all people from sin and death so that they can share in God's love. In *Pastoral Constitution on the Church in the Modern World* (*Gaudium et Spes,* 1965), an important document of the Second Vatican Council, the Church describes its mission as an expression of compassion:

> The joys and hopes, the griefs and anxieties of the [people of our time], especially of those who are poor or in any way afflicted, these are the joys and hopes, the griefs and anxieties of the followers of Christ. Indeed, nothing that is genuinely human fails to raise an echo in their hearts. (1)

This mission of compassion is carried out whenever the Church makes Christ's saving action present in word and deed, primarily through the celebration of the liturgy. But it does not end within the walls of church buildings. Having been transformed by Christ in the liturgy, the Church is called to bring Christ's saving presence

The Catholic Worker Movement

Dorothy Day founded the Catholic Worker movement in 1933 at the urging of her friend, Peter Maurin. Even today, the Catholic Worker movement is best known for its hospitality houses, where volunteers offer food, clothing, shelter, and welcome. Beyond hospitality, Catholic Worker communities are known for their strong support of labor unions, human rights cooperatives, and the development of a nonviolent culture. It is not uncommon for those involved to protest racism, unfair labor practices, social injustice, and war. The *Catholic Worker* newspaper still sells for a penny a copy, bringing awareness to social justice issues of the day. In a testament to their core principles, there has been no central leader of the movement since Dorothy's death in 1980. The Catholic Worker movement is an example of a group whose very mission is rooted in an understanding and living out of the principles of Catholic social teaching.

Dorothy Day and Peter Maurin, cofounders of the *Catholic Worker* newspaper.

> **This mission of compassion is carried out whenever the Church makes Christ's saving action present in word and deed. . . .**

into the world so that all people might be transformed by his love. Catholic social teaching and the action for justice that flows from it are therefore critical to the Church's mission. As the bishops of the world put it:

> Action on behalf of justice and participation in the transformation of the world fully appear to us as a [necessary part] . . . of the Church's mission for the redemption of the human race and its liberation from every oppressive situation. ("Justice in the World" ["Justicia in Mundo"], 6)

Some people might wonder why the Church needs special teachings to guide action for justice; after all, it already has Scripture. Yet the specific social situations of the world today are much different from those of the Mediterranean world some two to three thousand years ago when Scripture was written. Catholic social teaching serves as a kind of bridge, applying the timeless truths of Scripture—as well as the accumulated wisdom of the Church's **Sacred Tradition**—to the new and complex social situations of the modern world.

Catholic social teaching is the teaching of the Church that examines human society in light of the Gospel and Church Tradition for the purpose of guiding Christians as they carry on the mission of Jesus in the world. It is issued by popes and bishops in letters, statements, and official documents that are addressed to the whole Church and the whole world.

> The term *Catholic social teaching* implies that the Church attempts to be a teacher of society through its official documents. In your opinion, who are the most influential "teachers" of society in the world today, and what is their message?

The Church Responds

Understanding the historical context in which Catholic social teaching evolved is crucial to comprehending the principles the Catholic Church has established for guiding our efforts toward building a more just world. It was the signs of the times in the eighteenth and nineteenth centuries that first sparked the modern Catholic social teaching tradition.

Sacred Tradition Refers to the process of passing on the Gospel message. Tradition, which began with the oral communication of the Gospel by the Apostles, was written down in Scripture, is handed down and lived out in the life of the Church, and is interpreted by the bishops of the Church in union with the pope under the guidance of the Holy Spirit.

The Development of Catholic Social Teaching

The Age of Enlightenment brought dramatic growth, including new economic and political systems such as capitalism, socialism, and communism.

The eighteenth and nineteenth centuries saw dramatic change in the western world. In Europe and the United States, numerous scientific discoveries and applications led to new developments in navigation, medicine, communication, and manufacturing. These developments led to the rise of factories, an increase in international commerce, and the growth of ever-larger cities with working-class populations.

At the same time, leading thinkers were also proposing new economic and political systems, such as **capitalism**, **socialism**, and **communism**. There was a growing belief in society that the world's problems could be solved using human reason and scientific

---

capitalism An economic system based on the private ownership of goods and the distribution of goods determined mainly by competition in a free market.

socialism An economic system in which there is no private ownership of goods, and the creation and distribution of goods and services is determined by the whole community or by the government.

communism An economic and governmental system where goods are owned in common and are available to all as needed.

> "The Church responded by applying God's eternal moral truth to these new social challenges."

understanding. This thinking had its roots in the **Age of Enlightenment**, an eighteenth-century period in Western philosophy. During the Enlightenment, some people rejected the belief that any truth could be known through divine Revelation; they believed that all truth could be discovered solely through human reason.

These developments resulted in big changes in governments and economics. Kings and queens were replaced with popularly elected parliaments and congresses. Agricultural economies were replaced with manufacturing economies. Guilds and craftspeople were replaced with factories. Human society changed in dramatic and fundamental ways, bringing new opportunities for human growth and development and new moral challenges. The Church responded by applying God's eternal moral truth to these new social challenges.

For Review

1. What is Catholic social teaching?
2. Which economic and political system was the *Catholic Worker* newspaper and movement a reaction to?
3. In what way does the Catholic Church make Christ most present?
4. Why did the Catholic Church develop Catholic social teaching if Scripture already contains a guide to action for justice?

Age of Enlightenment A movement that began in the nineteenth century that considered human reason as supreme in the acquisition and development of knowledge and so questioned both the possibility of Revelation and the teachings of the Church.

Catholic Social Teaching Documents

In the middle to late 1800s, life in parts of Europe was miserable. In some countries, many people were unemployed and starving. Those with jobs were often little more than slaves, working seven days a week for wages that could barely put food on the table. Some factories were filled with children working in dangerous conditions for cruel supervisors.

In light of this social situation, Pope Leo XIII wrote the first modern social **encyclical**, "On Capital and Labor" ("Rerum Novarum"), in 1891. However, Leo XIII was not the first Catholic to address the injustices faced by the working class. Beginning in the early nineteenth century, many bishops around the world were actively supporting the associations and **unions** the workers were forming—even though labor unions were widely outlawed in the belief that they disrupted society.

Groups of Catholic thinkers and activists also worked on solutions to what was being called the social question. Twenty-year-old Frédéric Ozanam, for instance, started the Saint Vincent de Paul Society, a worldwide charitable organization for the poor. By 1886 many working Catholics in the United States were organizing into a controversial organization known as the Knights of Labor, a union supported by some of the US hierarchy, such as Cardinal James Gibbons of Baltimore.

Leo XIII was sympathetic to these early efforts; he himself had acted by establishing a savings bank for the poor. The foundation was laid for "On Capital and Labor" to appear in 1891.

Cardinal James Gibbons, 1834–1921.

> **encyclical** A teaching letter from the pope to the members of the Church on topics of social justice, human rights, and peace.
>
> **unions** Organizations of workers formed to protect the rights and interests of their members.

> **Work's primary purpose is to provide a decent life for workers and their families.**

"On Capital and Labor" was hotly debated when it was issued. Some praised it, and others scorned it, but it certainly was not ignored. Novelist Georges Bernanos would describe the impact of the encyclical in his fictional work *The Diary of a Country Priest* nearly forty years later:

> When it was published . . . it was like an earthquake. The enthusiasm! . . . The simple notion that a man's work is not a commodity, subject to the law of supply and demand, that you have no right to speculate on wages, on the lives of men, as you do on grain, sugar or coffee—why it set people's consciences upside down!

The Themes of "On Capital and Labor"

Like socialism, "On Capital and Labor" criticized the abuses of liberal capitalism that left the majority of workers with lives "little better than slavery itself" (2). But it opposed the socialist solution to that situation, which was for the workers to take over and abolish the private ownership of property so that it would be owned in common by all people.

"On Capital and Labor" offered an alternative solution, one based on the Gospel and Church Tradition. That Tradition includes the notion of **natural law**—the God-given need for creation, including human beings, to follow what God intended it to be. The following are some major elements of the solution offered by Pope Leo XIII:

- **Cooperation between classes.** The social system proposed by "On Capital and Labor" is based on cooperation between workers and capitalists, with rights and duties for both.

---

natural law The expression of the original moral sense that God gave us that enables us to discern by our intellect and reason what is good and what is evil. It is rooted in our desire for God, and it is our participation in his wisdom and goodness because we are created in his divine likeness.

- **The dignity of work.** Work's primary purpose is to provide a decent life for workers and their families. Workers are owed reasonable work hours, Sundays and religious holidays off, and safe working conditions, with strict limits on child labor.
- **The just wage and workers' associations.** Workers must receive a **just wage**—an amount sufficient to provide a decent life for a worker's whole family—and must be free to organize associations, now known as unions, to negotiate working conditions.
- **The role of the state.** Government should avoid interfering in private matters, but in some situations, government has to take action through laws for the good of society.
- **Private ownership of property.** All people have a right to own property, but private property must be fairly distributed and used responsibly for the good of all.
- **Defense of the poor.** Christians and governments should make protection of the poor a priority.

Christians and governments should make protection of the poor a priority.

Like all social teaching documents, "On Capital and Labor" provides general guidance for how society can become more just. Although that guidance has changed as the many challenges that face society have changed, Catholic social teaching since then has continued to echo the major themes of its first document.

Did It Work?

In the end, the Church's social teaching is only effective to the extent that people act on it. In the case of "On Capital and Labor," the short-term reaction was mixed.

Why did "On Capital and Labor" cause such a stir in its time, and why is it still so influential?

just wage A salary that recognizes the value of the work being performed and that is high enough to allow the laborer and their immediate family to live a life of human dignity. Minimally, this means a wage above the poverty line.

> **"On Capital and Labor" established a precedent for the Church to speak out on social matters.**

Consider your work experience, and talk to your parents and friends about theirs. Based on these experiences, what are some ways "On Capital and Labor" could be updated for modern workers?

Many Catholics ignored or misunderstood the teaching, but many others took it to heart. Catholic labor unions, mutual-aid societies, cooperatives, and other organizations flourished as a result of the encyclical. It also enabled various Catholic political leaders to more boldly suggest and support legislation to improve the lives of the common people.

Over time, "On Capital and Labor" indirectly led to the development of government policies such as minimum-wage laws and the right to strike. As Pope Pius XI would say forty years later, "Great credit must be given [to 'On Capital and Labor'] for whatever improvement has been achieved in the workers' condition" ("On Reconstruction of the Social Order" ["Quadragesimo Anno"], 28).

But perhaps most important, "On Capital and Labor" established a precedent for the Church to speak out on social matters. It observed that individual moral choices affect society, and society affects individual morality; the two cannot be separated. Therefore, the Church must be concerned with moral issues not only on the individual level but on the social level as well.

By making that claim, "On Capital and Labor" helped the Church shift its approach to helping poor and vulnerable people. The Church had always called for Christians to ease poverty through charitable giving. But now it was also asking Christians to look for the social causes of such problems as poverty, and to

© Christopher Penler / Shutterstock.com

change the way society was set up so that the root causes of those problems would be eliminated as much as possible. In doing that, "On Capital and Labor" opened the doors to more than one hundred years of social teaching and action in the Church.

A Dynamic Tradition

The major Catholic social teaching documents that followed "On Capital and Labor" continued to build on it and had similar core themes. At the same time, society has undergone considerable change since "On Capital and Labor," and Catholic social teaching has developed to respond to those changes. For instance, beginning in the 1960s, the documents became more concerned with global issues, rather than just focusing on Western society, because more of the Church's bishops were from poor, underdeveloped countries. This new global concern allowed the Latin American bishops to call the whole Church to a "preferential option for the poor," a theme that has been especially prominent in the Church's social teaching since then.

Another example is Catholic social teaching's special attention to international peace and the morality of nuclear weapons during the **Cold War**. This was the period between about 1945 and 1990, when the United States and the Soviet Union competed to dominate the world through military might.

Likewise, the Church has shifted its attitude toward private property. Leo XIII believed it was important to emphasize the right to own private property because socialism was challenging that right. Since then, however, the Church has seen that the Western world, despite its wealth, largely ignores most of the world's population that suffers from poverty. So, although the Church does not dispute the right to private property, it has put more emphasis on the responsibility to use the goods of the earth for the benefit of all.

Key Documents and Summaries

Since "On Capital and Labor," numerous papal and Vatican documents have added to the wealth of the Church's social teaching. The chart on the next two pages lists nine encyclicals and one pastoral constitution, with a few key points from each of them.

Cold War The period between about 1945 and 1990, when the United States and the Soviet Union competed to dominate the world through military power.

"On Capital and Labor" ("Rerum Novarum")
Pope Leo XIII

- addresses the Church's right to speak on social issues
- affirms that every person has basic rights that must be respected by society
- promotes the rights and just treatment of workers

"On Reconstruction of the Social Order" ("Quadragesimo Anno")
Pope Pius XI

- criticizes both capitalism and socialism
- criticizes the growing gap between the rich and the poor
- introduces the understanding that large organizations and governments have the responsibility to support the good of human beings, families, and local communities but should not take over responsibilities and decisions that can be handled by individuals and local organizations

"On Christianity and Social Progress" ("Mater et Magistra")
Pope John XXIII

- shows concern for workers and women
- criticizes the gap between rich nations and poor nations
- says that excessive spending on weapons threatens society

"Peace on Earth" ("Pacem in Terris")
Pope John XXIII

- warns against modern warfare, especially nuclear weapons
- says peace can be achieved only through a just social order
- gives a detailed list of the human rights necessary for a just social order

Pastoral Constitution on The Church in the Modern World (Gaudium et Spes)
Vatican Council II

- says the Church must serve the world and work with other organizations in promoting the common good
- condemns the use of weapons of mass destruction
- maintains that peace is not just the absence of war but is justice throughout society

Catholic Social Teaching Documents

1967

"On the Development of Peoples" ("Populorum Progressio")
Pope Paul VI

- calls for true progress toward the economic, social, cultural, and spiritual fulfillment of human potential
- teaches that the economic development of those who are poor and the moral development of those with material wealth are linked
- criticizes unrestrained capitalism where profit is the primary motive and where private ownership is an absolute right

1981

"On Human Work" ("Laborem Exercens")
Pope John Paul II

- teaches that work is at the center of social issues
- says all people who are able to work have both the right and the duty to work
- emphasizes the rights of workers; says that people are more important than profits or the things they make

2009

"On Charity in Truth" ("Caritas in Veritate")
Pope Benedict XVI

- says justice must be applied to every aspect of economic activity
- teaches that both the exclusion of religion from society and religious fundamentalism are obstacles to a just society
- says that technology should not drive our society but should serve the common good

2015

"On Care for Our Common Home" ("Laudato Si")
Pope Francis

- critiques consumerism and irresponsible development
- laments environmental degradation and climate change
- states that concern for the natural world is no longer optional but is an integral part of Church teaching on social justice.

2020

"All Brothers" ("Fratelli Tutti")
Pope Francis

- calls for more human fraternity and solidarity
- is written as a plea to reject wars and condemn the death penalty
- proposes an ideal world of fraternity in which all countries can be part of a "larger human family"

For Review

1. What are the six major elements of the solutions Pope Leo XIII offered in "On Capital and Labor"?
2. What has been one of the most important results of "On Capital and Labor" for the Church?
3. Have the core themes of modern Catholic social teaching changed much since "On Capital and Labor" was issued? Give an example of what has changed or what has stayed the same.
4. Why have the Church's documents on Catholic social teaching become more focused on global issues?
5. What is the main focus of the Church's teachings on the ownership of private property?

Themes of Catholic Social Teaching, 1–3

Although some scholars have listed ten, fourteen, or even twenty basic themes of Catholic social teaching, the US Catholic bishops have limited their list to seven. As you learn about the themes of Catholic social teaching, keep in mind that the themes do not stand alone; they cannot be separated from one another. Instead, they are interdependent, woven together to support and complement one another.

The Life and Dignity of the Human Person

Yevgeny Yevtushenko was only a child when he and his mother witnessed twenty thousand German prisoners of war being marched down the streets of Moscow in 1944. Crowds of women lined the streets to show their contempt for the defeated enemy who had taken the lives of their brothers, sons, and husbands, and who had caused them to suffer a long winter of near starvation. At first, the soldiers and police had to restrain them, so great was their anger. But as the enemy paraded by, the women encountered only bloody, exhausted men and boys who passed with their heads hung low:

> The street became dead silent—the only sound was the shuffling of boots and the thumping of crutches.

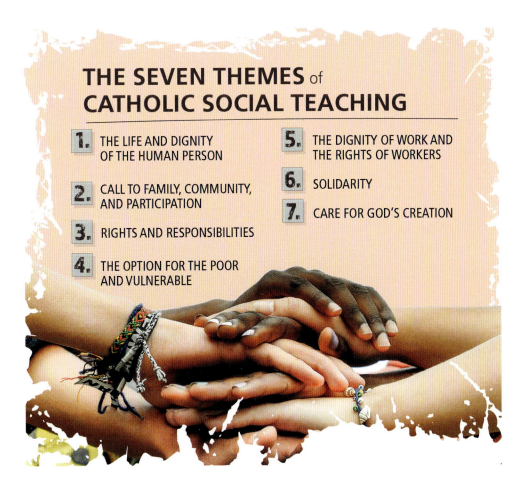

Then I saw an elderly woman in broken-down boots push herself forward and touch a policeman's shoulder, saying: "Let me through." . . .

She went up to the column, [and] took from inside her coat . . . a crust of black bread. She pushed it awkwardly into the pocket of a soldier, so exhausted that he was tottering on his feet. And now suddenly from every side women were running towards the soldiers, pushing into their hands bread, cigarettes, whatever they had.

The soldiers were no longer enemies. They were people. (Yevgeny Yevtushenko, *A Precocious Autobiography*)

German prisoners of war.

Those Russian women experienced a transformation on that cold day in 1944. The goodness within them overcame their deep pain and anger, allowing them to see their enemies not as monsters but as fellow human beings that suffered just as they did. And by caring for the men as God cared for them, the women became more truly people who reflected the image of God.

All Are Loved by God

In their compassionate response, the Russian women recognized and acted on the most basic principle of Catholic social teaching: All human beings have dignity because they are loved by God and made in his image. People, motivated by selfishness, fear, or hate, have always found reasons not to respect the dignity of others: race, gender, sexual orientation, ethnicity, disability, age, and history, just for starters. But Catholic social teaching insists that nothing can take away the fundamental dignity of any person, not even their own destructive actions.

The insight that *all* people have equal dignity because they are loved by God has major implications for

What does it mean to you to seek goodness for all people?

Christians. If God loves and wants goodness for every person, then how can Christians do anything less than loving and seeking goodness for all people?

For Human Life

In other words, Christians are called to be *for* human life. At the most basic level, this means allowing people to live. Respect for human life is the basis for the Catholic Church's opposition to abortion, the death penalty, euthanasia, and other forms of violence, including most wars.

But respecting human life means a lot more than simply allowing others to live—it also means helping others live to the fullest, experiencing all the dignity and goodness that God intended for them in the physical, social, mental, and spiritual aspects of their lives.

Specific examples of the principle of respecting human life and dignity might include the following:

- not using genetic engineering to manipulate human life for the creation of products
- giving poor, rural communities in underdeveloped countries access to clean water and the means to produce their own food
- placing human needs before profits when making business decisions

Promoting the life and dignity of human beings is the most fundamental of the Catholic social teaching principles. It is the one by which Catholicism judges the morality of social institutions and policy decisions, and it is the one on which all the other principles are based.

The Call to Family, Community, and Participation

In September 1957, nine Black students were enrolled at the formerly all-white, Central High School in Little Rock, Arkansas. Though their attendance was to be the first test of desegregation in response to the landmark Supreme Court case *Brown v. Board of Education*, the governor of Arkansas called in the

> **All human beings have dignity because they are loved by God and made in his image.**

> **Promoting the life and dignity of human beings is the most fundamental of the Catholic social teaching principles.**

> Who is marginalized in your community? In what ways do you contribute to or push back against this social injustice?

Arkansas National Guard to stop the Black students from entering the high school. Melba Pattillo, one of the nine, describes her experience:

> When we arrived at the school, the driver urged me to get out quickly. The white hand of a uniformed officer opened the door and pulled me toward him as his urgent voice ordered me to hurry. The roar from the front of the building made me glance to the right. Only a half-block away, I saw hundreds of white people, their bodies in motion and their mouths wide open as they shouted their anger. The roar swelled, as if their frenzy had been fired up by something. It took me a moment to digest the fact that it was the sight of us that had upset them.
>
> As I entered a classroom, a hush fell over the students. The guide pointed me to an empty seat, and I walked toward it. Students sitting nearby quickly moved away. I sat down surrounded by empty seats, feeling unbearably self-conscious. One of the boys kept shouting ugly words at me throughout the class. I waited for the teacher to

The Little Rock Nine monument is on the grounds of the Arkansas State Capitol building. The monument faces the governor's office window as an eternal reminder of the African American students who demonstrated courage and tenacity in the fight for integrated education.

speak up, but she said nothing. My heart was weeping, but I squeezed back the tears. I squared my shoulders and tried to remember what Grandma had said: "God loves you, child. No matter what, He sees you as His precious idea." (Melba Pattillo Beals, *Warriors Don't Cry*)

Once the students were able to attend school regularly under the protection of the 101st Airborne Division, they no longer had to contend with mob violence, but school life was not easy for Melba or the other eight students of the "Little Rock Nine." Throughout the year, classmates who wanted the students to quit or be expelled regularly harassed them. Melba was often pushed and tripped. At one point, someone squirted acid into her eyes.

Melba's struggle to be fully a part of society reflects the Catholic social teaching theme of **participation**—the right and responsibility of all people to participate in all aspects of human society—educational, political, cultural, religious, economic, and so on. Those who are not able to fully participate in society are often said to be **marginalized**, or forced outside the main group.

Relationships are an important part of being human. In fact, the human desire to be in relationship is a basic part of what it means to be made in the image of God, who is the relationship of three persons (Father, Son, and Holy Spirit) united in one divine love. That is why the popes and bishops say human beings "realize," or fulfill, their dignity in relationship with others and in community. To understand what the popes and bishops mean, just think about all the ways the person you are today has been shaped, in good and bad ways, by the people in your life (not to mention by God and the natural environment around you).

> Most of the time, the exclusion of people from mainstream society is not as obvious as it was in Melba's case. Do you see examples of people being marginalized, perhaps in more subtle ways, in your school? In your opinion, what are some of the reasons people are excluded?

> **The human desire to be in relationship is a basic part of what it means to be made in the image of God.**

participation The right and responsibility of all people to take an active part in all aspects of human society.

marginalized Those who have been relegated to an unimportant or powerless position within a society or group.

The Christian tradition places special importance on participation in the family. The family is society's most basic building block. It is the place where people are meant to care for and love one another most intimately, and, ideally, it is the place where people are able to realize all that God calls them to be. Catholic social teaching emphasizes the need for society to support families so that all people have an opportunity to participate in a family.

At the other end of the spectrum, participation at the international level means that all nations—whether they are rich or poor, weak or powerful—are able to share in making decisions for the global community.

Two aspects of participation—the common good and subsidiarity—are often listed as separate themes of Catholic social teaching. They are important enough to touch on here.

The Common Good

It is possible, of course, to participate in society in a negative way. But according to Catholic social teaching, people are called to participate in society positively, in ways that contribute to the common good. The

> In your local newspaper, find an article about a government, business, or organization doing something that affects society. Do you believe this organization is promoting the common good or not?

common good is the social condition that allows *all* the people in a community to reach their full human potential and fulfill their human dignity. The common good is *not* "the most good for the most people," which would suggest that some people might be left out or might have to live under unjust conditions for the good of the majority. Working for the common good implies paying special attention to groups and individuals that are excluded from the benefits experienced by the rest of society.

Subsidiarity

The way society is organized affects how well people can participate in it. Catholic social teaching says that large organizations or governments should not take over social responsibilities and decisions that can be carried out by individuals and small local organizations. But larger organizations or governments have a responsibility to coordinate and regulate society when individuals and smaller organizations do not or cannot

> Working for the common good implies paying special attention to groups and individuals that are excluded from the benefits experienced by the rest of society.

common good The social condition that allows *all* people in a community to reach their full human potential and fulfill their human dignity.

As individuals, we can take part in many activities that contribute to a safer and cleaner community.

When the level of need is beyond what we as individuals can handle, government organizations such as FEMA can step in to help alleviate suffering in the community.

carry out responsibilities necessary for the common good. This concept, known as **subsidiarity**, could also be explained by saying that governments and large organizations should exist to serve the good of human beings, families, and communities, which are the center and purpose of social life.

Rights and Responsibilities

God created every person with equal dignity and value. Because of that equal dignity, every person has the right to the things necessary to live a dignified life. **Rights** are those conditions or things that every person needs in order to be fully what God created them to be. The rights necessary for people to be able to live are known as **survival rights**: these include the right to live in safety, the right to adequate food and shelter, the right to medical care, the right to essential social

> *God created every person with equal dignity and value.*

subsidiarity The moral principle that large organizations and governments should not take over responsibilities and decisions that can be handled by individuals and local organizations, and that large corporations and governments have the responsibility to support the good of human beings, families, and local communities, which are the center and purpose of social life.

rights Those conditions or things any person needs to be fully what God created them to be.

survival rights The rights necessary for people to be able to live.

The right to a quality education is considered a "thrival" right.

services, and the right to equal protection under the law. But God does not want creation merely to survive but also to thrive and flourish. So beyond survival rights, Catholic social teaching insists that all human beings also have a right to those things necessary for them to fully recognize their God-given dignity. These **thrival rights** include such things as education, employment, a safe environment, and enough material goods to support a family. They also include the right to live by one's **conscience** and religion, to immigrate, and to live without discrimination.

In addition to the rights already mentioned, human beings' economic, political, and cultural rights must also be respected by other individuals and society. You might be surprised at how long the list of rights can become. One of the most complete lists of human rights in Catholic social teaching can be found in Pope Saint John XXIII's encyclical "Peace on Earth." Here are examples of the rights outlined in the encyclical:

> Make a list of the rights you think belong to all people. After each right, list the responsibilities that might limit it.

---

thrival rights The rights necessary for people to fully recognize their God-given dignity, such as education, employment, a safe environment, and enough material goods to support a family.

conscience The "interior voice" of a person, a God-given internal sense of what is morally wrong or right.

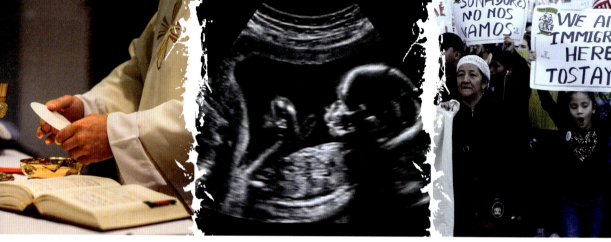

- the right to worship according to one's conscience
- economic rights
- political rights
- the right to life
- rights pertaining to moral and cultural values
- the right to choose one's state in life
- the right of meeting and association
- the right to emigrate and immigrate

Responsibilities: Limits on Rights

Though Catholic social teaching affirms the importance of rights, it also says that rights are not unlimited. An individual's rights are limited by their **responsibilities** for the good of others, as well as for the common good of the whole society. Out of responsibility for the common good, governments must regulate rights in particular instances.

---

responsibilities Those things a person is obligated to do.

The Influence of Women on the Universal Declaration of Human Rights

Human rights that are officially recognized (if not always respected) by most nations in the world are listed in a 1948 United Nations document that the Catholic Church has strongly supported as a tool for promoting justice, the Universal Declaration of Human Rights. Eleanor Roosevelt, former First Lady of the United States, was the first chair of the Commission of Human Rights and was instrumental in the drafting of the Universal Declaration of Human Rights. She was joined by Hansa Mehta from India, who succeeded in changing the text from "All Men" to "All human beings are born free and equal . . ." Minerva Bernadino, a diplomat from the Dominican Republic, pushed to include the wording, "the equality of men and women" in the preamble. Begum Ikramullah from Pakistan, championed Article 16 regarding equal rights in marriage. Bodil Begtrup

Former First Lady Eleanor Roosevelt, speaking at the United Nations in July 1947.

of Denmark advocated that the text refer to "all" or "everyone" rather than "all men." Not surprisingly, it was a woman, Marie-Hélène Lefaucheux of France, who ensured that gender equality was included in Article 2. Evdokia Uralova fought for the inclusion of "equal pay for equal work" in Article 23. And Lakshmi Menon from India was passionate about the principle of gender equality being included throughout the document.

For example, all people have the right to own property (land, cars, money, clothes, and so on). But Catholic social teaching says that everything in the world is a gift given by God for the good of *all* people, both now and in the future. So people have a responsibility to care for their property, and to use it to promote their own dignity as well as the dignity of their families and all members of society. When some people have more property than they really need, while others do not have enough to maintain a dignified life, then those with more have a responsibility to fulfill their neighbor's right to the necessities of a good life.

For Review

1. Define the following terms: *marginalized, common good, subsidiarity.*
2. What is the most basic principle of Catholic social teaching?
3. Define *participation*. What does participation mean for families and nations?
4. Define *rights*. What general responsibility do people have that limits their rights?

Themes of Catholic Social Teaching, 4–7

Elias took off his shoes to give to a homeless man who was wearing plastic bags tied around his feet in place of shoes. Elias has more shoes at home. His walk home was cold and wet, but he barely noticed because he was thinking about the man he helped.

Would the man be there tomorrow? Elias was going to spend his extra cash on ordering food for dinner. But then he thought about stopping to buy some new underwear and socks in case he saw the man again.

Shondra started packing extra items in her lunch because there was a girl at her table who never ate lunch. The girl said it was because she wasn't hungry, but Shondra was pretty sure it was because she couldn't afford lunch or there wasn't enough food to bring from home. Shondra asked around the table if anyone wanted her extra sandwich or chips, being careful not to single the girl out. Unsurprisingly, Shondra ended up providing lunch for this girl for several weeks. After that experience, Shondra focused on thinking of other ways to provide lunch or snacks for kids who needed them without embarrassing them.

Matt and Lauren are twins. They were excited for their senior year spring break trip to the beach with friends. But around Christmas, their youth minister handed out a flyer about a mission trip to the Dominican Republic that would take place the same week as their spring break. The twins both wanted to go on the beach trip, but the mission trip seemed like a good chance to help people and to see what issues affect people outside their community. The week of service was hard work. Matt and Lauren came home with sore muscles, bug bites, and dirty clothes, but also a lifetime of memories. They helped build a school, planted crops, learned phrases of conversational Spanish, shared meals and prayed with their host families, and, most importantly, learned how to put the needs of others before their own comfort.

In our daily lives, we are often presented with the opportunity to help others. It is not difficult to choose to offer a pregnant woman a seat on the bus or to share an umbrella with a man walking in the pouring rain. Yet to truly embrace Christ's example and the principles of Catholic social teaching, we are called to act to ensure the well-being of others—especially those most in need in our society—even if it sometimes creates temporary discomfort or inconvenience for us.

We are called to make the needs of the poor and vulnerable a priority. Here, people are lined up on the streets of New York for free food distribution.

> **The option for the poor and vulnerable is the choice to put the needs of society's most poor and vulnerable members first among all social concerns.**

In your opinion, what are the limits (if any) to helping poor and vulnerable people?

The Option for the Poor and Vulnerable

The **option for the poor and vulnerable** is the choice to put the needs of society's most poor and vulnerable members first among all social concerns. The term *poor and vulnerable* refers not only to those without money but also to those who are deprived of their basic rights or of equal participation in society.

Why does God call humanity to place the needs of the poor and vulnerable first? Simply put, their need is greater. Choosing to defend poor and vulnerable people does not imply that they are necessarily better or more valuable than others. Nor does it imply that people who are not poor are neglected by God, whose love does not exclude anyone. Society is called to place the needs of the poor and vulnerable first in the same way parents pay special attention to a sick child. The parents do not love the sick child more than the other children, but they make the sick child their top priority because of that child's greater need.

option for the poor and vulnerable The choice to put the needs of society's most poor and vulnerable members first among all social concerns.

A Call to Whole Societies

Although the option for the poor and vulnerable can be made by individuals, more often it refers to the choice of an organization, a community, or a society. In the pastoral letter "Economic Justice for All," the United States Conference of Catholic Bishops describes the option for the poor and vulnerable in this way:

> The primary purpose of this special commitment to the poor is to enable them to become active participants in the life of society. It is to enable all persons to share in and contribute to the common good. The "option for the poor," therefore, is not an adversarial slogan that pits one group or class against another. Rather it states that the deprivation and powerlessness of the poor wounds the whole community. These wounds will be healed only by greater solidarity with the poor and among the poor themselves. (88)

From the bishops' words, we can see that the option for the poor and vulnerable involves freely choosing to become friends or partners with those who are poor and taking on their problems as our problems. This is the choice to think of the poor as part of "us"—part of our community of concern—rather than as "those people." For those who are themselves poor or vulnerable, this choice means standing by other people in the same situation rather than trying to take advantage of them to get ahead. The option also involves a commitment to take action to transform the injustice that prevents poor and vulnerable people from actively participating in the life of society.

The Society of Saint Vincent de Paul

The Society of Saint Vincent de Paul began in 1833 in Paris, France. Frédéric Ozanam was a young law student when he was challenged during a debate to demonstrate what he and his fellow Catholic students were personally doing to help the poor in their community. Within a matter of weeks, Ozanam and five of his classmates formed the "Conference of Charity." They funded the organization with their own money and donations from friends. They visited the poor in their homes, providing aid. The conference was soon placed under the patronage of Saint Vincent de Paul, who had spent his life in France serving the poor. Twelve years after its founding in France, the Society of Saint Vincent de Paul was established in the United States. The most recognizable characteristic of the Saint Vincent de Paul chapters is their "home visits." The visiting Vincentians go to the homes of those who are poor to identify immediate and long-term needs, and provide emergency assistance with utilities, rent, food, and clothing.

The Dignity of Work and the Rights of Workers

> Make a list of the rights of workers that have come to your attention in the past several years. In what way, if any, are these issues being addressed?

In 1933, Frances Perkins became the first woman to serve in a presidential cabinet position. President Roosevelt asked Perkins to join his cabinet to formulate the New Deal. With his promise to back her priorities, she was able to pursue the issues of a forty-hour work week, minimum wage, unemployment compensation, abolition of child labor, and universal health insurance.

In 1937, autoworkers at several major factories initiated a sit-down strike. They successfully brought production to a standstill. After forty-four days of the company trying to freeze and starve them out, the company was forced to give in to the workers' demands, which included a fair minimum wage, protections for assembly-line workers, a grievance system, and the recognition of the United Auto Workers union.

In 1963, President Kennedy signed the Equal Pay Act, which was a win for both women and workers. The Equal Pay Act was an amendment to the Fair Labor Standards Act and banned pay disparity for equal work based on gender. Soon afterward,

President Johnson signed the Civil Rights Act, which, in part, banned workplace discrimination based on race, gender, religion, color, or national origin.

The rights of workers is an issue spanning the globe over centuries. In the fight for equality, safety, and equal pay, there have been both losses and victories. The victories have provided many of the working conditions that we take for granted today. This should give us good reason to keep pushing for justice in this area.

> Think about the jobs or work you have had. Have they promoted your human dignity, and, if so, how? How have they served the dignity of others? If they haven't done either, what would have to happen to change that?

Work Is for the Benefit of People

Traditionally, when we think about the value of work, we might think immediately of the amount of money paid for it, or the product that is the result of work—a new car, for example. Business executives might think of the value of work in terms of profit.

Catholic social teaching says, "The basis for determining the value of human work is . . . the fact that the one who is doing it is a person" ("On Human Work," 6). Work, and the economy in general, exists for the sake of people, not the other way around. In the context of justice, then, the value of work is measured by whether it promotes the human dignity of the worker.

The Dignity of Work

Work promotes human dignity by providing families with the things they need to live and flourish. Besides enabling people to live, good work also promotes human dignity simply because it reflects God's work of creation. As images of God, humans are made to be creative, to bring order and goodness to the world. When work is done well, whether it is cleaning a floor or creating a database, it contributes to the common good and, ultimately, to the work of the Father, Son, and Holy Spirit in the world. The **dignity of work** is the value that work has because it supports human life and contributes to human dignity.

> **Besides enabling people to live, good work also promotes human dignity simply because it reflects God's work of creation.**

dignity of work The value work has because it supports human life and contributes to human dignity.

Workers' Rights

The things necessary for dignified work are known as the **rights of workers**. Those rights include the right to employment, to decent and fair pay, to a safe workplace, and to anything else that is required for the basic life and health of workers. Workers also have the right to organize and join unions for the purpose of ensuring these basic rights. Because the dignity of work is about more than just ensuring necessities, Catholic social teaching also calls for workers to be given the freedom and responsibility to use their God-given creativity in their work.

Solidarity

Catholic social teaching says that a spirit of friendship—between individuals, groups, and nations—is the basis for a just world. The Church calls this **solidarity**: a constant commitment to the common good, based on the belief that "we are all really responsible for all" ("On Social Concern," ["Sollicitudo Rei Socialis"], 38).

Solidarity is based on the understanding that all people are part of the same human family, whatever their national, racial, ethnic, economic, or ideological differences may be. Because we are all children of God, we have the same responsibilities toward one another that any family members have. We are called to work for the good of our brothers and sisters in a spirit of friendship, whether or not they are part of our own social group.

The idea of solidarity may not seem remarkable. After all, we are taught the importance of friendship and cooperation from childhood. But to a great extent, modern societies are still based on the values of competition and conflict, not solidarity. Catholic social teaching rejects the idea of a winners-and-losers

> **Solidarity is based on the understanding that all people are part of the same human family, whatever their national, racial, ethnic, economic, or ideological differences may be.**

rights of workers The items necessary for dignified work, including fair pay, a safe workplace, and anything else necessary for the basic life and health of workers.

solidarity The union of one's heart and mind with all people. It leads to the just distribution of material goods, creates bonds between opposing groups and nations, and leads to the spread of spiritual goods such as friendship and prayer.

Solidarity calls us to come together to bring out the goodness in everyone.

society in which people focus on the good of their nation or group only, and proposes solidarity as an alternative. The Christian vision is one of a world in which all people cooperate to bring about goodness for everyone.

Care for God's Creation

Salpointe Catholic High School in Tucson, Arizona, is "a Laudato Sí" school, which means that it is a school that seeks to live and apply the principles in Pope Francis's encyclical on the environment. It all started with Sr. Jane Remson, O.Carm. She is the executive director of the Carmelite NGO (nongovernmental organization) and participated in the Carmelite Justice, Peace and Integrity of Creation program in Rome. She was so inspired that she invited Salpointe administrators and teachers to find ways to implement the encyclical into lesson plans and school projects. The initiative began in science and religion classes but soon spread to all areas of the curriculum.

Being a "Laudato Sí" school has come in handy in some unexpected ways. The school has reduced the amount of paper used by partnering with Google and becoming a one-to-one Chromebook school. Whenever possible, the school communicates digitally rather than by using paper.

The committee that spearheads the "Laudato Sí" project also takes into consideration the use, byproducts, and waste of all materials used at the school. For example, when the Chromebooks were delivered on pallets, the school made furniture with the wood rather than sending it to the landfill.

Salpointe created the curriculum, which was published in English and Spanish by the Carmelite NGO. The NGO freely provides access to the "Laudato Sí" curriculum. It has also published a study guide to help others understand the encyclical.

Catholic social teaching calls all people to care for God's creation—to live their faith in relationship with all creation by protecting the health of people and the planet. Most people are not necessarily trying to do malicious things to the earth, but they may not be aware of the actual consequences of their actions. Care for God's creation, in the words of the US Catholic bishops, "is not just an Earth Day slogan; it is a requirement of our faith" (*Sharing Catholic Social Teaching*). That requirement is based on God's call in the Book of Genesis for humans to "cultivate and care for" creation (2:15).

> **Catholic social teaching calls all people to care for God's creation— to live their faith in relationship with all creation by protecting the health of people and the planet.**

These Japanese cherry blossoms are a sign of the beauty of God's creation—from tiny bud to full blossom.

An Interdependent World

God's creation is intended to flourish in a world of interdependence and a world of peace because all its members—humans, animals, and elements—work together for the good of all. Christians are called to care for the environment not only because it is necessary for the full development of human beings but also because the environment, as a work of God, has beauty and value in itself. The beauty of creation can reveal to us something of the beauty of the Creator who made it.

> Go on a walk outside, alone or with some friends, in the area where you live. What might God's reasons be for making the things you find? How do they fit into the mutual interdependence of the world?

For Review

1. Define the terms *rights of workers* and *solidarity*.
2. Why does God call humanity to place the needs of the poor and vulnerable first?
3. In what two ways does work contribute to human dignity?
4. Why are Christians called to work for environmental justice?

3

LIVING JUSTICE

Faith in Action

In This Chapter

A Call to Action

Awareness: Friendship with the World

Analysis: Asking Why

Action: Bringing Life to the World

A Call to Action

A group of teens from Saint Thomas High School participated in a service project at a soup kitchen during their senior year. Many of them expressed hesitation about the long-term project at first. They asked questions such as, "Why are these people not able to provide food for themselves?" or "What can we do to help?" But as the students got to know the people they served and learned about the many factors and issues involved, they were both moved and overwhelmed. Many people have had similar experiences with other issues—they see the environment being destroyed, refugees seeking safety, or people struggling to survive on the margins of society—and they are moved with compassion. But they may ask, "My actions are needed, but what can I do?"

Scripture provides us with a vision for a world ruled by love, and Catholic social teaching guides us in applying that vision to modern-day situations. But neither offers a specific plan for pursuing justice in every situation we might face because each situation is different. How, then, do we figure out what to do? How can we make justice a reality in the world?

> God calls each of us to act for justice in the world. In what ways do you think God might be calling you to work for justice?

> When your actions are needed, what can you do to make justice a reality?

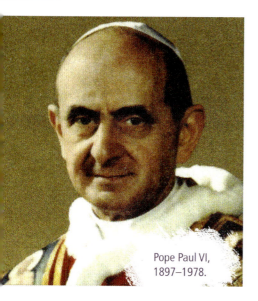

Pope Paul VI, 1897–1978.

The Circle of Faith-in-Action

In 1971, Pope Paul VI issued an apostolic letter, "A Call to Action" ("Octogesimo Adveniens"), that called Christians "to bring about the social, political and economic changes seen in many cases to be urgently needed" for justice. The letter offered a three-step process for taking action—a process always guided by "the light of the Gospel" and Church teaching. The letter suggested that Christians need not act alone, but could act with the help of the Church, other people "of good will," and "the help of the Holy Spirit" ("A Call to Action," 4).

At about the same time this letter was issued, other theologians were developing a similar approach to justice that is sometimes called the pastoral circle or the circle of **praxis**. Praxis means living according to one's beliefs, not just in private, but in a way that affects the world. You might say that Christian praxis involves putting faith into action for the world.

The approach to seeking justice we examine borrows aspects of both the circle of praxis and "A Call to Action." We call this approach the **circle of faith-in-action**.

> "Christian praxis involves putting faith into action for the world."

Awareness, Analysis, Action

The circle of faith-in-action involves three basic steps. Because true justice reflects the will of God, each step of the circle is guided by faith—in particular, by the Gospels' and the Church's teaching about justice:

1. **Awareness:** Before we can work for justice in the world, we must see, hear, and know the world in a spirit of friendship, just as God does. When we perceive the world from God's point of view, we are better able to recognize the ways it can be made a better place to live.

---

praxis Living according to one's beliefs, not just in private, but in a way that affects the world.

circle of faith-in-action The approach to working toward justice that involves three steps: awareness, analysis, and action.

2. **Analysis:** The next step is to ask: Why is the world the way it is? And how can it be made as good as God intends?

3. **Action:** Once we have answered the questions of analysis, we can act for justice in ways that make life better for everyone.

The action people take for justice will often lead them into a deeper relationship with the world, and thus a deeper awareness of it—especially if they reflect on and pray about their action. Consequently, the process starts all over again on a deeper level; in that way, it is less like a circle than a spiral.

The circle of faith-in-action is just one approach to bringing justice into the world. Many people did not have any plan when they started working for justice—they had only compassion and courage. However, the circle of faith-in-action represents the wisdom these leaders have passed on to us because of their experiences. That wisdom is a useful guide for those who follow in their footsteps.

> *The action people take for justice will often lead them into a deeper relationship with the world, and thus a deeper awareness of it.*

Putting the Circle into Motion for Teens

Every day, three to four hundred people come to a downtown soup kitchen for a hot lunch. That is where the group of teens from Saint Thomas High School volunteered for one year. The students swept, cooked, served food, and sometimes spent time talking or playing cards with the diners. We will follow the experience these students had during their volunteer project to take a deeper look into what faith-in-action looks like in real-life situations.

> What kind of volunteer work have you participated in? What opportunities are available to you through your school?

For Review

1. What should guide those seeking justice, according to the apostolic letter "A Call to Action"?
2. Name the three steps of the circle of faith-in-action, and provide a one-sentence description of each.
3. What might be some advantages of working for justice with other people rather than alone?

Awareness: Friendship with the World

The students at Saint Thomas had certain images and expectations around the sort of people they would be serving. They said they expected the soup kitchen diners would be "dirty," "unstable," "unappreciative," or "crazy." With such expectations, some of the students were naturally a bit afraid of going to the kitchen.

After visiting the soup kitchen for the first time, however, the students' perceptions of the diners changed. The students discovered a group of people genuinely grateful to see them and eager to interact. In fact, the students couldn't wait to come back for the next visit. This raises some questions.

Why did the students initially have a negative image of homeless and hungry people? Why did their first perceptions not accurately reflect who the soup kitchen diners really were?

These questions are important because the way the students approached the problems of hunger and homelessness would have been very different if their visit to the soup kitchen had not caused them to alter their initial perceptions. How we perceive a situation will determine whether and how we will pursue justice in it. That's why justice begins with awareness: seeing, hearing, and knowing the world in a spirit of friendship, as God does.

What are some preconceived ideas you might have about those who are homeless and how they came to be in that situation?

> Who in your life, if anyone, perceives you as you really are? If someone wanted to get to know who you really are, what would be the best way for them to do that?

Do You See What I See?

At the most basic level, being aware involves interpreting the information provided by our senses in a way that gives us an accurate picture of the world. The differences that arise between people because they interpret the same reality in different ways is a constant reminder that we each have our own awareness of the world—we each perceive it and make sense of it in different ways.

The following story about how photographer Jana Taylor teaches poor and orphaned children in Los Angeles to see their world in a new way illustrates that point:

The kids often come from dismal and chaotic surroundings. On the first day of the program, Taylor asked them, "What is beautiful in your home?" The typical response was, "Nothing."

For six weeks, Taylor taught them photography. "The message of my photography and my teaching is that life is good, even though many of the children got off to a shaky start, and goodness is the foundation of everything," Taylor said. By the end of the program, she received a completely different response to her question about what is beautiful. "They told me they found beauty in the way 'light hits the kitchen table,' 'dirt reshapes the pattern on the floor,' and 'birds sing in the trees outside the window.' They saw beauty in simple things."

Jana Taylor helps her students see beauty in the ordinary through the lens of a camera.

Where have you witnessed beauty in the ordinary in the world around you?

"I can see things I never saw before," said Elisa Sanchez, one of the participants. "I also found ugly can be turned into beautiful." Added Rafael Hous: "The camera can help take you beyond what you see in front of you—[to] see beauty in a piece of wood or even the trash." (Based on Daniel B. Wood, "Poor No More")

Worldviews: Guides for Relating to the World

What enabled the photography students to see their world in a new way? Their eyesight didn't change, but they learned a new way of seeing, one based on Jana's belief in the basic goodness of everything. Their story demonstrates an important point: our basic beliefs about the world guide the way we relate to it.

The basic beliefs that guide the way someone relates to the world can be said to be their **worldview**. Someone's worldview might include their responses to basic questions such as these:

- What is most important in life?
- Do all people have the same rights?
- What responsibilities do individuals have to society, and vice versa?

> Think of a room in your house. Write a detailed description of the place from memory. What can you see, hear, smell, or feel? Then go there and spend ten minutes doing nothing but carefully observing it. After you are finished, write down everything you noticed for the first time. What prevented you from noticing these things before?

worldview The basic beliefs that guide the way someone relates to the world.

> What does your own worldview look like? Write down your perspective on each of the worldview questions listed on the previous page and here. Then list any other important beliefs or values that define who you are and how you act.

- Are most people basically good or bad?
- Is there a God, or is life determined by random chance? What is God like?

A particular worldview is made up of the answers someone gives to these and other important questions about life in the world.

At first, the photography students' worldview included the basic belief that nothing in their world was beautiful. Jana Taylor's worldview, on the other hand, included the basic belief that goodness is the foundation of everything. Taylor invited the kids to see through her worldview because she knew that doing so could profoundly change the way they lived. Being able to *see* beauty in their world could enable them to *create* beauty in their lives.

Because our worldview has such a profound effect on the way we relate to one another—and therefore on our approach to justice—it makes sense to understand where our worldviews come from.

Awareness: Friendship with the World 79

Have you had an opportunity to work with homeless people like the students from Saint Thomas High School did? What was your experience like?

Experience

One way we develop our unique worldview is by learning from our experience of the world. For instance, people who grew up in poverty during the Great Depression often value thriftiness and financial security. Similarly, the kids' experiences with Jana Taylor and photography altered their basic perception of the world around them.

It is likely that the first perception the students at the soup kitchen had of hungry and homeless people resulted in part from their experience, or lack of experience, with such people. They may have seen homeless people on the street and assumed that all homeless and hungry people were similar. But their one-on-one experience with the soup kitchen diners provided them with a more realistic picture.

> Describe one of the most significant experiences of your life. How has this experience affected your values and beliefs?

Culture

Personal experience is not the only factor that affects worldviews. Often, our most basic beliefs do not come from our own experience, but from the culture in which we live. **Culture** can be described as all the shared values, beliefs, and ways of relating and living

> Think of some symbols of youth culture. What does each symbol say about young people? How does youth culture affect how young people view the world and justice?

culture The shared values, beliefs, and ways of relating and living together that characterize a particular group of people.

> **Culture shapes worldviews by teaching its members to adopt the beliefs and behaviors of the group.**

Make a list of the five most important values or beliefs of the culture in which you live. After each item, consider whether or not you share the value or belief and why.

together that characterize a particular group of people. A shared culture enables members of a group to work and live with one another with less conflict and misunderstanding.

Each of us belongs to many different groups, so we are influenced by many different cultures. For example, the dominant culture of the United States includes things like the English language, a certain set of laws, belief in the freedom of individuals, the mass media, and a capitalist economy. Within that dominant culture are many subcultures, such as youth culture, which includes young people's clothing, attitudes, social rules, and music. Youth culture can, in turn, be divided into even more subcultures.

Culture shapes worldviews by teaching its members to adopt the beliefs and behaviors of the group. For instance, *peer pressure* is a term often used to describe the pressure young people might feel to change who they are to fit in with the culture of a particular group. But all people, even adults, experience peer pressure. From the time we are children, others in our social group teach us, whether it is intentional or not, what is "normal" for that culture—the ways of thinking and acting that people must follow to fit into the group's culture. At first, it is our families who teach us what is culturally normal. Later, friends, teachers, and the media all push us to adopt the beliefs, values, and practices of the cultures they represent. As we learn these beliefs, values, and practices, consciously or unconsciously, they become part of our worldview.

Blind Spots

Together, experience and culture give us our unique way of relating to the world. Just as sight helps us get around the physical world, our worldview helps us navigate the social world. But just as our sight has its limitations, so does our worldview. Being aware of the limitations of our worldview can help us avoid being blind to injustice.

Jesus often pointed out such blindness: "You blind ones . . ." Jesus said to the scribes and Pharisees, "you hypocrites . . . have neglected the weightier things of the law: justice and mercy and fidelity" (Matthew 23:19–23).

Unfortunately, history is full of examples of people who were blind to injustice. The practice of slavery, for instance, was regarded as normal by most cultures around the world throughout human history. Not all people were blind to the injustice of slavery, but few had the imagination to envision a world in which all would be free. Indeed, many became abolitionists, but those who were willing to take decisive action to end slavery were not as numerous. The poet and essayist Ralph Waldo Emerson was among the strident abolitionists with clear ideas about what must be done. In a speech in 1851, opposing the Fugitive Slave Law, Emerson said, "An immoral law makes it a [person's] duty to break it at every hazard." Yet slavery existed from the founding of the United States of America until the passage of the Thirteenth Amendment in 1865. And the legacy of slavery continues to influence American history through the civil rights movement until the present day.

> **If seemingly well-intentioned people—whole nations, even—can be blind to glaring injustice, then each of us suffers from a certain amount of blindness to injustice too.**

It would be nice to think that had we lived then, we would have known better—that we would have fought the injustice of slavery. But history repeatedly teaches us that otherwise good and intelligent people are capable of being blind to even the gravest injustice.

If seemingly well-intentioned people—whole nations, even—can be blind to glaring injustice, then each of us suffers from a certain amount of blindness to injustice too. What can we do about it? We can do what the blind did in the Gospels: turn to Jesus, who can help us see.

Seeing the World as Jesus Does

Jesus can help us "see" a vision of justice for the world if we view the world from his perspective, in which love, not selfishness, is the most important value. A love-centered worldview relates to the world in a spirit of friendship, a spirit of solidarity. The following are some of the characteristics of that worldview:

- **Seeing, hearing, and knowing with respect.** True friends really want to get to know one another on a deep level, in much the same

What does a love-centered worldview look like to you?

way that God knew the people of Israel before leading them into the Promised Land: "I have *witnessed* the affliction of my people. . . . [I have] *heard* their cry. . . . I *know* well what they are suffering," God told Moses (Exodus 3:7, italics added). People who see through a love-centered worldview enter into solidarity with the world by respectfully seeing, hearing, and knowing it.

- **A vision of abundant life.** True friends want one another to have a good and abundant life. Jesus said, "I came so that they may have life and have it more abundantly" (John 10:10). He brought abundant life by healing the sick, reaching out to those on the margins of society, restoring relationships through forgiveness, and by giving his own life to overcome death. People who see through a love-centered worldview envision the Reign of God—a world in which peace, justice, and goodness bring abundant life to everyone.
- **Compassion.** True friends experience compassion when one of them is suffering, and that compassion moves them to act—just as God entered the world through Jesus to save us from sin.

Seeing, Hearing, and Knowing with Respect

Admittedly, the Saint Thomas students did not go to the soup kitchen with the intention of becoming friends with anyone there—at least not at first. But as they listened to the diners' stories and opened their eyes to who the diners really were, they found it increasingly difficult to lump "the poor" or "the homeless" into one generic group. Instead, the students recognized the diners as individual human beings. They were people's mothers, fathers, sisters, brothers. They were someone's child.

That realization was possible because the students related to the soup kitchen diners with respect. *Respect* is a word that means "to look again." The

> **True friends experience compassion when one of them is suffering, and that compassion moves them to act.**

Everyone, even the homeless and marginalized, is someone's child.

> **Respect acknowledges that the world is good because the world was created from God's own goodness.**

photography students mentioned earlier "looked again" at the world around them, but instead of looking at it in their usual way, they looked for the goodness in it. To see, hear, and know the world with respect is to look beyond outer appearances and first impressions to see the goodness that is the foundation of all God's creation. Respect acknowledges that the world is good because the world was created from God's own goodness.

Although at first they were nervous about getting to know the diners, the students were willing to see, hear, and know the diners' goodness. The students' attitude of respect allowed them to relate to the diners not simply as strangers too poor to feed themselves, but as people with whom they could have a human relationship.

One student's experience demonstrates how mutual respect builds human relationships. He left the kitchen to visit the diners and was invited to play cards. He shared that the small action of showing he cared by his willingness to spend time created a relationship with people. It wasn't about the game they were playing; rather, it was about treating the diners with dignity and respect by showing they had something in common. It meant they were all just people.

Why do you think *respect* means "to look again"? How does looking again or looking deeper help you see and understand someone?

A Vision of Abundant Life

Jesus desires that all people live an abundant life, full of goodness. Many of the Saint Thomas students began to develop a similar vision as their relationship with the people at the soup kitchen deepened. As a result, they became more aware of ways the people were prevented from living full, abundant lives.

"Why am I so fortunate and they aren't?" "What will their future be?" "How can people make plans to better themselves when they don't have enough food to eat?" The student volunteers posed these types of questions regularly.

Jesus' worldview invites us to question what our culture considers to be normal, asking, Is life being lived as abundantly as God intended? The themes of Catholic social teaching are a good guide to the types of questions we can ask to determine whether society fosters a full and good life for all:

- Is all human life being protected and fully supported so that it can thrive? Is everyone's dignity being respected?

- Is everyone able to participate in the life of the community? Are all families being strengthened?

- Are human rights and responsibilities being respected?

Voting is one way to participate in the life of the community.

Catholic Charities USA
Serving Compassion

The National Conference of Catholic Charities (NCCC) was established in 1910, when nearly four hundred people gathered to bring about solidarity among those working in charitable ministries. The Great Depression gave the NCCC the motivation to call on the government to provide relief and pass legislation to protect economic security, safe labor conditions, and public housing. Eventually, the NCCC would take the name Catholic Charities USA to have a stronger advocacy voice. Almost immediately, they were tasked with coordinating domestic disaster response efforts on behalf of the Catholic Church in the US. The priorities of Catholic Charities USA today include affordable housing, immigration advocacy and refugee services, mental and physical health care, food assistance and nutrition programs, advocacy and social policy initiatives, disaster relief, as well as Catholic identity and ministry resources.

- Do all people have good work that respects their dignity and provides them with a good life?
- Are the care and protection of poor, vulnerable, and marginalized people a top priority for society?
- Is the integrity of God's creation being respected and protected?

The students found that for many of the soup kitchen diners, the answer to these questions was often no. The student volunteers identified that an inequity existed—a wrong that needed to be set right. The diners at the soup kitchen were struggling just to survive. To live life to their full potential, the diners needed to be able to thrive.

Compassion

Friendship can be risky because it implies sharing not only the friend's joy but the friend's pain as well. Relating to the world through a love-centered worldview is like that. If you have ever had a friend who was in trouble, then you know that the problem was not just your friend's; to a certain extent, it was your problem too. If you were moved to help your friend, then you experienced compassion.

Compassion isn't always a comfortable emotion. But Christians are called to follow Jesus and share in his ministry of compassion and healing to others, even when to do otherwise might seem to be the easier path. Because the Saint Thomas students had developed a relationship of solidarity with the diners,

© Catholic Charities USA

compassion led them to be deeply dissatisfied with the situation the diners' faced. But it also prompted them to take action to change the situation.

Compassion led the students to question the underlying causes of the situation faced by poor people. This questioning is critical, as it often reveals what actions need to be taken for justice.

For Review

1. Define the term *worldview*.
2. Explain how experience and culture shape a person's worldview.
3. How can we avoid being blind to injustice?
4. Describe the characteristics of a love-centered worldview.
5. How can we become more aware of where we are being called to do justice?

Analysis: Asking Why

If we truly care about the world and its people, then eventually we will ask, "Why are so many people unable to live out their human dignity as fully as God intended?" We already know that injustice doesn't "just happen," nor does it come from God. Rather, people continue to promote injustice whenever they choose to seek their own self-interest at the expense of the good of others. Injustice is the result of human choices. That insight allows us to focus the question more narrowly: What human choices cause injustice, and what do people need to do to promote justice?

These are powerful questions with the potential to reveal not only the root causes of injustice but a vision of justice worth working toward. These questions are the beginning of **social analysis**, which is the process of understanding how people's lives are affected by the relationships that shape the society in which they live.

The Art of Asking Questions

The students of Saint Thomas High School had questions once they began their volunteer experience. They wanted to understand who or what was responsible for homelessness and hunger. This very question sparked their analysis of the problem of homelessness and hunger. Questions are perhaps the most important tool of social analysis. When we ask questions, we are acknowledging that we do not know enough about a problem to solve it. And that allows us to consider the problem at a deeper level, where we might find ways to pursue justice that we had not thought of before.

The type of questions we ask about a problem will determine the sort of answers we get. Good questions are based on a love-centered awareness of the world. For instance, several students answered the question of responsibility for homelessness by focusing on the responsibilities of the poor. Personal responsibility is an important building block of justice. But because they related to the diners in the soup kitchen in a spirit of respect, many of the students took a deeper look at the problem and realized that the causes of homelessness and hunger are more numerous and complex than simply a lack of responsibility on the part of the poor. That awareness led them to ask more questions.

As the students continued to analyze the problem of homelessness and hunger over the course of the year, one question led to another. Soon they

---

social analysis The process of understanding how people's lives are affected by the relationships that shape the society in which they live.

The problem of homelessness and hunger involves a wide range of issues.

were considering a wide range of issues: unemployment, business ethics, government, the criminal-justice system, discrimination, education, drugs, affordable housing, the minimum wage, and teen pregnancy, to name a few. The fact that all these issues are somehow related to the problem of homelessness and hunger might seem surprising, but it reveals an important reality: our world is one of interdependent relationships.

Finding the way to justice requires identifying the relationships that make it possible—as well as those that prevent it.

> **Finding the way to justice requires identifying the relationships that make it possible—as well as those that prevent it.**

A World of Relationships

Independence is a prime value of our culture—and one that is necessary for human dignity. But sometimes the emphasis our culture places on independence blinds us to the reality that human beings do not and cannot live in complete independence from one another. Rather, all creation is **interdependent**: we depend on one another for our existence.

Almost anything we do is possible only because of our life-giving relationships with other people and creation. Just think of all the relationships that make your life what it is: relationships with parents, siblings, friends, and teachers come to mind immediately. But your life is affected by thousands of other people as well, even if your relationship with them is not so personal. Think of the hundreds of people involved in bringing you the clothes you wear, for instance, or the water from your faucets or the food you eat.

Moreover, the people who shape your life are themselves affected by their relationships with other people. Our lives are shaped by an intricate web of relationships that connect us, directly or indirectly, to millions of other people.

> Take a few minutes to engage in a social analysis of your own relationships. How are they affected by the community or society you live in? What would the outcome be if you were more intentional about your relationships?

interdependent The state of things or people depending on one another.

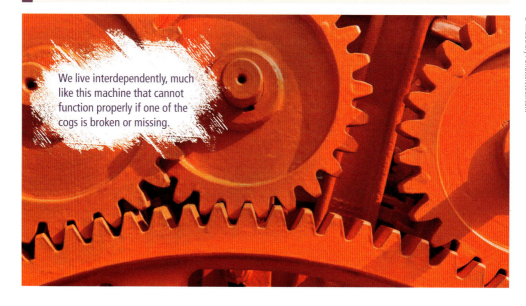

We live interdependently, much like this machine that cannot function properly if one of the cogs is broken or missing.

The Relationship Map: A Blueprint for Justice

Justice itself is made possible by many interdependent, life-giving relationships. When those relationships do not exist, or when instead of giving life they suppress or harm life, then injustice results.

To build justice, we need to ask, What life-giving relationships are necessary to make justice happen? Let's analyze the injustice of hunger as an example. We can begin with the very basic question, What is necessary for people to be well fed every day?

The most basic answer is food. Obviously, the next question is, Where can people get food? Again, the answers are simple: people can get food from their family, from a food shelf or soup kitchen, from a store, or, in a limited way, from a garden.

If a food shelf or soup kitchen is not available, people need money to buy food. How do people get money? The government's food stamp program is one source; family members might be another. But most people prefer to get their income from a good job.

Our analysis continues by asking, What do people need in order to get jobs? Here's where the student volunteers found that the seemingly simple issue of

> **Justice itself is made possible by many interdependent, life-giving relationships.**

What is the average cost of childcare in your city? What do parents of young children do for childcare when they work in the evenings or overnight?

Imagine that you are homeless and hungry and have no money. How would you find food? If possible, check around the community by calling or visiting the places you think would be most likely to provide you with food.

homelessness and hunger suddenly got more complicated. Many things are needed to get a job: transportation to work, a home, job training, childcare (if the person is a parent), nearby job openings that pay a living wage, and food.

We could take our analysis even deeper by continuing the questioning process: How do people get transportation, shelter, job training, childcare, and food—especially when they don't have money? What happens if an area lacks good job openings? Our questions have begun to reveal that getting enough food every day is not as simple as it might seem—not for those people who lack the basic life-giving relationships that most of us take for granted. Those who are poor struggle with these questions daily, as do those who, in solidarity, try to help them.

This analysis of how people's lives are affected by the various relationships that shape society is an example of a **relationship map**; just as a road map shows the connections between places, a relationship map

relationship map A map showing the connections between people that shape our society.

shows the connections between people that shape our society. Of course, our analysis of what people need to be well fed is limited. More questions would provide a deeper and more detailed analysis. But even at this basic level, a relationship map can provide us with a vision of what justice for the hungry might look like.

Social Structures

Society is shaped by the quality of its relationships and the way they fit together. The patterns of relationships that shape any society are known as **social structures**. The relationship map we just envisioned shows part of the social structure that enables most of us to eat every day. Government, business, labor, education, families, law—all these are social structures too, because their existence is sustained and shaped by the relationships among them.

We usually take the relationships that structure our world for granted. For example, our earlier analysis of homelessness and hunger does not consider the basic structures of production and distribution that make food readily available—the natural environment, transportation networks, processing factories, farms, and so on. But these structures are what keep people from going hungry. It is because some of these basic structures are broken that close to 800 million people globally, many of them children,

Cycle of Poverty

The cycle of poverty is created by broken social structures. Poor health and living conditions lead to a lack of education or education at a school that doesn't have much funding or resources. Lack of education creates a lack of opportunities. When you are not well educated, many doors of decent-paying jobs with insurance and benefits are closed. Lack of opportunity leads to low income. When you lack disposable income, new clothes and shoes, groceries in the cupboard and refrigerator, and housing in a safe neighborhood seem out of reach.

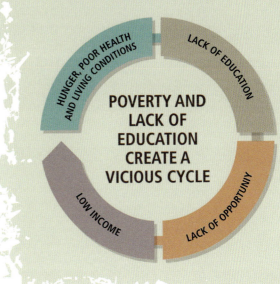

POVERTY AND LACK OF EDUCATION CREATE A VICIOUS CYCLE

---

social structures The patterns of relationships that shape any society.

Structures of sin lead to generations being born into poverty.

suffer from chronic hunger. The structure of our social relationships influences a great deal in our world: who is rich and who is poor, who is included and who is left out, even who lives and who dies.

Building or Blocking Justice?

People often view social structures as permanent. Confronted by images of hungry children, they might be tempted to say, "That's just the way things are." However, the structures that shape society are not inevitable. They are the result of the decisions that people make every day.

Each of the relationships that contributes to justice for the hungry, for example, is made possible by individual decisions. Individual decisions also contribute to the social structures that block justice, which the Church calls **structures of sin**. Structures of sin can be identified by asking, What are the barriers to life-giving relationships? In the relationship map about hunger, the barriers that prevent people from having good jobs, a good education, shelter, affordable childcare, supportive families, and so on, are the structures of sin that cause the poverty that leads to hunger.

> What are the barriers to life-giving relationships in your life? What happens when you intentionally try to work on your relationships rather than carelessly interacting with those around you?

structures of sin The effects of personal sin over time, which can affect social structures and institutions.

The social structures that lead to injustice are not shaped by chance. They do not "just happen." People have the power to build the structures that shape their world. It is how people choose to use that power that determines whether those structures promote justice or injustice.

Power: Shaping Our World

Human **power** is the God-given ability everyone has to affect their own life, the lives of others, and the world around them—including its social structures—in either positive or negative ways. Power builds relationships.

All people have power because all people can cause change, at least on some level, although some people have more power than others. To say that power is God-given means that the ultimate source of all power is God. But not all people agree with this perspective. Often, people view human beings as the source of all power. Each of these perspectives has important implications for how people choose to use power.

Power-over

The belief that human beings are the source of their own power is reflective of the belief that people get power by working to acquire it. Think about limited resources like oil or electricity. Those who acquire power may believe they "own" it and have "earned" the right to use it for any purpose, even at the expense of others. Moreover, if power is something that can be acquired, then it also can be taken away, and that would mean it needs to be defended from others.

This is known as a **power-over worldview**. Dr. Seuss cleverly depicts this worldview in his book *Yertle the Turtle*. Yertle, king of the turtles, believes he rules all that he can see. To see farther—and therefore

> **People have the power to build the structures that shape their world.**

---

power The God-given ability everyone has to affect their own life, the lives of others, and the world around them—including its social structures—in either positive or negative ways.

power-over worldview An outlook in which power is seen as something acquired to be used for any purpose, even at the expense of others.

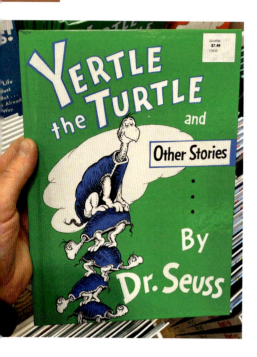

increase the extent of his rule—he commands the turtles to form a tall stack by standing on one another's backs. Yertle then makes his throne at the top of the stack, from where he can rule over an even greater expanse of land. In the worldview reflected by Yertle's attitude, power is gained at the expense of others. Only one person can sit at the top of the stack, while everyone else must remain below.

Such power is often acquired at the expense of the needs of those who are poor and vulnerable. The result is a structure of sin that fosters injustice. In Seuss's story, the turtles at the bottom of the pile experience pain and hunger from bearing the weight of all the turtles above them.

Ironically, those who abuse their power harm not only those at the bottom of the pile but themselves as well. The oppressed may live in fear of the powerful, but the powerful also live in fear that the oppressed may take away their power. The division the powerful create between themselves and those they dominate deprives both sides of the solidarity or friendship that would otherwise allow them to experience each other's gifts and insights.

Power-with

A love-centered worldview, in contrast to the power-over perspective, understands that God is the source of all power. Therefore, our power—our ability to affect the world around us—is not something we own, but something God has given us to use for the good of the world and ourselves.

According to this worldview, everyone has God-given power, and because we live in an interdependent world, that power is meant to be shared in relationship with others. This is called the **power-with worldview** because it sees power as something to be used with and for others to bring about the good of everyone.

A power-with worldview does not deny that some people might exercise more power than others. For

> **Everyone has God-given power, and because we live in an interdependent world, that power is meant to be shared in relationship with others.**

---

power-with worldview An outlook in which power is seen as something to be used with and for others to bring about the good of everyone.

Do you think striking is an effective tool for improving working conditions?

example, business leaders often have a greater ability to affect society than do low-level employees, and dictators have more power than their subjects. But the extra power these people have is not their own; it comes from others.

Similarly, people who rely on the support of others for their power—such as the business owner—would lose much of their power without that support. For instance, the business owner gets power from customers and employees. If the customers stopped paying for the company's products, the business owner would lose the economic power they received from the customers. This is what happens during a **boycott**. And when employees refuse to work for their employer during a **strike**, the employer loses the physical and mental power gained from their work.

It is not necessarily bad for some people to have more power than others. In democratic countries, people elect leaders who have more political power than ordinary citizens do because it would be impractical for all political decisions to be made by the entire

boycott The practice of refusing to support something, such as a person, a store, or an organization, to express disapproval and create pressure for change.

strike An organized work stoppage whereby workers refuse to work in order to gain public support and to pressure their employer to address their rights.

population. However, leaders who have a power-with worldview know that their extra power comes from the people, and that they are called to use it with and for the people.

Power for Justice

Eventually, the students of Saint Thomas wanted to go beyond asking why? Soon they were asking, "What can we do to make life better for hungry and homeless people?" But perhaps even more important, they wondered whether they, as high school students, had enough power to do anything. The students raised good questions, such as: "Just how much power does any one person—especially a young person—have to change injustice?"

The Catholic Church believes that God is the source of our power to do justice. When people open themselves to the grace of the Holy Spirit and share their power in solidarity with others, their combined power to bring justice into the world is great. Shared power strengthens relationships among people rather than causing divisions among them—and it is the key to transforming structures of sin.

Together, we *do* have the power to change the world. But we need to understand the best way to use that power to act for justice.

> **Together, we *do* have the power to change the world.**

Do teenagers have the power to work for justice? Use a specific example to support your response.

If a problem seems overwhelming for you, remember that when people band together to pool their energy, change is possible.

For Review

1. Explain what it means to say that "all creation is interdependent."
2. What does a relationship map show?
3. What is a social structure?
4. Explain the difference between the power-over and power-with worldviews.

Action: Bringing Life to the World

Once the process of social analysis reveals the individual choices and social structures that cause injustice in a particular situation, the next step in the circle of faith-in-action is to change the situation in a way that allows all people involved to experience the good life that the Creator planned for them. This is action.

As the students from Saint Thomas who volunteered at the soup kitchen recognized though, acting for justice is not easy. You might think, "I'm only one person, and the world is huge!" Many people—especially those who benefit from unjust social structures—often actively resist any change to those structures. In a big, often hostile world, how does one start taking action for justice?

Opportunities for Action

Let's review how the circle of faith-in-action brings us to the point of acting for justice. In the first step of the circle, relating to the world in a spirit of solidarity makes us aware of the reality the world faces. In the second step, analysis provides a vision of what justice for the world might look like. In the third step, we can compare the reality to our vision of justice by asking, What relationships need to be built, and what structures of sin need to be transformed for the reality of the world to become more like the Kingdom of God?

Let's return to the problem of hunger for the diners at the soup kitchen as an example. Examining their reality revealed where action was needed to build life-giving relationships or to transform structures of sin so that people might no longer go hungry. The students found that unemployment, low-wage jobs, homelessness, and a lack of family or community support were among the barriers to justice the soup kitchen diners faced.

Consider some of the following actions that might help the hungry overcome those barriers:

- By volunteering at the soup kitchen, the students created life-giving relationships that helped to overcome the diners' lack of money or family support.
- Supporting job training programs or minimum-wage laws would be two ways to overcome the barriers of unemployment and jobs that don't pay enough to cover both rent and food.
- Recognizing the relationship between hunger and homelessness, some students participated in a demonstration demanding more federal support for affordable housing.

These are just a few possibilities. The opportunities to create life-giving relationships that build justice are limited by our imagination only.

Direct Action and Social Action

Given all these choices for action, you might wonder which is best. For some people, the best action might be that which involves the least work or expense. In a love-centered worldview, however, the best course of action is the one that is the most life-giving for all the people involved in the situation.

We can divide all the opportunities to act for justice into two categories:

- **Direct action** occurs on the level of individual relationships and is usually aimed at meeting an immediate need. The students' volunteer work at the soup kitchen would be an example of direct action.

> *The best course of action is the one that is the most life-giving for all the people involved in the situation.*

direct action Action that occurs on the level of individual relationships and is usually aimed at meeting an immediate need.

social action Action that attempts to change the behavior of society and its institutions in a way that promotes justice.

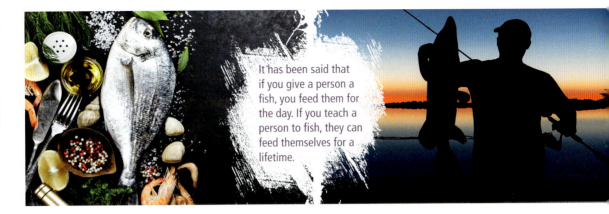

It has been said that if you give a person a fish, you feed them for the day. If you teach a person to fish, they can feed themselves for a lifetime.

- **Social action** occurs on the level of social structures. Social action attempts to change the behavior of society and its institutions in a way that promotes justice. The students' attempts to influence federal policy on affordable housing would be an example of social action.

The Two Feet of Justice

Often, the approach that will allow poor and marginalized people to truly live out their human dignity involves both direct action and social action. Without one or the other, efforts to change injustice may fall short. For example, if the students did not provide food at the soup kitchen (direct action), hundreds of people would have gone hungry. Distributing meals met a real need—satisfying the diners' immediate hunger.

On the other hand, the students clearly recognized that direct action alone was not sufficient to bring the soup kitchen diners the full and abundant lives they deserved. Creating full and lasting justice for all those who go hungry requires action to change the social structures that cause chronic hunger in the first place.

So both direct action and social action are needed to address the injustice of hunger. Direct action is needed to satisfy people's hunger today; social action is needed so that people will not become hungry tomorrow. Because direct action and social action work together to move justice forward, they are often called the two feet of justice.

> **The approach that will allow poor and marginalized people to truly live out their human dignity involves both direct action and social action.**

Adapted from USCCB, *Poverty and Faith Justice*

Create a list of at least three direct actions and three social actions that teens can take to address needs and promote justice.

Action: Always for Human Life and Dignity

The life and dignity of human beings is the foundation of justice, so the goal of any action for justice is always to protect and promote human life and dignity. This basic goal has certain implications for the ways we act for justice. It implies acting in solidarity with those who experience injustice, but it also means confronting those who promote injustice with love rather than hostility.

Acting in Solidarity

What does it mean to act in solidarity? Recall that solidarity is like friendship—it is an ongoing commitment to the good of others. A clear example that illustrates the difference between action that respects the dignity of those who are poor and action that does not is Project Five-Two.

Project Five-Two—named after the Gospel story of the multiplication of the five loaves and two fish—was

Project Five-Two helps families provide for others in their community while they need assistance.

formed in communities in Brazil. When unemployment and poverty were at an all-time high, groups of five employed families adopted two unemployed families and provided them with basic food items—beans, rice, and eggs. This direct action sustained the unemployed families while they looked for work. When they found work, they then shared food with others.

But Project Five-Two didn't stop there. It also encouraged the unemployed people to unite and prayerfully examine the underlying causes of their situation, find solutions, and take social action. Some of the solutions they enacted were to urge lawmakers to pass legislation to ensure unemployment benefits. This aspect of Project Five-Two was crucial because the problem was one that involved social structures and couldn't be solved by food charity alone.

When a popular TV show host heard about the project and shared the story on air, positive attention came to the community in the form of food donations. However, the Project Five-Two community politely refused the food collected as a result of this publicity. Representatives were concerned that people thought the only situation that needed to change was a food shortage when what was really needed were jobs and other policy changes so that people could feed themselves. The organization wanted to stay true to its mission of raising people's consciousness about the need to change faulty social structures. Its purpose was larger than acting as a social aid fund. Of course, food assistance could temporarily relieve the effects of unjust social structures, and the donations to Project Five-Two were offered with good intent. But food donations didn't get to the root causes of the larger issue. The Project Five-Two community knew that changing social structures was the only way to bring about lasting change.

> **Solidarity, on the other hand, acknowledges the interdependence of human relationships.**

Solidarity: Partnership and Commitment

Why would the project leaders reject the help? From their point of view, the action of only securing food donations did not reflect a desire to enter into solidarity with poor people. Real friendship is a two-way street in which both sides benefit. A true friend doesn't act as if they are doing the other person a favor by offering their friendship or help.

Solidarity, on the other hand, acknowledges the interdependence of human relationships. Poor people may depend on rich people for assistance, but the economic power of rich people comes in part from poor people. The interdependent nature of relationships means that when poor and oppressed people are helped, ultimately all people benefit, including rich and powerful people. Rather than viewing assistance for poor people as an optional favor, solidarity says: "We're in this together. Your grief is my grief, your joy is my joy."

In rejecting the aid, the project leaders were calling the donors to make a fundamental change in the way they related to poor people: to go beyond a superficial relationship and enter a life-giving relationship of mutual respect. They were calling for a basic change in social structures.

> Make a pros and cons list of the consequences of refusing the food donations. Brainstorm a way for the Five-Two Project to accept the donations and still try to get their message out.

Solidarity says, "your grief is my grief, and your joy is my joy."

Acting in Love

Solidarity is the key to overcoming unjust social structures. But remember that those structures don't just happen; they are the result of human choices, whether these choices are intentional or not. Attempts to change unjust social structures are often met with economic, political, or even violent resistance from those who benefit from them. How should those who work for justice respond to such resistance?

One option would be to take a power-over approach: terrorists, for example, use fear and violence to bring about social change. But the Christian justice tradition takes a power-with approach. That approach is grounded in the belief that as Jesus announced, "The kingdom of God is among you" (Luke 17:21). God's love has already begun to overcome sin and injustice through Christ. God's love, not violence, is the source of all power. Although the human instinct is to fight one's enemies to defeat them, the way of Jesus is to love one's enemies in a way that brings them into God's Reign.

"Love Your Enemies"

The commandment to love one's enemies has long been considered one of the most challenging aspects of the Gospel. Much of this teaching is collected in the Sermon on the Mount (see Matthew 5:1–7:29 or Luke 6:20–49). You are probably familiar with the following passage:

Cycle of Poverty

A person who took seriously Jesus' instruction to love the enemy was the Hindu spiritual leader Mohandas Karamchand Gandhi (1869–1948). His approach to loving the enemy has been imitated by many others since then, including the leaders of the US civil rights movement.

Gandhi believed that all aspects of life should be guided by the principle that nothing is more important than respect for human life and dignity. That principle had two important implications for how people ought to live, Gandhi said. At a minimum, it meant living nonviolently—never harming the life or dignity of another person—not even hating an unjust enemy.

Gandhi also thought people should respect human life and dignity by refusing to cooperate with anything that harms it. Injustice doesn't just happen; it arises from the ways people choose to use their power. Gandhi believed that if enough people refuse to cooperate with injustice, it will not have the power to exist.

Gandhi's approach, often called **nonviolent noncooperation**, led him to organize strikes, boycotts, and acts of **civil disobedience**—intentionally breaking laws that are unjust—during India's long struggle against British rule. Ultimately, India won its freedom, largely without using violence against the British.

---

nonviolent noncooperation A way to respect life and dignity by refusing to cooperate with anything that harms it.

civil disobedience Intentionally breaking laws that are unjust.

> Think about who your "enemy" is—perhaps someone you don't like or have been hurt by. Without naming the person, brainstorm a list of actions you could take that would be good for them. Then consider whether you would be willing to take any of those actions. If so, how might "loving your enemy" change the two of you? If not, what would need to change before you could take any of the actions?

"You have heard that it was said, 'You shall love your neighbor and hate your enemy.' But I say to you, love your enemies, and pray for those who persecute you, that you may be children of your heavenly Father." (Matthew 5:43–45)

Here is another way of stating Jesus' message: In the world created by humans, it is ordinary to love our friends and family while shunning our enemies. But the world that Christ has opened for us—the Kingdom of God—is different. Everyone is invited into the Kingdom, even people we don't like. God's grace is offered to all people, regardless of whether they are just or unjust.

Is Jesus suggesting that we must accept and even encourage injustice, or "be nice" to those who harm others? The Gospels provide a clear answer. We need not choose between justice and love; rather, like Jesus, we can be committed to both. Throughout the Gospels, Jesus' commitment to the truth of his Father's love for all people leads him consistently and boldly to challenge injustice whenever he encounters it.

Challenging injustice is not inconsistent with loving those who are responsible for that injustice. Love is not always the same as "being nice." For example, taking the car keys away from a drunk friend would be a better way of loving them than avoiding a confrontation by letting them drive drunk, because taking away the keys could save their life. Similarly, when an enemy is challenged in love, the goal is not to defeat them or have power over them; rather, the goal of action based in love is to restore the enemy's relationships—with their own dignity, with other people, and with God.

For Review

1. Explain the difference between direct action and social action. Why are both necessary for justice?
2. What does it mean to act for justice in solidarity?
3. How does action based in love confront those who promote injustice?

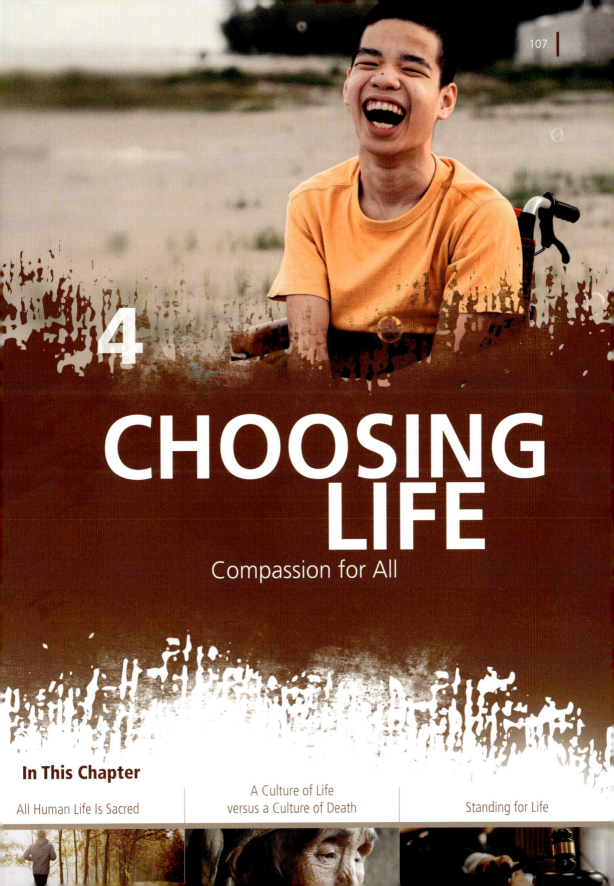

4

CHOOSING LIFE

Compassion for All

In This Chapter

All Human Life Is Sacred | A Culture of Life versus a Culture of Death | Standing for Life

All Human Life Is Sacred

During her freshman year of college, Mary started dating a boy from her history class. They had a lot in common and started studying together and making regular weekend plans. One night they had sex. Neither of them had planned for it, and even though Mary tried not to think about it, she was worried that she might get pregnant. The week before Christmas break, she got sick and went to the campus health center. The nurse asked her a few questions and ran a few tests. Ten minutes later she came into the exam room and bluntly said: "You aren't sick. You're pregnant. You have some choices, but you will have to make them quickly. Having a baby will change everything. You can have an abortion, but if you do, it will need to be soon." Abortion? Mary was still trying to wrap her mind around the word *pregnant!*

A seven-year-old girl was kidnapped while she slept in a tent with her siblings during a family camping trip. She was held captive for a week before she was killed. When they found the man responsible, the girl's parents were overcome with rage. Her mother said: "I would have killed him myself if we had been in the same room. Knowing the fear and pain our daughter endured was all-consuming. I could think of nothing else." The girl's parents deeply felt the need for justice, but was the death penalty the answer?

Bryce was a healthy, active young man who had just gotten married and was training for a half-marathon. One morning, while preparing to go for a run, he felt dizzy, and his vision was blurred. His wife drove him to the hospital, and what had begun as a normal morning had become a terrible nightmare. Bryce had a brain tumor. It was cancerous and aggressive. The doctor was blunt—Bryce had only months to live. Each day he would become weaker, eventually unable to see or walk or feed himself. While his wife talked with the doctors and his parents, Bryce felt the room closing in around him. This couldn't be the way his life would end. He envisioned spending some cherished time with his family before going to one of several places where he could legally be prescribed medications that would end his life. But was this the best choice? Is it okay to actively seek an early death to avoid inevitable challenges and suffering? What might be the reasons Bryce should choose life even under these difficult circumstances?

> Choose one of these three scenarios, and consider how you might respond. What is the main motivation in your decision about how to handle the situation?

> Think about a time you had to make a moral decision. What was your motivation for the decision you made—fear? vengeance? anger? concern for others? love? Did your community or environment impact your decision-making?

Each of the preceding situations present some key moral questions: Is abortion ever okay? Is it right to see the death penalty as a form of justice? Is ending one's life of suffering a good choice? The Catholic Church applies its social teaching to these and all issues of life and provides solid guidance for our response.

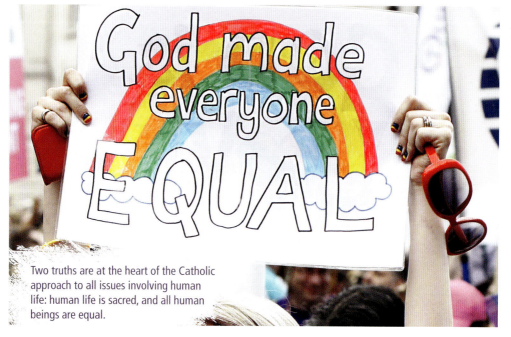

Two truths are at the heart of the Catholic approach to all issues involving human life: human life is sacred, and all human beings are equal.

A Consistent Life Ethic

Issues of life involve some extremely difficult situations, and these difficult situations cannot be dismissed or ignored. Christians are called to have compassion for *all people*—including those who are not yet born, those with disabilities, those who have little education or who live in poverty, those who are elderly or ill, and those who are guilty of crimes. Two convictions— that human life is sacred and that all human beings are equal—lie at the heart of the Catholic approach to issues involving human life.

Human life is sacred. Each human life is **sacred** because it comes from God, it is always loved by God, and it is meant to return to God. "God alone is the Lord of life from its beginning until its end" (*CCC*, 2258). Respect for the sacredness of human life and respect for human dignity are closely linked, as this passage from *The Church in the Modern World* indicates:

> Each human life is sacred because it comes from God, it is always loved by God, and it is meant to return to God.

---

sacred A place, object, or person that is considered holy because it is dedicated to God or set aside for religious purposes.

Whatever is opposed to life itself, such as any type of murder, genocide, abortion, euthanasia, or willful self-destruction . . . whatever insults human dignity, such as subhuman living conditions, arbitrary imprisonment, deportation, slavery, prostitution, the selling of women and children; as well as disgraceful working conditions, where [people] are treated as mere instruments of gain, rather than as free and responsible persons; all these things and others of their like are infamies indeed. They poison human society, but they do more harm to those who practice them than [to] those who suffer from the injury. (27)

> What do you think the Church means when it says these actions "do more harm to those who practice them than to those who suffer from the injury"?

All human beings are equal. Because all people are created in the image of God, all people have equal dignity and an equal claim to fundamental human rights (adapted from *The Church in the Modern World*, 29). That all people have equal dignity and an equal right to life is the foundation of Christian justice and the Catholic social teaching principle called the life and dignity of the human person.

Whenever society decides that one person or group is less human than another, or not human at all, it suggests that human dignity is not given by God but depends on the judgment of others. Once society accepts that notion, all people, especially those with less power, become vulnerable.

Therefore, protecting the life and dignity of any person or group requires that we protect the life and dignity of all people. Cardinal Joseph Bernardin of Chicago (1928–1996) called this the **consistent ethic of life**. It is also called the **seamless garment**, after Jesus' seamless tunic in John's Gospel account of the Crucifixion. The soldiers could not divide the tunic

---

consistent ethic of life A system of pro-life principles claiming that protecting the life and dignity of any person or group requires that we protect the life and dignity of all people.

seamless garment Another name for the consistent ethic of life, taken from the image of Jesus' tunic in the Gospel of John, which refers to the ethical, religious, and political threads of moral issues that are unified in one vision.

> **The right to life is the most important human right because all other rights depend on it.**

among themselves by tearing it apart because it was made of a whole cloth, and ripping it would have ruined it. The Church's teaching is a consistent whole (like the seamless garment) in which the ethical, religious, and political threads of moral issues are unified in one vision.

The right to life is the most important human right because all other rights depend on it. That right is most threatened by violence. But it is also threatened by *anything* that undermines it. Like the seamless garment that cannot be torn apart, Bernardin argued that we cannot "tear apart" the issues of abortion, poverty,

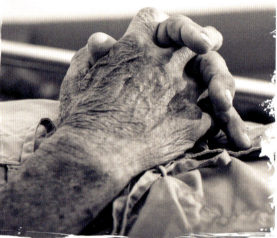

the death penalty, human trafficking, racism, war, and anything else that affects human life and dignity:

> If one contends, as we do, that the right of every fetus to be born should be protected, . . . then our moral, political, and economic responsibilities do not stop at the moment of birth. Those who defend the right to life of the weakest among us must be equally visible in support of the quality of life of the powerless among us: the old and the young, the hungry and the homeless, the undocumented immigrant and the unemployed worker. . . . Consistency means we cannot have it both ways. We cannot urge a compassionate society and vigorous public policy to protect the lives of the unborn and then argue that compassion and significant public programs on behalf of the needy undermine the moral fiber of the society or are beyond the proper scope of governmental responsibility. ("Cardinal Bernardin's Call for a Consistent Ethic of Life")

Cardinal Bernardin brought the interconnectedness of all life and dignity issues into sharp focus. The seamless garment represents consistency. If we value life, we must support it at every turn. The consistent ethic of life suggests that far from being in competition with one another, the well-being of each person and the well-being of all people are really interrelated.

Catholic Guardian Services

Catholic Guardian Services (CGS) is a multiservice organization that functions under the umbrella of Catholic Charities of the Archdiocese of New York. CGS addresses the fundamental needs of families that are disadvantaged, underserved, and impoverished, as well as people with special needs. As a member of Catholic Charities, CGS values all life. The focus of CGS is the family as the main unit of society, and a preferential option for the poor. CGS runs the Parenting Resource Center. The goal of the Parenting Resource Center is to improve maternal and child health. The Parenting Resource Center conducts in-home visits and offers maternity classes on breastfeeding, budgeting, and developmental milestones. The center also provides support groups. The goal is to prevent families from being in crisis and support them when they do experience crisis.

In keeping with the principle of valuing the life and dignity of all people, CGS provides foster care and child welfare services, family support services, and disability services. CGS also sponsors an unaccompanied minors' program for children immigrating from Central and South America. Many of these minors are sent to the US by their families to escape abuse in the form of human trafficking, gang violence, and forced labor. CGS shelters many of these children in home-type residences where they have access to health care, education, trauma counseling, and all necessities. They offer pro bono (free) legal representation to try to reunite families if possible and provide transitional homes during the process.

For Review

1. What is the term first used by Cardinal Bernardin to explain why protecting the life and dignity of any person or group requires that we protect the life and dignity of all people?
2. What two convictions lie at the heart of the Catholic approach to issues involving human life?
3. Name several of the right-to-life issues that affect human life and dignity according to the Catholic Church's teaching.

A Culture of Life versus a Culture of Death

For most people, choosing life over death might appear to be the obvious choice, but the widespread practice of all types of killing, legal and illegal, and the oppression of others suggests that the choice is not as simple as it might seem. What does it mean to "choose life"?

In his 1995 encyclical "The Gospel of Life" ("Evangelium Vitae"), Pope Saint John Paul II identifies the ways two different cultures answer that question. Each culture bases its answer on a different understanding of what it means to be fully alive.

- One culture says we are fully alive when we have what we want.
- The other culture says we are fully alive when we are true to who we are.

Examining these different worldviews can help us better understand the way our society approaches a wide range of justice issues.

The Culture of Death: We Are What We Have

From the perspective of the first worldview, "choosing life" would appear to be the main message of US culture. Advertisements for soft drinks, beer, shoes, and cars urge us to live life to the fullest—a life of excitement, luxury, and convenience. We are told we should have what we want because we deserve it. The way to live this abundant life is by buying the products being advertised.

According to this worldview, we are what we have. The more we have—in terms of possessions, abilities, good

A Culture of Life versus a Culture of Death

Where do you see the message "having an abundant life means having nice things"?

looks, or power—the more fully human we are. So when we start out in life, we are "less human" because all we "have" is our body, and not much of a body at that. A body or mind "flawed" by physical or mental disabilities is considered less human still. In this worldview, the soul is not part of what it means to be human because new life is only the result of a biological process, not a gift from God.

If we are what we have, then being fully alive means having what we want—not just in terms of material items but also in terms of doing what we want. In this view, the basis of human rights is not the sacredness of life and the dignity of the human person, but the ability of people to get what they want.

This worldview is called the **culture of death** because the culture views human life as separate from God, who is its source. It is a worldview that leads to death for those who are considered less valuable.

- The culture of death claims that it is the right of people to have more than they need, even as poverty causes death for other people.

> If we are what we have, then being fully alive means having what we want—not just in terms of material items but also in terms of doing what we want.

culture of death A worldview that fails to respect and protect human life in all its stages.

> In a culture of death, those who cause a burden to others are thought of as having less worth. Other than the unborn, who would be considered "less worthy" of living? What is the danger in this way of thinking?

- It views people who cause a burden to others as less worthy of life.
- It views the quality of a life as the only measure of whether it is worth living. As a result, the intentional killing of someone whose life is deemed to be no longer worth living—called euthanasia—is preferred over a natural death that may involve suffering.

It is *not* wrong to have things or to want an enjoyable life. Wanting a better life becomes a problem only when it is viewed as the *only* goal of life. In the Christian view, choosing life is about much more—it is about choosing love.

All Human Beings Have Worth

Pope Francis has spoken bluntly about the deconstruction of our societal values and how that is reflected in our policies and practices. Think of life issues such as abortion, stem-cell research, capital punishment, euthanasia, and suicide, as well as human trafficking, access to adequate health care and education, oppression of civil rights, and equality for all races, genders, ages, income levels, and abilities. Pope Francis challenges modern societies that often lack respect for the life and dignity of all human beings in these areas and points out the marks of a culture of death. "[Ultimately,] persons are no longer seen as a paramount value to be cared for and respected, especially when poor and disabled, 'not yet useful'—like the unborn, or 'no longer needed'—like the elderly" ("Address to the Diplomatic Corps").

This mindset, that human beings are dispensable, takes many forms:

> This way of discarding others can take a variety of forms, such as an obsession with reducing labour costs with no concern for its grave consequences . . . a readiness to discard others finds expression in vicious attitudes that we thought long past, such as racism, which retreats underground only to keep reemerging. . . . It frequently becomes clear that, in practice, human rights are not equal for all. (Pope Francis, "All Brothers," 20, 22)

All human beings have worth, no matter their age or ability.

As a society, when we don't provide resources for the education and care of all young people, we are sending a clear message that some are not as valued as others.

Recognizing that we do not have a social structure that supports a consistent life ethic is an important starting point. And identifying our personal biases and attitudes about specific moral issues can help us understand whether we truly support a culture of life or a culture of death.

> Brainstorm a list of ways we treat people as dispensable in society.

The Culture of Life: We Are Images of God

If we are only what we have, then life can only end in death, because cars, careers, and even "the perfect body" will eventually pass away. But in Christian belief, we are more than what we have, and death is not the end of the story. According to the following Scripture passage, we are images of God:

> God did not make death,
>   nor does he rejoice in the destruction of the
>   living.
> For he fashioned all things that they might have
>   being,
> . . . .
> For God formed us to be imperishable;
>   the image of his own nature he made us.
>   (Wisdom 1:13–14, 2:23)

In Christian belief, we are more than what we have, and death is not the end of the story.

Those who require extra care are also considered to be special gifts of God.

> Describe messages you receive from the media about what is valuable and life-giving.

We are more than just our bodies; we have souls too. United, our body and soul make us fully human, no matter what we have or what we look like. Being fully alive means reflecting the image of God within us by imitating the perfect image of God, Jesus Christ, in loving God and one another. If we do this, we are complete; we need nothing more. Even death cannot take life away from us, because we hope to share in the resurrected life of Christ in heaven.

This worldview is referred to as the **culture of life** because it recognizes that all human life comes from God and is meant to return to God. Rooted in love, this worldview brings life to the world:

- It calls people to share what they have with others, especially those who do not have enough to live.

- It views all people as gifts of God, even those who require extra care.

- It sees life as worth living even if it involves suffering, because love can transform suffering into something good.

culture of life A worldview that recognizes that all human life comes from God and is meant to return to God; it respects and protects human life in all its stages, from conception to natural death.

For Review

1. What is the difference between a culture of life and a culture of death?
2. How does the culture of death define who we are as human beings? What does it say we must do to be fully alive?
3. How does the culture of life define who we are as human beings? What does it say we must do to be fully alive?
4. Describe how a culture that claims "we are what we have" might affect the way someone views issues related to life and death.

Standing for Life

Because God wills every human being into existence in a unique, loving act of creation and creates each person in his image and likeness, every person's life must be respected and protected from the moment of conception until natural death. Let's look more deeply at some of the key issues related to this foundational Catholic social teaching principle: abortion, artificial conception, genetic engineering, euthanasia, suicide, and capital punishment. Of course, many other issues threaten or disrespect the life and dignity of the human person, such as poverty, human trafficking, and racism. In fact, this Catholic social teaching principle that calls us to honor and protect life provides guidance and wisdom for many moral decisions and is foundational to working toward a world of justice.

Abortion

Abortion is the deliberate termination of pregnancy and ending of life of an unborn child in the womb. Any abortion performed to intentionally end a pregnancy and the life of an unborn child at any stage is strongly opposed by the Catholic Church. If a critically ill mother requires a medical procedure to save her life, but that procedure indirectly results in the death of her unborn child, the tragic situation would be morally acceptable because the death of the child is not directly intended.

The Beginning of Human Life

The Catholic Church's position on abortion is based on the understanding that sacred human life begins at conception and therefore is protected by rights that should be defended. The fact that human life begins at conception is

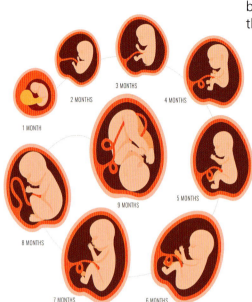

not just a religious stance. It is supported by modern biology and particularly the study of genetics. Consider these medical facts:

- From the moment the sperm and ovum meet, the cell they form has its own unique human DNA, different from that of any other human being. Left to its natural development, this cell will develop into an adult human being.

- The embryo's body is clearly differentiated from its mother's body. Although the mother's body provides oxygen and nourishment, as the embryo develops, it has its own intact and separate body. Its blood is not shared with the mother, and it often even has a different blood type.

- As early as twenty-one days after conception, the embryo's heart begins to beat. At nine weeks, the embryo has fingerprints. At twelve weeks, the fetus sleeps, exercises, curls its toes, and opens and closes its mouth. At eighteen to twenty weeks, the fetus is fully capable of feeling pain.

These facts and others lead to the inevitable conclusion that a unique human life begins at the moment of conception.

The value of a human being does not depend on its stage of development. You were not less human as a baby than you are now. Neither does the value of human life depend on the circumstances surrounding it. Though the evil of rape cannot be overstated, the child who is conceived by rape has the same dignity and rights as any other child. Abortion cannot erase rape, but it does end the life of the unborn child.

One of the arguments people make in support of abortion is that a pregnant woman has the right to make choices about her own body, including the baby growing inside her womb. However, science provides clear proof that the baby's body, while dependent on the mother's body, is a distinct human being. Therefore, a sacred human life has begun that also has rights that must be ensured.

In opposing abortion, Catholics cannot ignore the hardship and suffering that pregnancy causes for many

What circumstances might cause a woman to consider abortion as an option? What feelings might she experience? How would you respond if a friend told you she was pregnant and wasn't sure what to do?

A unique human life begins at the moment of conception.

women. Often, those who consider having an abortion are frightened of the consequences if they choose to keep the child. Perhaps their families are not supportive. Maybe they don't have any money or a stable place to live. The pregnancy may be a result of violence. It might be that they have discovered their child has a genetic disease or birth defect. But the Church calls us to respond to these difficult situations with love, not violence. We should provide support for women facing this choice, ensuring they have a safe place where they can share their stories—their deepest hopes and their greatest fears. We should be strong advocates for pregnancy and prenatal coaching, financial planning, counseling services, and any number of other support services that can support women in bringing their unborn child to life. And if, for whatever reason, a woman has an abortion, we should reach out to her with love to assist in her healing.

Pope Francis has been very clear about the Church's message of mercy and forgiveness for women who have had abortions:

> I am well aware of the pressure that has led them to this decision. I know that it is an existential and moral ordeal. I have met so many women who bear in their heart the scar of this agonizing and painful decision. . . . The forgiveness of God cannot be denied to one who has repented, especially when that person approaches the Sacrament of Confession with a sincere heart in order to obtain reconciliation with the Father. ("Letter Regarding the Jubilee of Mercy")

Abortion and Mercy

Though the Church calls us to defend the lives of unborn babies, it also calls us to respect and care for the many women who have had abortions. Because our society often does not support families, and especially single mothers, many of these women do not feel they have any other choice. Many women feel tremendous shame, guilt, and grief following abortion. The Church has responded to the grief of these women by offering parish-based programs like Project Rachel, through which trained counselors can help women to heal.

> In an effort to follow our call to a consistent ethic of life, why must we respond to unwanted pregnancy with options other than abortion?

Other Beginning-of-Life Moral Issues

Modern advances in genetics research have resulted in other beginning-of-life issues. One of these issues is using artificial means of conception to bring new human life into the world, such as in vitro fertilization. This artifical means of conception creates a fertilized ovum in a laboratory and then implants it in the woman's womb. Another means is artificial insemination, a fertility technique that artificially implants sperm in a woman's womb. A third artificial means is the use of a surrogate mother—placing a fertilized ovum from one woman in another woman's womb and letting the baby grow inside the other woman, usually to be given to the biological parents after birth.

As well-meaning as these techniques may be, they all share a serious flaw. The dignity of sexuality requires that children be created naturally. Children must be the outcome of the loving union of a husband and wife in sexual intercourse and not conceived through some artificial means. The Church, knowing that the pain of married couples who are unable to conceive children through natural means is very real, has great sympathy for husbands and wives who struggle with infertility. The Church encourages research and medical treatments that increase the chances of natural conception for these couples.

Another beginning-of-life issue is prenatal testing, which involves testing the embryo or fetus for diseases or birth defects while it is still in the womb. The Church teaches that prenatal testing is permissible if it

In vitro fertilization involves fertilizing the ovum in a lab like the one shown here.

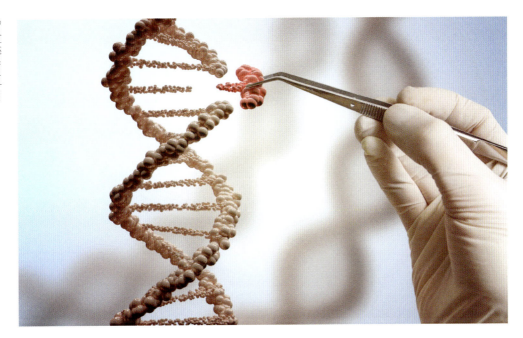

does not cause any harm to the embryo or fetus and is done for the purposes of safeguarding and healing the developing baby in the womb or after birth. But prenatal testing for the purpose of deciding whether to abort the baby is morally wrong.

Genetic engineering for the purpose of creating a person with predetermined qualities (eye color, hair color, gender, and so on) is wrong because it falsely puts human beings into God's role of determining the uniqueness of every human person. And stem-cell research that uses aborted embryos and fetuses is also not acceptable due to its reliance on abortion for material.

These beginning-of-life issues are clear examples of an important moral principle: just because human beings have the technology and knowledge to accomplish certain actions does not mean those actions are morally right. Justice calls us to defend the rights of human beings from conception through all stages of life. For that reason, we must defend, care for, and heal the unborn as we would any other human being.

> **Just because human beings have the technology and knowledge to accomplish certain actions does not mean those actions are morally right.**

What other situations might be included in the moral principle stating that just because we *can* do something doesn't mean it is morally right?

End-of-Life Issues

We now turn our attention to moral issues concerned with the end of our life on earth. In "The Gospel of Life," Pope Saint John Paul II identified the growing acceptance of euthanasia and suicide in developed countries as another sign of the rise of a culture of death. He wondered how many people in countries that have promoted human dignity in so many other ways—reducing poverty, protecting workers' rights and women's rights, promoting racial tolerance, and so on—could so easily accept attacks on human life at its beginning and at its end. He proposed this answer to the question:

> When he denies or neglects his fundamental relationship to God, man thinks he is his own rule and measure, with the right to demand that society should guarantee him the ways and means of deciding what to do with his life in full and complete autonomy. It is especially people in the developed countries who act in this way: they feel encouraged to do so also by the constant progress of medicine and its ever more advanced techniques. . . . In this context the temptation grows to have recourse to euthanasia, that is, to take control of death and bring it about before its time, "gently" ending one's own life or the life of others. In reality, what might seem logical and humane, when looked at more closely is seen to be senseless and inhumane. Here we are faced with one of the more alarming symptoms of the "culture of death," which is advancing above all in prosperous societies, marked by an attitude of excessive preoccupation with efficiency and which sees the growing number of elderly and disabled people as intolerable and too burdensome. (64)

As we consider these end-of-life issues, remember that death is only the end of life for our physical body. Because our compassionate and loving Father sent his only Son for our eternal salvation, our souls live on,

What is at risk when we value people only for their health or usefulness?

and we will know eternal life in resurrected bodies. If we focus on the promise of this ultimate destiny, we will more easily make the right moral choices at the end of life.

Euthanasia

An end-of-life issue we might hear about in the news is **euthanasia**, also called mercy killing. Euthanasia is an action against the Fifth Commandment. Intentionally causing the death of a human being is murder, regardless of the motive or circumstance. The person choosing to die by euthanasia and the people helping them are committing a serious sin.

Proponents of euthanasia make it an issue of human freedom, saying that people who have a serious physical disability or who are terminally ill and in severe pain (or their families, if the people are incapable of making their own decisions) have a right to choose to end their suffering. This sounds like a good and noble intention, but does it ever make euthanasia right? Euthanasia violates human dignity and the respect we owe to our Creator, the author of human life. Even the best of intentions—for example, sparing family members the burden of providing care through a long and painful disease, or easing a sick person's suffering—do not justify euthanasia.

When discussing euthanasia, it is important to understand the Church's teaching on natural death. Rejecting euthanasia as a moral choice does not mean we must use extraordinary measures to prolong the life of a person who is near death. When a person is near death, it is legitimate to reject extraordinary treatments whose only use is to prolong life. Likewise, the use of painkillers is allowed even if their use risks bringing death more quickly, because the direct intention is to relieve the dying person's suffering, not to cause their death.

> Why is euthanasia morally wrong even when done to end suffering near the end of life?

euthanasia A direct action, or a deliberate lack of action, that causes the death of a person who is disabled, sick, or dying.

Terri Schiavo became the face of the euthanasia issue when her husband petitioned the court to be able to remove her feeding tube after she suffered cardiac arrest that left her without oxygen for an extended time.

Rejecting euthanasia does not represent a lack of compassion for people who are suffering and dying. To the contrary, it rejects the false solution offered by euthanasia in favor of the sometimes harder but morally right response: placing our trust in God until the natural end of our days on earth. We do this with the help of God's grace and the compassionate support of others.

Christians have an outstanding history of caring for people who are sick, disabled, or dying. Through hospice programs, medical advances in pain relief, and spiritual support, we help one another make that transition from death to new and eternal life with God.

Suicide

Suicide is also a sin against the Fifth Commandment. Sacred though life is, for some people, it can at times seem overwhelming, and they seek desperate solutions. But the answer is not suicide. By ending one's own life, a person takes over a decision that is God's alone to make—when and how we die. It is always God's will that we preserve our own life as well as the lives of others. Suicide is the ultimate rejection of God's gifts of hope and love. It causes devastation to the surviving family and friends, and it also wounds the greater human family, which is prematurely deprived of the gift of the life of the person who dies by suicide.

Although suicide is always wrong, the Church recognizes that serious mental illness or suffering can contribute to the decision a person makes to take their own life. If you know someone who is thinking about suicide, it is essential that you do what you can to get the person the medical, psychological, or spiritual help they need, even if it breaks a promise of confidentiality. If you know someone who has taken their own life, you should not consider them lost to the love of God. The Church prays for those who have died by suicide, placing them in God's love and mercy.

The Death Penalty

Think back to the scenario of the little girl who was kidnapped and murdered while on a family camping trip. Her parents, grieving and heartbroken, considered wanting capital punishment for the perpetrator. This emotional response is understandable. But our laws and principles cannot be led by emotion. We establish our laws and principles to relieve us of the burden of making decisions fueled by our gut reactions. Consider the effect if this perpetrator is executed by the penal system:

> When the state, in our names and with our taxes, ends a human life despite having non-lethal alternatives, it suggests that society can overcome violence with violence. The use of the death penalty ought to be abandoned not only for what it does to those who are executed, but for what it does to all of society. (United States Conference of Catholic Bishops, "A Culture of Life and the Penalty of Death")

> *Our laws and principles cannot be led by emotion. We establish our laws and principles to relieve us of the burden of making decisions fueled by our gut reactions.*

> **The consistent ethic of life maintains that every person is worthy of life and basic dignity.**

What does the death penalty do to society? If we are to embrace a consistent life ethic, what is an alternative to capital punishment?

What does the death penalty do to society? In considering **capital punishment**, we must be clear that the death penalty is not solely about the criminal. In many ways, it is about us: "the actions taken in our name, the values which guide our lives, and the dignity that we accord to human life" ("A Culture of Life and the Penalty of Death"). Taking the life of another as retribution or punishment makes anyone who supported candidates, laws, or policies in favor of capital punishment, complicit in the act itself. When we devalue some lives, we devalue all life.

The consistent ethic of life maintains that every person is worthy of life and basic dignity. This even includes murderers. When our laws and policies treat some people as unworthy of protection, we have damaged the belief that all life is sacred. The Church's teaching is clear. It does not mean that there are no consequences or punishment, but if all human life has value, then we, as a society, do not have the right to take a life. Everyone has a right to life because we are human beings.

capital punishment The practice of killing people as punishment for serious crimes.

Supporters of capital punishment do not deny that those being executed are human beings—at least not from an objective, biological point of view. But they make two basic arguments to justify their position:

- Certain crimes are so violent that in committing them, the offenders basically forfeit their human rights, including the right to life.
- Certain crimes harm society so much that the only way of restoring justice is to make the offender experience the same level of harm they caused society.

This approach to criminal justice, in which the emphasis is on hurting the offender, is known as **retributive justice**. "An eye for an eye and a tooth for a tooth" is the slogan of retributive justice, which embraces the idea that a person can do something so heinous that they surrender their right to life. Is this possible? Can a person surrender their most basic human right? The Church draws a hard line here and says that no one can surrender their right to life, even if they commit a horrible crime. If we apply the consistent ethic of life principle, everyone's life has value. Our worth isn't dependent solely on our actions or attitudes. We have worth because God loves us.

Catholic Mobilizing Network

The Catholic Mobilizing Network is a national organization that mobilizes Catholics, and all people of goodwill, to value life over death. They seek to end the use of the death penalty and to transform the US criminal justice system from punitive to restorative. How does the Catholic Mobilizing Network promote **restorative justice**? It's all about relationships. Groups such as the Catholic Mobilizing Network and Prison Fellowship take the approach that crime harms people, relationships, and community. Restorative justice provides avenues to heal those relationships. Sometimes that means a convict will write to, talk to, or meet with their victim or the victim's family. It allows willing prisoners and victims to meet and explore topics such as personal responsibility and making amends. These meetings can lead to the transformation of people and relationships. Restorative justice can heal trauma and give a life meaning from woundedness. In opposing capital punishment, the Catholic Mobilizing Network does not advocate for a lack of consequences. To the contrary, they promote accountability. They hold that it is only through acknowledging that we are mutually responsible for one another and for our actions that transformation can begin.

restorative justice An approach to dealing with convicted criminals in which they are urged to accept responsibility for their offenses through meeting victims or their families and making amends to victims or the community.

retributive justice The approach to those who have committed crimes that is concerned with punishing or rewarding an individual.

Catholics are called to advocate for the abolition of the death penalty through their civil actions, such as voting for representatives who run on a platform opposing capital punishment.

Ending Capital Punishment

The US Catholic bishops sum up the Church's opposition to capital punishment in one sentence: "The antidote to violence is love, not more violence" ("Living the Gospel of Life," 21). In 2018, Pope Francis revised the *Catechism of the Catholic Church* to reflect the consistent life ethic by describing the death penalty as "an attack on the inviolability and dignity of the person"[1] that is "inadmissible" in all cases (2267). Then, in 2020, he issued a new encyclical "All Brothers," which solidified the Church's position against capital punishment. The encyclical calls all Catholics to advocate for the **abolition** of the death penalty worldwide.

Pope Francis formally stated what has been the long-held belief of the Church. Everyone has a right to life. Everyone has a right to be treated with basic dignity. Using the death penalty as punishment for even the most heinous crimes violates these basic principles. Implementing the death penalty as a method of vengeance does not right the wrong that was committed. Using the death penalty for retribution will not heal the victims of capital crimes. We must find a punishment suitable to the crime without reducing ourselves to the level of taking the life of another.

> "Pope Francis formally stated what has been the long-held belief of the Church. Everyone has a right to life. Everyone has a right to be treated with basic dignity."

abolition The action of terminating a system, practice, or institution.

A Call to Live More Fully

Although we have focused on a few specific issues in this chapter, the call to choose life is at the heart of all justice issues. The rest of this course continues the discussion about how to build a culture of life.

It would be wrong to suggest that choosing life does not involve sacrifice, pain, or suffering. And it would be dishonest to suggest that people who choose to live following Catholic social teaching principles live happily ever after without struggles and difficulties. However, the Church believes that choosing to solve difficult situations through violence, while perhaps easier, is not life-giving to anyone involved.

The Christian choice for life is based on the choice Jesus made to suffer and to sacrifice his life so that all might have new life eternally. It was a choice he struggled with in the garden at Gethsemane. Even after the Resurrection, Jesus kept the wounds of his suffering. Choosing life does not take away suffering, but it does make us more fully alive.

> Reflect on the statement, "Choosing life does not take away suffering, but it does make us more fully alive." What does it mean to be fully alive?

> What is the difference between vengeance and consequence? Think about why vengeance cannot be a fair motivator for punishments such as the death penalty.

For Review

1. Name some medical facts that support the understanding that life begins at conception.
2. How is refusing extraordinary measures to prolong the life of a person near death morally acceptable?
3. Define *retributive justice* and *restorative justice*.
4. What reason does Pope Francis give to explain that capital punishment is inadmissible at all times?

- Develop your own culture of life by treating everyone with dignity and respect—even those with whom you disagree on key issues. Avoid supporting media that promote violence and degrade human sexuality.

- Organize a drive to collect baby supplies for parents who need material assistance. Use the drive to educate others about the need for social changes that will make these issues less common.

- Volunteer at a local crisis pregnancy center or homeless shelter. Young people are almost always welcome to help.

- Practice restorative justice in relationships with others by focusing on healing rather than revenge.

- Ask yourself, how does my high school (or future college) support pregnant students? Then work with school officials and other students to create support networks.

- Join the Catholic Mobilizing Network or Amnesty International USA's campaign to abolish the death penalty.

- Contact your Catholic diocese to find out how you can help lobby for legislative change.

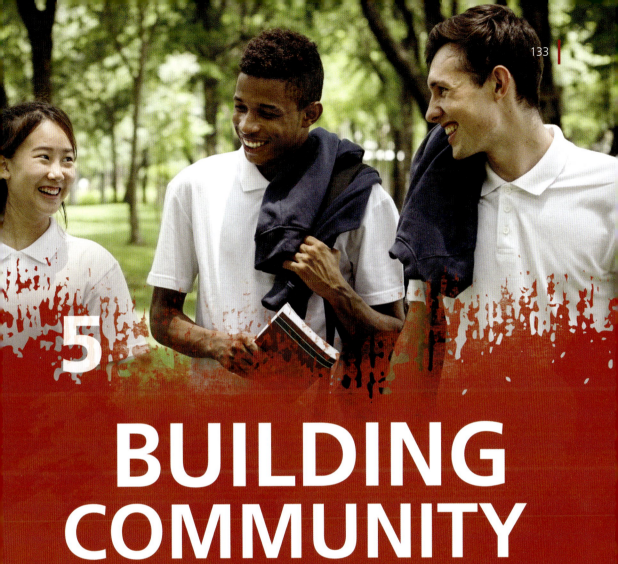

5

BUILDING COMMUNITY
Celebrating Unity and Diversity

In This Chapter

Mixing It Up | What Makes a Community? | The Anatomy of Exclusion | Building Inclusive Communities

Mixing It Up

Mix It Up at Lunch Day is an international campaign that encourages students to identify, question, and cross social boundaries. Any school can host a Mix It Up event. Students and administrators identify the divisions in their school that are clearly drawn. During a Mix It Up event, students are asked to move out of their comfort zones to try to connect with someone new over lunch. It's a simple act with profound implications. This program encourages educators to promote healthy, welcoming school environments as a year-round effort. Interactions that bridge the gap between groups can help reduce prejudice. Here is what it looks like in practice.

Once a year, students are invited to break out of their cliques and join their classmates in the courtyard to socialize and learn about a game designed to help them "mix it up." Students each receive a colored sheet of paper with a letter on it. The challenge is for each student to find six other students with letter combinations that spell the words *Mix It Up*. As soon as they have found the right combination of letters, the group stands in line in the correct order to spell out the words.

Some students are skeptical about the event, but in the end, everyone genuinely has a good time. Most of the feedback from the program includes reactions from students who affirm that they met peers that they might have otherwise never engaged with. And the experience of connecting with even one new person is valuable to them. Every school has cliques, of course. But the hope is that the event helps break the ice between groups. It's not easy to meet new people, but after this event, it becomes easier for students to get to know someone new.

Two Approaches to Community

In a way, the Mix It Up activity forces students to answer an important, if unspoken, question: How will we define our community? It is a question whose answer has a huge impact on human life and dignity. As you have already learned, choosing life means more than protecting people from being harmed; it also means ensuring that people are able to live in a way that reflects their dignity as images of God. Of the many things that allow people to live full and dignified lives, one of the most basic is participation in a community. "Human dignity can be realized and protected only in community," the US Catholic bishops say in their pastoral letter "Economic Justice for All" (14). This is true not only because we depend on our relationships with others to provide us with what we need for a life of dignity but also simply because human beings are **social**: as images of God, we are made to be in loving relationship with one another.

Our nature draws us together to form **communities**, groups of people who relate to one another based on common characteristics, circumstances, or interests. The Mix It Up event reveals two ways of thinking about community. **Exclusion** attempts to determine who does and does not belong to the

The **National Catholic Board** on Full Inclusion

The experience of just one person or family can make a difference for an entire community. When Beth Foraker gave birth to her son Patrick, he was diagnosed with Down syndrome. One of the challenges Beth faced was that Patrick would not be able to attend the school where his older brother and sister went because there was no programming for children with Down. However, she was determined that Patrick would have every opportunity possible, and through her work with a local Catholic organization, she was able to see Patrick become the first student with Down syndrome to be fully included in a Catholic school. However, Beth realized that there was no national Catholic organization working toward inclusive classrooms in all Catholic schools. As Patrick was set to finish middle school, Beth decided to create this organization herself—the National Catholic Board on Full Inclusion (NCBFI). The NCBFI provides families, educators, administrators, and faith-filled people with resources that support and promote the inclusion of students with disabilities in Catholic schools.

---

social A characteristic of human beings that recognizes they are made to live in relationship with one another.

communities Groups of people who relate to one another based on common characteristics, circumstances, or interests.

exclusion The act of determining who does and does not belong to a community by focusing on the differences that separate people from one another.

What can you do to make your school community more inclusive?

community by focusing on the differences that separate people from one another. The Mix It Up participants offered many examples of ways students often define community by excluding others based on differences such as grades, clothing, or race. **Inclusion**, though not ignoring the differences that make each person unique, recognizes that those differences are small compared to the dignity people share as images of God. The way we live together should also be a reflection of God, who is the relationship of the Father, Son, and Holy Spirit united by love in one God. In inclusive communities, love overcomes the differences among people, which the students began to realize when they participated in the Mix It Up event.

> What is your vision of a strong and united community? What exactly would make it strong and united?

For Review

1. Why is participation in community essential to human dignity?
2. What does it mean to say that human beings are social?
3. Define *exclusion* and *inclusion*.

inclusion The act of recognizing that the differences that make each person unique are small compared to the dignity people share as images of God.

What Makes a Community?

Participation in community is both a right and a responsibility. The US Catholic bishops say in their pastoral letter "Economic Justice for All": "Social justice implies that persons have an obligation to be active and productive participants in the life of society and that society has a duty to enable them to participate in this way" (71). Each person has a right to participate in community to live out their God-given dignity more fully. Each person has a responsibility to participate because the good of others in the community depends on it.

> Each person has a right to participate in community to live out their God-given dignity more fully.

Just what does it mean to participate in a community? Saint Paul frequently addresses that question in his letters to the early Christian communities.

Varieties of Gifts, Same Spirit

In his First Letter to the Corinthians, Paul describes the Christian community—the church—using the image of the Body of Christ. He says that the Christian community consists of many members who have a variety of gifts:

> There are different kinds of spiritual gifts but the same Spirit; there are different forms of services but

Aside from your school community, what other communities are you part of?

the same Lord; there are different workings but the same God who produces all of them in everyone. To each individual the manifestation of the Spirit is given for some benefit. (12:4–7)

Paul goes on to compare the community, with its variety of gifted members, to the human body. The body has many parts—a hand has a different function than an eye, and the feet cannot take the place of the ears—but the parts work together as one. In the body and in the community, "if [one] part suffers, all the parts suffer with it; if one part is honored, all the parts share its joy" (1 Corinthians 12:26). In the church, all are united in relationship with one another through Christ. Paul's image of community provides a model for Christians to build community in the world as well. Three key themes are evident in Paul's teaching:

> **Although we all have different gifts, we are all loved equally by God.**

1. **Although we all have different gifts, we are all loved equally by God.** No two people are alike; each has different gifts to offer the community. In the excerpt from First Corinthians, Paul celebrates the **diversity** of the community but points out three times that

diversity The inclusion of people of different races and cultures in a group or organization.

differences among people do not mean that one person is less valuable than another. Catholic social teaching echoes Paul:

> Since all [humans] possess a rational soul and are created in God's likeness, since they have the same nature and origin, have been redeemed by Christ and enjoy the same divine calling and destiny, the basic equality of all must receive increasingly greater recognition. (*The Church in the Modern World,* 29)

2. **We need one another.** All the different members of a community, like the parts of the body, are vital for the common good (the well-being of the entire community) because each brings a unique contribution to the whole. If one person's gifts are ignored or disposed of, the whole community suffers. But when gifts are offered and received, both the recipient and the giver are enriched. Participating in community is necessary for us to give our gifts to others and to benefit fully from the gifts of others.

3. **Solidarity is key.** Solidarity is what holds a love-centered community together. You may have experienced the sort of solidarity of which Paul speaks if you have a close-knit family or group of friends: if one is hurt, all hurt; if one is happy, all are happy.

Living Together in Community

In defining what makes a community, Catholic social teaching echoes and expands on the teaching of Paul. In "Economic Justice for All," the US Catholic bishops identify several basic requirements for community life (see 79–84). When any of these are ignored, the dignity of individuals and groups within the community is violated, and the well-being of the whole community suffers.

Read the full description of community found in 1 Corinthians, chapter 12. Using Saint Paul's analogy of the human body and community, consider one of the communities you are a part of. What are the different roles people fulfill in that community? How do all the different roles work together to form a community? What does the community represent as a whole?

> **Solidarity is what holds a love-centered community together.**

What structures allow the members of your community to live a more abundant life?

> Think about a community to which you belong. What gifts do you receive from it? What gifts do you contribute to it?

The right and responsibility to contribute to the common good. Justice happens when everyone is actively working for the good of everyone else. Therefore, everyone has a right and a responsibility to use their gifts and talents to contribute to the good of the whole community. For its part, the community needs to ensure that all people can contribute. When the gifts of members and groups are not recognized because some are considered too young or too old, for instance, everyone loses.

The right to access the benefits and resources of the community. When people or groups are denied access to the community's benefits and resources, such as adequate education, their ability to live as God intended is threatened. When members are threatened, the community as a whole is threatened as well. Communities have a duty to organize structures that allow each member to live an abundant life.

Human rights. The requirements of participation listed above are fulfilled in basic **human rights**. Those rights "include the rights to fulfillment of material needs, a guarantee of fundamental freedoms, and the protection of relationships that are essential to participation in the life of society[1]" ("Economic Justice for All," 79).

When individuals or groups are prevented from participating in community in these ways, they become excluded and marginalized. An inclusive community makes sure everyone can live life fully:

> The ultimate injustice is for a person or group to be treated actively or abandoned passively as if they were nonmembers of the human race. To treat people this way is effectively to say that they simply do not count as human beings. . . . The poor, the disabled, and the unemployed too often are simply left behind. ("Economic Justice for All," 77)

These are only the minimum requirements for a just community. Ultimately, love and solidarity are the glue that holds community together: "Only active love of God and neighbor make . . . community happen" ("Economic Justice for All," 64).

Human Rights
Minimum Requirements

To respect human life and dignity, we must respect each person's human rights. In our society, human rights are regarded as absolute, or unlimited. But Catholic social teaching stresses that the human rights of each person are balanced by a responsibility to respect the rights of all other people in the community.

Following are some of the most important human rights identified in "Economic Justice for All" as essential to ensuring human dignity and participation in community:

- **Basic rights necessary for the protection of human dignity.** These include the rights to life, food, clothing, shelter, rest, medical care, and basic education.
- **Rights necessary to ensure basic human rights.** People also have the right to earn a living and the right to security in the event of sickness, unemployment, and old age.
- **Rights that enable participation in community.** Full participation in the life of the community requires economic rights, including the rights to employment, healthy working conditions, wages, and job benefits that allow workers and their families to lives of dignity, and the possibility of property ownership. Civil and political rights are also necessary for participation; some of these include the right to freedom of speech, the right to freedom of assembly, the right to worship, and the right to political participation.

human rights The fundamental rights that belong to all humans.

For Review

1. Why do people have a right and a responsibility to participate in community?
2. Describe three themes in Paul's teaching about community.
3. In your own words, summarize the requirements for participation in community.
4. What can happen when the basic requirements for community life are ignored?

The Anatomy of Exclusion

Even though justice demands participation for all, the opportunity to participate is often denied. To find out why, let's look at some examples. More than likely, each of us has had some experience of being excluded from a community.

Mei: Mei experienced exclusion because she was one of few Asian students in her middle school. "I was treated like an outsider because I didn't share the same culture and ethnicity as most of the other kids in my school. It wasn't just comments made behind my back. Kids would say things right to my face! I could hear kids calling out racial slurs in the hallway when there were no teachers around. I was teased about the way I looked and talked. It hurt my feelings, and then I got angry. After a while, I just tried to ignore it."

Have you ever been treated like an outsider? What do you think is the root issue for some members of the community excluding others?

© bgrocker / Shutterstock.com

Addison: "I went to a house party with a group of my friends. There was alcohol and marijuana available. I chose not to drink or smoke. Someone called me out in front of the group, and I just said that I didn't think it was good for me. I guess I could have just said 'I don't feel like it' or 'I don't want to,' but saying that it wasn't good for me made it seem like I was judging them for doing it. I felt embarrassed when they were laughing at me, and my friends were too drunk to do anything about it. Basically, I stayed to make sure they got home safely, but I felt so uncomfortable for the rest of the night."

Elliot: "Things got worse for me when I started high school. As a gay student, I was the subject of constant bullying. Whenever I was not with my friends, I tried not to be in crowded places like the cafeteria. The kids who bullied me would love to mock me in front of a big group. It used to be just words, but I was pushed and shoved and had my school clothes stolen out of my gym locker. It takes a lot of energy trying to avoid the people who seem to hate me."

Notice that teens excluded Mei, Addison, and Elliot for one aspect or perceived aspect of who they are. These students have been hurt by what has happened, but the whole group is hurt too. Mei, Addison, and Elliot are so much more than the qualities that have been used as the rationale for their exclusion—each has dreams, talents, and gifts to share with the whole community. If we consider exclusion at a societal level, we see that it causes serious harm to individuals, groups, and whole societies.

Those who wish to exclude others try to make the case that some people "just don't belong," or that some people, by nature, are "just not fit" to take on certain roles within the community. Even if these excuses are never spoken aloud, they have the potential to influence the way we relate to one another. When we consider the excuses given for excluding people, we come to the complex issues of stereotypes, prejudice, and discrimination.

> Think of a time you were excluded from a community. How did it affect your sense of dignity? How did you respond to the exclusion?

> **If we consider exclusion at a societal level, we see that it causes serious harm to individuals, groups, and whole societies.**

> Who is excluded from a community you belong to? Why are they excluded? How does their exclusion hurt them? How does it hurt the whole community?

> **The way we treat others is based on the way we view them.**

Stereotypes: Harmful Assumptions

The way we treat others is based on the way we view them; our views are in turn influenced by our culture and personal experience. But as we discussed earlier in this course, the limitations of our experience and culture cause us to view the world in a way that is often inaccurate or incomplete. When our view of a person or group is based on inaccurate or incomplete knowledge, it is a **stereotype**.

Stereotypes can be positive or negative. Either way, stereotypes are too broad. It is impossible for stereotypical characteristics to apply to all members of a group. Basing our attitudes toward others on stereotypes demonstrates disrespect for the uniqueness of individuals.

Direct Experience, Faulty Logic

Many stereotypes develop from direct experience of others. But the conclusions represented by these stereotypes are the result of faulty logic. In the following examples, the conclusions, which are stereotypes, do not necessarily follow from the observations:

- The only parents in my neighborhood who stay home with their little kids are women; therefore, men have inferior parenting skills.

stereotype A positive or negative characterization applied to a group of people that is developed by assumptions, lack of direct experience, or biased thinking.

How is the stereotype "men have inferior parenting skills" reinforced in the media?

What harm can come from stereotypes based on faulty logic?

- Some terrorist attacks are committed by Muslims; therefore, all Muslims cannot be trusted.
- Catholic high school costs a lot of money; therefore, Catholic high school students must be rich.

Obviously, all these conclusions represent faulty logic. You may have a dog that's a collie, but it doesn't mean that all dogs are collies. Yet, such logic is the basis for much stereotypical thinking.

> Consider stereotypes you have developed based on the direct experience of others. In what way do these stereotypes disrespect a person or group? What is the faulty logic that creates these stereotypes?

Learned from Our Culture

Another source of stereotypes is the culture in which we grew up. Many stereotypes are learned from the people around us, such as parents, friends, and teachers. Children can be taught to view certain groups as inferior just as easily as they can be taught that everyone is equal.

News reports tend to be biased based on who is sponsoring their content. This can end up promoting stereotypes. Social institutions such as businesses, churches, and schools may also promote stereotypes, often because of the way such institutions are structured. According to the Bureau of Labor Statistics, women have never held more than 30 percent of the

CEO positions of Fortune 500 companies. This statistic could erroneously lead some to believe that women somehow lack the skills to run large corporations. However, this would ignore the influence that history and traditional business structures have in this area. This is an example of how institutions can influence or create stereotypes.

Stereotypes and Participation

Stereotyping is an everyday occurrence. Many stereotypes, especially positive ones, seem harmless. So it is easy to lose sight of how much they limit the right of some individuals and groups to participate in the community as they choose.

Other stereotypes can fuel deep-seated negative attitudes that make efforts to include everyone difficult. For example, Tania was diagnosed with major depressive disorder and anxiety. Some kids at her school noticed when she was going through a rough time. They saw the dark circles under her eyes from exhaustion, her disheveled clothes, her lack of interest in activities, and her observable anxiety before tests. Rather than treating her with kindness and compassion, they whispered behind her back. They called her weird and crazy. Unfortunately, this behavior isn't random unkindness. These actions perpetuate the stigma people with mental illness face every day. The way Tania was treated could be the tipping point toward further marginalization. When we exclude and demean those who are suffering, we are actively preventing them from being full members of our community.

Prejudice and Discrimination

When stereotypes are combined with fear or selfishness, they can become **prejudice**: an attitude of hostility directed at whole groups of people. Prejudice involves prejudgment, or judging someone before knowing all the facts or without considering the facts. The hostility of prejudice blinds one to the dignity all people share, creating a kind of poison in relationships.

Nura experienced religious prejudice against Muslims in her new high school when she wore a hijab to school. She was unprepared for the ugly, hateful comments that other students made to her and about her. She kept a journal of all the comments from that day and gave it to her Middle Eastern Studies teacher. Her teacher was distressed but not surprised and said, "I have deep concern that this fear and hatred will become associated with patriotism."

Prejudicial attitudes harm the human dignity of both those who hold the attitudes and those at whom the attitudes are directed. But there is a distinction between prejudice and the power to impose restrictions on other people based on that prejudice. Even if *all* people have some prejudicial attitudes toward people of another race or ethnicity, only *some* people have the power to actively exclude others from resources, activities, and organizations. The greater the level of power combined with prejudice, the greater the potential for damage.

When people who are motivated by prejudice use their power to deny individuals or groups the right to participate in community, **discrimination** results. Discrimination can be seen in actions on an individual level, such as when those motivated by prejudice have refused to sell a house or rent an apartment to certain people.

> **prejudice** An attitude of hostility directed at whole groups of people. Prejudice involves judging someone or something before knowing all the facts or without considering the facts.
>
> **discrimination** The act or practice of treating others as less than or unequal and using power to deny individuals or groups the right to fully participate in community.

> Suppose you overheard someone making prejudicial comments about another person or group. How would you respond? How would your response be different if the comment was directed at your own group?

Discrimination can be based on any of the many issues that make people different from one another: gender, age, class, ethnicity, religion, sexual orientation, and so on. But one of the most explosive, widespread, and deep-seated examples of discrimination in the United States is racism.

The Sin of Racism

In their pastoral statement "Moving Beyond Racism: Learning to See with the Eyes of Christ," the Catholic bishops of Illinois define **racism** as "a personal sin and social disorder rooted in the belief that one race is superior to another. It involves not only prejudice but also the use of religious, social, political, economic or historical power to keep one race privileged."

Although there has been some progress addressing racism, it is unfortunately clear that it has not yet been eradicated. It continues to be a serious social justice concern, and we are called to confront its many manifestations and refuse to participate in racial discrimination of any kind.

> In what ways does racism or some other form of prejudice persist in your city or town today?

Discrimination on a Social Level

When people discriminate against one another on an individual level, patterns of discrimination will build to create social structures. Sometimes such structural discrimination is consciously chosen by an institution or society, as in the case of apartheid in South Africa, in the reservation system that segregated Indigenous Americans in the United States, or in the denial of voting rights to US women before 1920.

Such consciously chosen discrimination is much rarer in the United States today than it once was. But discriminatory social structures persist as the indirect result of many individual acts of discrimination. The following are some examples of structural discrimination.

> In what ways does race affect the way you interact with people?

---

racism The belief that one race is better than another, which is based in prejudicial thinking and often leads to discrimination.

John Howard Griffin

In 1959, John Howard Griffin embarked on a daring experiment to explore the relationship between Blacks and whites in the segregated South. After being blinded in an accident and later regaining his sight, Griffin realized just how much the ability to see could be an obstacle to true perception—especially when sight allowed people to discriminate based on skin color. He was challenged by his Black friends to "walk in the skin" of a Black person to truly understand their experience.

Griffin agreed. With the help of drugs, dyes, and radiation, he darkened his skin. For two months, he traveled through the Deep South, a white man in black skin. Griffin's disguise was so effective that not a single person of either race ever suspected that he was not Black.

Griffin became the target of racism. The attitudes he encountered from white people ranged from genuine kindness that was apparently free of racism to open hostility. Mostly, though, he was habitually scorned and rebuffed. He was harassed by teenagers, threatened by others, stared at with open hatred, and routinely denied service that he had received when his skin was light.

As he reflected on his experiences, Griffin realized that at the root of the racism he experienced was fear of the other—that is, fear of those we do not know. Although his understanding of the effects of racism was still limited in many ways, his experience helped him more fully appreciate the dignity that all people have in common.

The wage gap. The **wage gap** is the difference between the amount paid to different groups of people for their work. Much of this wage gap cannot be explained by differences in education, experience, or other qualifications. The gap applies between men and women as well as people of different races.

One cause of the gap between wages for women and men is historical. In the past, certain occupations were thought of as "women's work." Work that had fallen to women in the home, such as cooking, caring for children, sewing, and nursing, became the only work open to women seeking employment. Because the assumption was that women did not need to be breadwinners, these fields paid less than other comparable careers. It is only in recent decades that the salaries of teachers and nurses have begun to rise.

wage gap The difference between the amount paid to different groups of people for their work.

Do you perceive structural discrimination as an issue in your school community?

Assess how well the social structures of your school provide all students access to the benefits or resources of the school.

> **Discriminatory actions, prejudicial attitudes, and stereotyped images all work together to form a cycle of exclusion.**

Educational inequalities. Another example of structural discrimination can be found in the education system. As a group, the academic achievement of nonwhite students tends to lag that of white students, not because they have less academic potential, but for a complex variety of reasons, many of which can be traced to patterns of discrimination. Many schools whose students are largely nonwhite do not receive adequate levels of funding, for instance. And stereotypes sometimes cause teachers to have lower expectations of nonwhite students.

Housing discrimination. Although laws prohibiting housing discrimination have been in effect for decades, many people still face barriers when they try to buy or rent a home. Studies have shown that in some areas, Black people applying for housing are treated differently than white people with similar incomes about half the time. Discrimination ranges from being shown fewer housing units than white applicants, to being given worse rental terms, to being denied housing that was later offered to whites with the same or worse qualifications. Such widespread discrimination helps explain why many communities remain segregated along racial lines. Housing discrimination contributes to other types of structural discrimination because the barriers to good housing prevent people from moving to locations where more jobs are available, or where schools are better funded.

A Cycle of Exclusion

Discriminatory actions, prejudicial attitudes, and stereotyped images all work together to form a cycle of exclusion: a widely held stereotype combines with fear or selfishness to create a prejudicial attitude, which leads to discrimination on an individual level and then becomes incorporated into the structures of society. Structural discrimination leads to conditions that reinforce negative stereotypes. All people are called to work for an end to this cycle:

> Racism is not merely one sin among many; it is a radical evil that divides the human family and denies the new creation of a redeemed world. To struggle against it demands an equally radical transformation, in our own minds and hearts as well as in the structure of our society. ("Brothers and Sisters to Us")

For Review

1. What is a stereotype? How do we develop stereotypes?
2. Define the terms *prejudice, discrimination,* and *racism.*
3. What is structural discrimination? Briefly describe one example.
4. Describe the cycle of exclusion, illustrating your explanation with a specific example (either a real one or one you make up).

Building Inclusive Communities

To break the cycle of exclusion, we must reconsider the questions, Who belongs to our community, and who does not? Jesus was asked a similar question. Remember that Jesus taught that no commandments were greater than love of God and love of neighbor. In the Gospel of Luke, however, a questioner asked Jesus, "And who is my neighbor?" (10:29). In other words, the questioner wanted to know who deserved his love and who didn't.

Who Is My Neighbor?

The term *neighbor* refers to those who are "nigh," or near to us. This can refer

> **Jesus was teaching that love of neighbor means love of all.**

Jesus used a "good Samaritan" to challenge the self-righteousness and stereotypical thinking of his listeners. Who might appear as the "good" person in the story if Jesus were teaching today? Why would the choice of this person surprise and challenge modern listeners?

to physical nearness or to people with whom we have something in common. Often, however, we are tempted to think of "something in common" in narrow ways, such as having the same skin color or the same faith.

Jesus offers a different definition of *neighbor,* responding to the question by telling the parable of the good Samaritan, in which a Samaritan helps a wounded traveler after a priest and a Levite have walked by the man (see Luke 10:30–37). At the end of the story, Jesus asks, "Which of these three . . . was neighbor to the robbers' victim?" (10:36). Jesus' questioner reluctantly admits that the neighbor was the Samaritan.

That answer surprised Jesus' listeners. The priest and the Levite were prominent members of the Jewish community. The people of Samaria, on the other hand, were looked down on as believers in a distorted, even heretical, form of Judaism. As a result, they were usually shunned. Jesus was teaching that love of neighbor means love of all. At the same time, he was challenging his listeners' deeply held stereotypes.

Jesus Embraces Humanity

For Jesus, *neighbor* referred to anyone who deserved his love—even those who might be considered enemies (see Luke 6:27). Christ's mission of salvation was universal—that is, meant for all people. By example, Jesus taught that the ability of all people to participate in the life of the community is an important dimension of the Kingdom of God:

- The Pharisees and the scribes were reported to have said, "This man welcomes sinners and eats with them" (Luke 15:2).

- Those suffering from leprosy were especially singled out as outcasts in Jesus' day, and to even touch a leper would cause "ritual impurity." Yet, when a man covered with leprosy asked Jesus to heal him, "Jesus stretched out his hand, touched him, and said, . . . 'Be made clean'" (Luke 5:13).

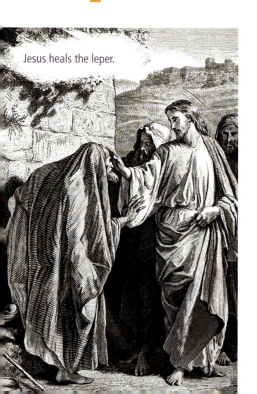

Jesus heals the leper.

- Jesus treated women with respect and included them in the life of his community. For instance, although women were not provided with religious instruction, Jesus taught them (see Luke 10:39–42).

The Christian faith teaches that Jesus' very being represents an acceptance of **humanity** because he is God incarnate, fully God and also fully human. A still greater demonstration of Christ's embrace of humanity is his death. He willingly shed his blood for the forgiveness of all. He excluded no one.

The community of people gathered in Christ—the Church—continues Jesus' mission of uniting all people in love, primarily by uniting people with God through the celebration of the liturgy. When people are truly united with God, they are united with one another. This is why the US bishops write: "Let all know that [racism] is a terrible sin that mocks the cross of Christ and ridicules the Incarnation. For the brother and sister of our Brother Jesus Christ are brother and sister to us" ("Brothers and Sisters to Us").

Although perfect unity among people cannot be achieved as long as the world is marked by sin, we can move toward that reality by opening ourselves to Jesus Christ, whose grace has the power to open our hearts to one another.

Searching the Heart

To change exclusive communities into inclusive ones, we must redefine our notions about who belongs and who is excluded; we must change our definition of *neighbor*. We need to experience **conversion**—a change of heart—on both the personal and the social level. We can begin to make that change by closely examining our own heart and the heart of society.

> Think of someone you have encountered who is often excluded from social activities. Imagine how Jesus might interact with that person. Then say a prayer asking for the ability to be more like Jesus in your daily interactions with others. Be as specific as possible.

> "To change exclusive communities into inclusive ones, we must redefine our notions about who belongs and who is excluded; we must change our definition of *neighbor.*"

---

humanity The quality or state of being human and being created in God's image with shared dignity; all human beings collectively.

conversion A profound change of heart; a turning away from sin and toward God.

Examining Our Own Heart

- **Attitudes about difference and diversity.** When we are around people who are unlike us, how do we feel deep down? Is our behavior different than when we are around people who are more like us, with whom we may feel more comfortable?

- **Self-acceptance.** People who have a hard time accepting themselves often fail to accept others. They make a show out of what they think is wrong with others to bolster a false sense of superiority.

- **The roots of our fear and hatred.** Do we fear that others will harm us in some way? Do we believe that their differences somehow hold a threat or a challenge to our way of doing things? Do our fears have any basis, or are they irrational? Are we taking out our anger toward an individual who has harmed us by hating all those who seem to be like them?

- **Responding to prejudice.** How do we respond to prejudice directed against us? Do we passively accept it or lash back in anger? Or do we follow the way of Jesus, nonviolently asserting our dignity in a way that encourages the other person to better reflect their dignity?

> Read over the five areas we need to search in our hearts. Reflect on one area you want to focus on in changing your heart.

Do our fears keep us from changing the narrative of discrimination and exclusion?

- **Our basic approach to life.** Do we put most of our efforts into serving our own needs? Do we have any concern about other people or about contributing to the common good of our communities? To what extent are we guilty of the sins of greed and **apathy**?

Examining the Heart of Society

- **Historical patterns.** Because the cycle of exclusion is deeply rooted in history, we need to ask, How have past inequalities affected the ability of people to participate in society today?
- **Patterns of power.** Who holds power in society, and how does that affect the ability of all to participate? Are all types of people represented in government, religious, and business leadership positions? Who lacks the material resources for a life of dignity, and why?
- **Opportunity for all.** Do all people have access to the benefits of society, such as a good education? Can all contribute their gifts to society, for instance, by having access to jobs that reflect their talents?
- **Honesty.** Do we as a community honestly acknowledge patterns of exclusion so they can be addressed, or do we pretend they do not exist? Do we recognize and celebrate the gifts of diversity?

> We also can build a cycle of inclusion. Once we include others, it is easier to see them as neighbors.

Working to Create Inclusive Communities

We have seen how exclusion is fed by negative stereotypes and how it continues to promote the stereotypes as well. But we also can build a cycle of inclusion. Once we include others, it is easier to see them as neighbors; seeing them in this light encourages us to further include them.

apathy The state of showing little concern or interest.

Between Individuals

The first step in creating inclusive communities is often simply getting to know "the other," those we might have fears or misconceptions about because of our lack of knowledge.

> What social group in your community do you most need to know better? Either by talking with someone from that group or by doing some research, make a list of the unique gifts people from that group bring to the community, for example, a special kind of food or music or a unique way of seeing things.

Michael Bravly and Forsan Hussein offer a good example of how personal conversion can support efforts to change structures of discrimination at a social level. Both met at Brandeis University in Massachusetts, but they came from worlds apart: Michael is a former officer in the Israeli Defense Forces, while Forsan is a Palestinian. The hostility between Israelis and Palestinians runs deep, the result of more than fifty years of conflict over land Israel now occupies.

The fear and distrust on both sides of the conflict might have been a barrier between the two, but any barrier was soon bridged by the sarcastic sense of humor each had. They quickly developed a friendship. By the end of their first semester at the school, they had formed an informal dialogue group with four other students, two Israelis and two Arabs, for the purpose of bridging the divide between the two cultures.

The group was called Children of Labaneh—an intentionally silly name that reflected something that unites rather than divides the two cultures: a love of *labaneh,* a type of thick yogurt enjoyed throughout the Middle East. At the group's weekly meetings, the students ate olives, pita bread, and, of course, *labaneh,* as they learned about one another's cultures. Each week, a student delivered a paper explaining some aspect of his or her culture, which the group then discussed. Sometimes discussions turned political and heated; other times, students just hung out and had fun. (Guy Raz, "Partners for Peace")

What started as a small group of friends eventually developed into an organization called Shalam ("Peace"). Through Shalam, Michael and Forsan began helping other people around the world create dialogue groups based on their experiences with Children of Labaneh. The friends' work was based on the belief that getting to know one another can help build peace among people, and that, in turn, can contribute to peace among nations. It was their hope that Jews and Palestinians could find a way to share the Holy Land and live together in peace. Though the Shalam organization no longer exists, Forsan has continued this work through the World Economic Forum as a Young Global Leader. The forum is a unique and diverse community of the world's most outstanding, next-generation leaders. These individuals commit their time to jointly shaping a better future and improving the state of the world.

On a Community Level

Sometimes, changing society so everyone can participate requires a cooperative effort. That is what happened in Syracuse, Indiana, when concerned students acted to support racial minorities in their mostly white community.

In 1999, racial tensions flared in Wawasee Community Schools, which serves Syracuse and two other communities, as the number of Hispanics living there steadily increased. A lack of communication led to distrust between the Hispanic community and the school system, which for a while excluded Hispanic kids from standardized testing and classes for gifted students. Racist comments from two teachers made matters even worse.

That's when some high school students formed a group called Wawasee Cares. They started with a petition drive. After collecting signatures from 1,100 of their peers, they took out a full-page ad in the local newspaper that began, "We condemn all messages of hatred and racism that have surfaced in our school and community." The group then organized a rally and spoke to teachers about their concerns during a week of diversity training.

Things began to change. The school district spent three years training teachers about diversity issues, for instance. And a local radio station started to air school closing and late-start announcements in Spanish—despite the threat of

Do you think student-led action, such as a petition, can be an instrument for change?

> **Reconciliation is an important part of creating inclusive communities.**

advertisers to pull their ads. "It's in the interest of every member of our community that every child is in school," said the radio station manager. "Some kids were missing school because of communication problems. It's a problem we could solve, and we did." (Adapted from Mary Harrison, "Awakenings in Wawasee")

Reconciliation is an important part of creating inclusive communities. As the Catholic Church advocates participation for all people, it attempts to acknowledge its own contributions to the cycle of exclusion. In a letter entitled "Heritage and Hope," the US Catholic bishops offer an apology to **Indigenous** peoples for the Church's role in perpetuating injustice:

> As Church, we often have been unconscious and insensitive to the mistreatment of our Native American brothers and sisters and have at times reflected the racism of the dominant culture of which we have been a part. . . . We extend our apology to the native peoples and pledge ourselves to work with them to ensure their rights, their religious freedom, and the preservation of their cultural heritage.

Indigenous A name given to the first known peoples who inhabited a place.

The Bismarck Indian School, which opened in 1908, was one of two off-reservation boarding schools located in North Dakota. The primary goal of these schools was to assimilate Indigenous children into non-native society.

On the National Level

Governments play a key role in breaking the cycle of exclusion when they enact legislation that promotes participation and justice. It may seem that access to buildings, health care, education, and mobility aids (walkers, canes, and crutches) should be readily available to anyone who has a disability. In truth, securing access to services is often neglected or denied. **Ableism** is the discrimination that people with disabilities face, and it encompasses practices that oppress, discriminate against, and stigmatize those who have a disability.

The government has made strides to address ableism with the Americans with Disabilities Act (ADA). This act addresses the rights of disabled Americans to participate in society by seeking to guarantee their access to schools, workplaces, and so on. Yet, the ADA did not become law until 1990. It is one of the most comprehensive pieces of civil rights legislation that prohibits discrimination and ensures that people with disabilities have the same opportunities as everyone else to participate in society. To fall under the protection of the ADA, one must have a physical or mental disability that significantly limits one or more major life activities. Though the ADA does not name all the disabilities covered, it is the role of the government to break the cycle of exclusion by enacting legislation that promotes participation and justice.

The US Catholic bishops make clear their support for legislation that encourages greater participation by attempting to correct the inequalities that were built into the structures of society because of past discrimination:

> Judiciously administered affirmative action programs in education and employment can be important

ableism Discrimination that oppresses, discriminates against, and stigmatizes those who are not "able-bodied."

The first New York City Disability Pride Parade, held in 2015.

> **Economic inequality must continue to be addressed to ensure the full participation of all nations in the global community.**

expressions of the drive for solidarity and participation that is at the heart of justice. Social harm calls for social relief. ("Economic Justice for All," 73)

On the Global Level

Exclusion on the global level needs to be addressed too. The voices of poorer, smaller nations are often ignored by global organizations determining international agreements: "Whole nations are fully prevented from participating in the international economic order because they lack the power to change their disadvantaged position" ("Economic Justice for All," 77). Furthermore, the participation of developing countries in the world economy is hampered by their huge debts to rich nations. These debts prevent the poorer countries from providing for the basic needs of their citizens. Efforts by the Church and other organizations in recent years have encouraged some nations to forgive, or write off, a portion of these burdensome debts. But economic inequality must continue to be addressed to ensure the full participation of all nations in the global community.

> Brainstorm some specific ways to build more inclusive structures at the local, national, or global level.

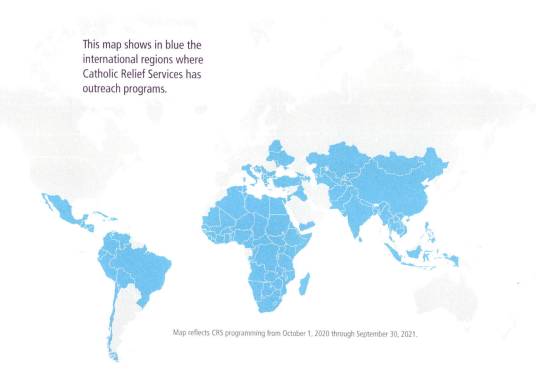

This map shows in blue the international regions where Catholic Relief Services has outreach programs.

© Catholic Relief Services

Map reflects CRS programming from October 1, 2020 through September 30, 2021.

Toward a Community of Love

We began this chapter with a question: How do we define *community?* The example of Christ reveals that true community is the place where the sharing of gifts and talents among all people makes each person more fully alive. It is a place where differences among people are not a source of division but a source of celebration.

The limitations of human sinfulness may make such a community sound like an impossible dream. In fact, the US Catholic bishops acknowledge that the fullness of love and community will be achieved only when God's work in Christ comes to completion in the Kingdom of God. This Kingdom has been inaugurated among us, but God's redeeming and transforming work is not yet complete (see "Economic Justice for All," 67). But the more we open ourselves to the Holy Spirit and to one another, the closer we come to experiencing God's Kingdom.

For Review

1. According to Jesus, who is our neighbor?
2. Name three questions that can help us examine our own heart and three questions that can help us examine the heart of society about exclusion.
3. What are three levels through which we can build inclusive communities?

WHAT CAN YOU DO?

- ☐ Make a conscious effort to get to know and respect people who are different from you. If you feel uncomfortable getting to know someone who is different, search your heart to find out why.

- ☐ Challenge stereotypes and prejudicial statements when you hear them.

- ☐ Reach out to those who are excluded from your school community and help them become more involved in a way they are comfortable with.

- ☐ Start a group in which people from different backgrounds can discuss what they have in common as well as how to break down the barriers that divide them.

- ☐ If you are part of a group that is excluded by others, help others get to know your group better by speaking out about the gifts it has to offer and the ways it is excluded. At the same time, work to change structures of exclusion.

- ☐ Organize an event that builds greater understanding of groups typically excluded from society—a celebration of diversity that showcases the gifts of different cultural groups in your community, or a presentation by someone from an excluded group.

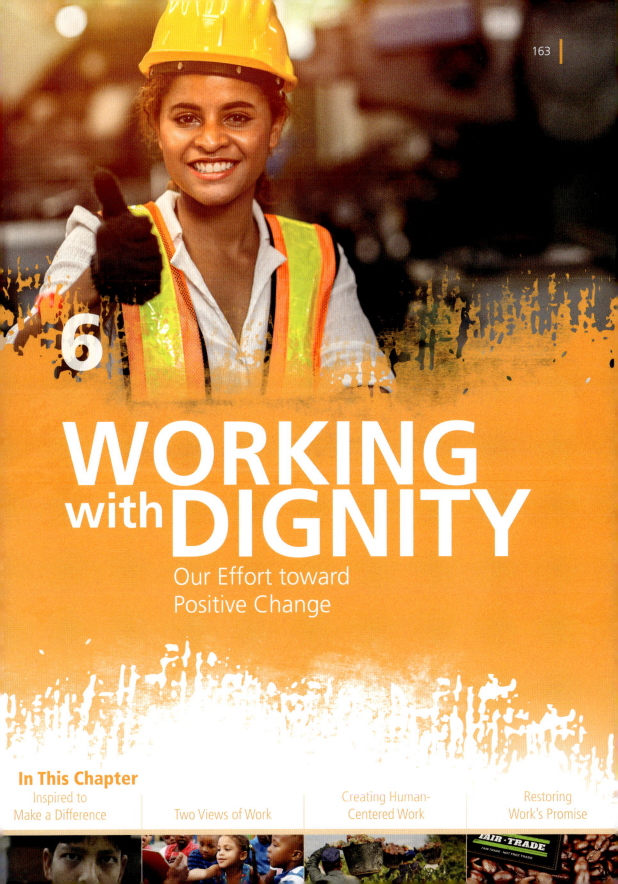

6

WORKING with DIGNITY
Our Effort toward Positive Change

In This Chapter

Inspired to Make a Difference | Two Views of Work | Creating Human-Centered Work | Restoring Work's Promise

Inspired to Make a Difference

Twelve-year-old Craig Kielburger was looking for the comics in the *Toronto Star* when a front-page headline caught his eye: "Battled Child Labour, Boy, 12, Murdered." Craig read the story about a boy his age who had been working in debt bondage since he was four years old to pay off a small loan his parents had received. The boy's name was Iqbal Masih, and his parents had borrowed 600 rupees (about $12) from the owner of a carpet factory. In exchange, Iqbal was forced to work in the factory until the loan was repaid. For twelve hours a day, six days a week, Iqbal, and children just like him, crouched before carpet looms tying tiny knots to make carpets for the European and North American markets. If the children made mistakes, they were beaten. They were also fined for every mistake they made. By the time Iqbal was ten, his family actually *owed* 13,000 rupees to the factory owner. Unfortunately, this situation is not unique. Debt bondage is often passed down from generation to generation. These corrupt employers force children of employees to labor to help pay off their parents' debt.

Iqbal was rescued by human rights activists, only to be murdered later by leaders of the carpet industry who didn't want their abusive practices to become public. It was after Iqbal's murder that Craig became aware of child labor. He began investigating what it was and what could be done to stop it. He eventually started an organization called Free the Children and began his pursuit of justice for child laborers. Craig later founded WE with his brother, an organization that works to empower youth to raise their voices and make a difference in their communities and around the world.

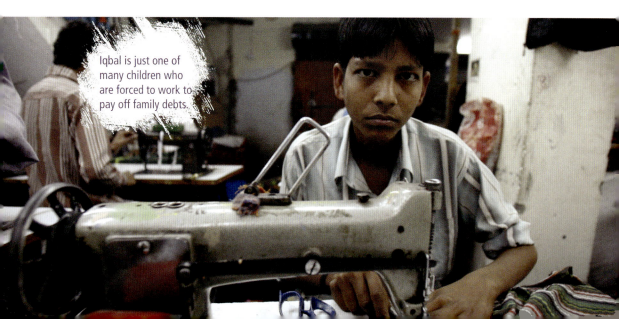

Iqbal is just one of many children who are forced to work to pay off family debts.

Workers Face Significant Challenges

Forced child labor isn't the only abuse surrounding work. Some other issues include unsafe working conditions and the problem of discrimination in the workplace. Unfortunately, these issues are more common than you might think. Some laws and policies protect workers, and some organizations exist to highlight and enforce strong workplace protocol, but the challenges continue.

For example, two teenagers were killed at a grain-storage facility in the Midwest when they were sent into a grain bin to break up clumps of corn by walking on it. They were not provided safety harnesses, and the machinery used to empty the bin was running. Rescue crews worked for hours to save the trapped teens, ages 14 and 19, who suffocated before they were freed. When the investigation of this tragedy was completed, the grain company was cited for twenty-five violations. In addition, they were found to have ignored child labor laws by hiring a worker under the age of 18 to perform a hazardous job. This failure on the part of the grain company became a warning beacon for other agricultural companies.

Migrant farmworkers also often experience labor abuses. They can be exploited when their employers confiscate or falsify immigration and work documents. In addition, the work of bending, picking, and filling buckets over and over is exhausting and can lead to long-term health problems. During harvesttimes, workers usually

Craig Kielburger
Making a Difference

Craig Kielburger was born in Ontario, Canada, in 1982. While he was attending Blessed Scalabrini Catholic School, Craig started an activist organization called Free the Children. Craig, his brother Mark, and a small group of their friends began by collecting signatures on a petition calling for the release of an imprisoned child labor activist. Craig was so determined that he eventually traveled with a family friend to Bangladesh to see the condition of child laborers for himself. The charity raised money to raid factories and free children. They eventually shifted their focus to begin funding school building projects and an international development model focused on education, clean water, health care, food security, and income generation. Craig and his brother continue their activism work today through the WE charity, an international charity and educational partner. WE functions both domestically and internationally to provide a yearlong service-learning program that nurtures compassion in students and gives them the tools to create transformative social change.

Mark and Craig Kielburger.

> Would you feel able to speak up for yourself if you were asked to work in hazardous conditions? What would you do if proper safety equipment was not provided for you?

work ten to twelve hours a day, seven days a week, with no overtime pay. In between harvests, their work disappears for weeks or months, leaving them without the means to support their families. In addition, many times workers are not provided bathroom breaks or access to clean drinking water. Many are afraid to demand fair treatment because they know they could be fired and replaced.

Labor abuses in the form of discrimination can occur in the workplace as well. Trish was told by her manager that he wished she would hurry up and retire because she was too old and there were already too many women in the office. In her work as a waitress, Jasmine experienced sexual harassment, had things thrown at her, and was called racial slurs. Her boss didn't do anything about it, and Jasmine was afraid if she pushed the issue she would be fired. Keith was the first Black police officer in a small, mostly white rural town. A short time after beginning his job, he found a piece of paper on his coat that said "Ku Klux Klan."

People deserve more than being used as tools to produce and generate profit, and labor abuses and discrimination have no place in a just society. Until workers are recognized as human beings with worth and dignity, these abuses will continue.

> **People deserve more than being used as tools to produce and generate profit, and labor abuses and discrimination have no place in a just society.**

Labor abuses can happen in any business. The abuse can come from management, coworkers, or customers. Who would you go to if you experienced workplace harassment?

© Bangkok Click Studio / Shutterstock.com

Many organizations work to provide better environments for workers. For example, the Occupational Safety and Health Administration (OSHA) is a United States agency dedicated to protecting all US workers. They investigate reported violations and put protocols in place or enforce consequences when existing laws to protect workers are broken.

The Coalition of Immokalee Farm Workers (CIW) is a worker-based organization founded in 1983 that is recognized for its achievements in the fields of corporate responsibility, community organizing, and combating modern-day slavery and other labor abuses common in agriculture. The CIW founded the Fair Food Program as a partnership between growers, workers, retailers, and consumers to transform agriculture in the United States through the power of prevention. The Fair Food Program is necessary because farm labor is one of the lowest-paid and least-protected jobs in the US. The CIW and the Fair Food Program know that **wage theft** and poverty are only part of the issue. Every day workers go to the fields knowing they may experience physical hazards, sexual assault, beating, sex trafficking, visa and document fraud, and death

> What do you think is a fair hourly wage? What basic rights do you think workers should be entitled to?

> **wage theft** The denial of wages or employee benefits rightfully owed to employees. It can occur in various ways, such as failing to pay overtime, violating minimum-wage laws, forcing employees to work "off the clock," and misclassifying employees as independent contractors to avoid paying benefits.

threats to themselves and their families. Before the CIW was formed and began advocating for farmworkers, the wage for picking a bucket of tomatoes had remained the same for more than three decades!

Many people do not feel empowered to speak up or advocate for themselves when they are asked to work in hazardous conditions or suffer the effects of discrimination, so advocating for laws that protect workers and supporting organizations that fight for workers' rights is important. When we become aware of dangers to workers' safety and dignity, at a minimum, we can share that information to increase awareness for others. We can also support businesses that have strong workplace policies or participate in programs that certify their commitment to and record of ensuring workplace safety, equity, and respect for workers.

> **In Catholic social teaching, work has a value that goes beyond what it produces.**

What Is the Value of Work?

In Catholic social teaching, work has a value that goes beyond what it produces. Work is a basic human right because it is necessary for human life, and it enables people to participate in the life of the community. But in the view of Catholic social teaching, work has value even beyond those basics: it is an expression of the creativity we possess as images of God. For these reasons, the Church affirms the dignity of work and the rights of workers.

Wage theft occurs when employers don't fully pay employees for their labor. This can be in the form of paying less than minimum wage, withholding overtime pay, or requiring employees to continue to work after they clock out.

The examples presented earlier illustrate that not everyone holds that view. When work is valued only for what it produces, rather than for the people who perform the work, workers often lose out. In these cases, work might actually harm a worker's life, dignity, and ability to participate in the community.

> Think of one way you have been affected by a worker this week. Write a paragraph reflecting on how this person's work affected your life and dignity, and how it might affect the life and dignity of the worker.

For Review

1. List three ways the dignity of work and the rights of workers are violated.
2. Name at least two organizations or institutions that are concerned with the dignity of work and the rights of workers.
3. What does Catholic social teaching say the value of work is? What is an alternate view of work that can harm workers?

Two Views of Work

Work is any sustained effort expended for a purpose that makes a difference in the world. People often view work as a chore, a necessary but not very enjoyable reality of life. In this view, work is toil—it is difficult, challenging, and wearing. This view legitimately reflects part of the reality of work. But Christian justice has a different view of work, one that says work still has the potential to be very good.

> *Christian justice . . . says work still has the potential to be very good.*

The Goodness of Work

Listen to how the following people approach their work:

- "Teaching isn't just a job. Of course, it pays the bills, but teaching is also about serving my

work Any sustained effort expended for a purpose that makes a difference in the world.

students. I truly care for my students and try to help them reach their potential. Though I don't always see immediate effects, I know I am filling a need in the lives of my students." —Sylvia, elementary school teacher

- "I'm sure many people wouldn't think that being a checkout clerk at a grocery store is a way to care for others. But to me, the most important part of my job is how people feel after interacting with me. I hope they leave the store with a smile on their face or feeling just a little bit better after I speak to them with genuine respect and kindness." —Dallas, grocery store clerk

- "Some people don't think of engineering as a field where the employees are concerned with people in addition to process and materials. And it's true, some contracting companies don't seem to be too concerned with how their product affects the environment. I try to reduce the impact of construction and pollution in both the short and long term because I'm trying to be mindful of the people and surroundings that our products affect."—Elizabeth, structural engineer

These workers' comments reflect the Church's attitude toward work. The US Catholic bishops sum up that attitude in their pastoral letter titled "Everyday Christianity." In it, they list four basic aspects of work:

> In the Catholic tradition, work is not a burden or just a way to pay bills. Work has a deeper, personal meaning. Work is a way of supporting our family, realizing our dignity, promoting the common good, and participating in God's creation.

A closer look at each of these points reveals the deeper value of work.

> Reflect on some work you have done for the pure pleasure of the activity (a chore, an artistic endeavor, or some volunteer work). What made it enjoyable? What did you gain from doing it?

Work should enable people to meet the basic needs of their family. Why is the minimum wage slow to increase while the cost of living continues to rise?

Family Needs

When we speak of a person's work, we often use the term *livelihood*: work that provides the basic necessities of life. The income from work enables a family to maintain a home and to buy food and clothing. Work also can provide these things directly. Workers can build shelters, grow food, and make clothing for themselves and their family. Work is a foundation for family life, meeting the family's survival needs. If a family remains in need even though one or both adults are working, work is not achieving its fundamental purpose.

In addition to providing for the family's material needs, work educates the children in the family. Parents can show their children how to be creative with their lives through work and help their children achieve the fulfillment of their potential.

Human Dignity

Besides providing a livelihood, work allows us to grow as people, learning and putting our natural talents to use.

> **Work is a foundation for family life, meeting the family's survival needs.**

Talk to a few adults in your life about the work they do for their livelihood. Do they view their work as fulfilling? Why did they make this career choice? Do they believe their work gives them dignity because it helps them provide for themselves and their families, or does their work make them feel not valued? Why?

> **Work is the primary means by which each of us becomes all God calls us to be.**

Have you ever been responsible for babysitting, raising a pet, housesitting, or caring for a garden? In what way does this responsibility give you a sense of dignity or worth?

What gives dignity is work. People who do not have a job, feel that something is missing, they lack that dignity that work properly gives, that anoints with dignity. Work expresses and nurtures the dignity of the human being, allows them to develop the capacities that God gave them, helps them to weave relationships of exchange and mutual help, allows them to feel like a collaborator of God to care for and develop this world, makes them feel useful to society and in solidarity with their loved ones. (Adapted from Pope Francis, "Video Message from Holy Father Francisco on the Occasion of the Fifty-Seventh Colloquium of the IDEA Foundation")

Work is the primary means by which each of us becomes all God calls us to be. We do this through our work, in part by contributing to the common good and participating in God's creation.

The Common Good

Every worker is a member of the larger society, so work enhances the common good. "Work serves to add to the heritage of the whole human family, of all the people living in the world" ("On Human Work," 10). In a class discussion about the value of work, one student's face lit up with sudden insight:

> Now I understand why my dad is such a perfectionist about his work! He's a carpenter, and he says that if he's going to put in a door, it will be a door that works perfectly. Now I see that it's not

so much the door he cares about; it's the people who will use it. He wants to give them something that's perfect because that's what they should have.

This student spoke with unmistakable pride; she had not realized before what a valuable contribution her father was making to others' lives. A door that works perfectly is a simple thing we might not appreciate unless we had to struggle with a poorly crafted door. Work is a way for us to provide something good and useful for others.

Sharing in God's Work

The Creation narratives in the Book of Genesis tell us that work is central to who we are as persons. Because we are created as images of a God who creates, we are invited to share in his creative work:

> [Humankind], created to God's image, received a mandate to subject to [themselves] the earth and all it contains, and to govern the world with justice and holiness. . . . While providing the substance of life for themselves and their families, men and women are performing their activities in a way which appropriately benefits society. They can justly consider that by their labour they are unfolding the creator's work. (*The Church in the Modern World*, 34)

Whenever our work makes the world a better place, it reflects the work of God. It is for this reason that the Church says work has a natural dignity.

> Whenever our work makes the world a better place, it reflects the work of God.

Pope Francis
on Participating in God's Work

We collaborate with the creative work of God when, through our work, we cultivate and preserve creation; we participate, in the Spirit of Jesus, in his redemptive mission, when by our activity we give sustenance to our families and respond to the needs of our neighbor. (In Hannah Brockhays, "Pope Francis Says Work's Not Just an Occupation")

When Good Work Is Denied

Notice that each of the dimensions of the value of work reflects basic relationships necessary for justice: the relationships with one's dignity, family, community, and God. Because work is necessary to maintain these life-giving relationships, all people have a responsibility to work. But justice says that whenever people have a responsibility to do something, they also have a corresponding right to do it. The responsibility to work is balanced by the right to work.

> "The responsibility to work is balanced by the right to work."

What would we expect work to look like if it reflected the values of the Christian worldview? Some of the characteristics associated with good work might include the following:

- a wage sufficient to support a family
- a fair opportunity for advancement, regardless of ethnicity, gender, or personal beliefs
- a workplace where health and safety guidelines for the industry are observed
- medical and retirement benefits
- ongoing training
- the ability to join a union or association to protect worker rights and privileges
- an employer who respects their employees, seeking their input and adjusting for the demands of their personal lives
- work that benefits others, or at least does not harm them

All these are characteristics of good work. But many workers around the world are denied even the most basic benefits of work. In turn, the significance of their work, and the dignity and satisfaction they should receive from their work, is absent. Many workers don't earn enough to support themselves, have no health or retirement benefits, and work in environments that are unsafe or unhealthy. In developing nations, the situation can be even worse: for many workers there are no rest periods, few days off, and hardly any free time. Some workers are not even free to leave the premises where they work. And, of course, many of these workers are children.

Treating workers like machines signals a dehumanization of the workforce. Workers are seen as tools, not as people, and their treatment is determined solely by economic considerations. In this view, the length of the workday is determined by the number of hours a worker can stay at their job without collapsing. No consideration is given to the worker because their worth is measured only in terms of what they can produce.

In many countries, labor laws afford little protection to workers. According to the International Trade Union Confederation, many countries allow unions and support laws meant to guarantee minimum wage, set maximum work hours, and require disability compensation, but in other countries, such as Argentina, Egypt, India, and Panama, union activity is repressed, and

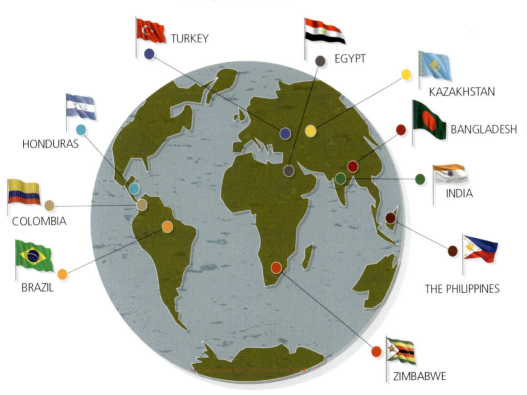

> **Another consequence of unemployment is the loss of a sense of personal dignity.**

workers' protections can be tenuous. Laws supporting workers are almost impossible to enforce in places such as Brazil, Zimbabwe, Colombia, the Philippines, and Saudi Arabia, where there is violent repression of strikes and protests, and threats and intimidation of union leaders.

Similar violations of existing laws are widespread, as in sweatshops in the United States, where many workers are illegal immigrants, and as such are unable to bring violations to the attention of the authorities without risking deportation. Others, such as domestic workers, may fall outside the protection of laws because they are hired "off the books."

Unemployment

Of course, many people are unable to find any productive work at all. The consequences of unemployment can be devastating. In emerging nations, employment may mean the difference between survival and starvation. Developed nations provide some financial support for the unemployed, but for many workers, the loss of a job can result in poverty.

Another consequence of unemployment is the loss of a sense of personal dignity. "Very few people survive long periods of unemployment without some psychological damage even if they have sufficient funds to meet their needs[1]," the US Catholic bishops

Unemployment not only creates a financial strain but also can negatively impact a person's physical and mental health.

note in the pastoral letter "Economic Justice for All" (141). Long-term unemployment has the potential to cause great harm to families. According to a study published in the *International Journal of Mental Health Systems*, the longer a person is unemployed, the more difficult it becomes to reenter the workforce. Numerous studies show a significant link between chronic joblessness and negative physical and mental health. Unemployed individuals are more likely to suffer from depression, anxiety, and other mental illnesses. They are more prone to develop stress-related conditions such as arthritis, heart attack, and stroke. These health issues are magnified by the fact that they often don't have access to the same health insurance that employers offer to employees.

Barriers to Work

Those who are excluded from full participation in society face special challenges in finding good work. Discrimination based on race and gender form one barrier; poverty is another. Welfare reform legislation passed in 1996 requires aid recipients to find work or lose benefits. But many welfare recipients lack the education and skills to find good work. Take Maria Ortega's story, for example, which has been documented in the book *Climbing the Walls*. Maria is a single mother living in southern California who never finished high school. As part of the effort to move welfare recipients into jobs, her county provided her with two years of basic education and computer training. During that time, Maria began volunteering in various neighborhood offices doing clerical work. After the two years were up, she was expected to find a job—or eventually face the loss of her benefits. She looked for work for four months, filling out three applications a day with no results. It was a challenge to even receive a reply to a job application, much less to secure a fair-wage job, with little experience.

Maria eventually did find work with a landscaping company, although she had to commute over an hour each way. As is often the case, jobs are not located near the highest concentrations of unemployed people. Because she began working, her food stamps

> Consider the conditions necessary for Maria Ortega to get and maintain good work.

were cut, even though the job paid only seven dollars an hour. That left very little for living after she paid for the transportation and childcare necessary to maintain the job. Unfortunately, Maria's case is not unique. Low wages are a major obstacle to good work for millions of families.

For Review

1. In your own words, restate the four purposes of work identified in Church teaching.
2. Why do people have a responsibility to work?
3. What does it mean to treat workers as a means of production?
4. Name at least three ways people are prevented from having good work.

Creating Human-Centered Work

Good work is a basic foundation for justice in the world. The lack of good work not only leads to poverty but also prevents people from participating in society and becoming all they are meant to be. How can we provide good work for all people? According to Catholic social teaching, the key is ensuring that work serves people before products.

A Parable about Work

Jesus himself was a worker, living in a culture that tended to equate a person's means of livelihood with their value as a person. Manual labor was not highly regarded in itself, yet Jesus worked as a carpenter before he began teaching. He clearly directed his message to workers, using all manner of human work to illustrate his teachings: tending sheep, baking bread, making wine, fishing, farming, and housekeeping, for instance.

Jesus told a parable about work that says a lot about what work is meant to be in a just world. As you read the parable of the laborers in the vineyard, pay attention to how the workers are treated:

> The kingdom of heaven is like a landowner who went out at dawn to hire laborers for his vineyard. After agreeing with them for the usual

Creating Human-Centered Work 179

If you were one of the first laborers hired, how would you feel about being paid the same as those hired late in the day?

daily wage, he sent them into his vineyard. Going out about nine o'clock, he saw others standing idle in the marketplace, and he said to them, "You too go into my vineyard, and I will give you what is just." So they went off. [And] he went out again around noon, and around three o'clock, and did likewise. Going out about five o'clock, he found others standing around, and said to them, "Why do you stand here idle all day?" They answered, "Because no one has hired us." He said to them, "You too also go into my vineyard." (Matthew 20:1–7)

At the end of the day, each of the laborers is paid. The usual arrangement would be to pay each laborer according to the amount of work he did. But in Jesus' parable, the landowner pays each worker the full daily wage. The laborers who worked all day complain:

"These last ones worked only one hour, and you have made them equal to us, who bore the day's burden and the heat." He said to one of them in reply, "My friend, I am not cheating you. Did you not agree with me for the usual daily wage? Take what is yours and go. What if I wish to give this last one the same as you? [Or] am I not free to do as I wish with my own money? Are you envious because I am generous?" (Matthew 20:11–15)

Is the landowner's payment of the workers fair?

Work Is for People

On the deepest level, the parable of the laborers in the vineyard is about God's generosity toward all—even those who, according to the world's standards, do not seem to deserve it.

But the parable also teaches us about the nature of just work. The landowner is concerned with justice, agreeing to pay "whatever is just." He pays all the workers the "usual daily wage"—a wage that is sufficient for living—because, in the landowner's view, the worker is more important than the quantity of work being done.

This is a basic insight of Catholic social teaching. The Church draws a distinction between the **subjective aspect of work**, which is what the worker experiences, and the **objective aspect of work**, which is what the worker produces. In his 1981 encyclical "On Human Work," Saint Pope John Paul II says that the subjective aspect of work is more important than the objective aspect:

> The basis for determining the value of human work is not primarily the kind of work being done, but the fact that the one who is doing it is a person. . . . This does not mean that from the objective point of view human work cannot and must not be rated and qualified in any way. It only means that . . . in the first place work is "for man" and not man "for work." (6)

And Pope Francis echoed that sentiment when he spoke to the managers and workers of the Terni Steel Mill in Italy:

> Work, in fact, directly concerns the human person, his life, his freedom and his happiness. The primary value of work is the good of the human person since it fulfills him as such, with his inner talents and his intellectual, creative and physical abilities. Hence the scope of work is not only profit and economics; its purpose above all regards man and his dignity.

> Using an internet job site, search for job postings in your area. Write down ten different types of jobs listed. Rank the jobs from 1 to 10, with 1 being the job generally considered the most prestigious. Does our society tend to equate a person's means of livelihood with their value as a person?

subjective aspect of work What the worker experiences in the action of working.

objective aspect of work What the worker produces as a result of their work.

The final result of the work is secondary to the fulfillment that the person achieves by doing the work.

Imagine a five-year-old working with poster paints. He shows his mother the masterpiece he has created, looking for approval. Only the most insensitive mother would criticize the artistic merit of the painting. It is the subjective aspect of the work that would be important to the mother; the child's joy in painting and presenting the picture has more value to her than the picture itself. This is not to imply that work has no objective value, but because the mother loves her child, the child is more important; the painting, though the mother may treasure it, is secondary.

In a similar way, because God loves us, *we* are important to him; our work is secondary. Simply put, work should serve the good of the people doing it. When it does not, then it is not just.

> In a similar way, because God loves us, we are important to him; our work is secondary.

The Rights and Responsibilities of Workers

The Church's view that work should serve the good of workers leads it to claim that workers have certain rights that should not be violated. These can be divided into rights that protect workers' responsibility to meet family needs and rights that protect workers' dignity.

Meeting Family Needs

Obviously, when people cannot work, families will suffer. But to speak of work that is just means more than earning money. Catholic social teaching on work and the family can be summarized in three ways:

- **The right to work.** Catholic social teaching affirms that everyone has the right to work. Work is the means by which people fulfill their responsibility to provide for themselves and their families, as well as a way to find fulfillment and to benefit others. It is also the primary way people take part in God's work of creation. Clearly, if people are denied work, they are missing out on something important to their humanity.

- **A just wage.** Because Church teachings identify work as the basis for family life, the pay for work can be considered just only if it is enough to support the worker's family. In any agreement between employer and worker, only a **living wage**—a wage that enables workers to support a decent life for themselves and their families—can be regarded as a just wage.

> *Work is the means by which people fulfill their responsibility to provide for themselves and their families, as well as a way to find fulfillment and to benefit others.*

living wage A wage that enables workers to support a decent life for themselves and their families.

Do you think the shift to many people working from home impacts families in a positive or negative way?

Why do you think the Catholic Church is supportive of the accessibility of unions for workers?

- **Respect for the worker's family.** As part of the whole person, the worker's home life should be considered too. This is particularly true for working women, who are sometimes "punished" for attending to the needs of the family. People should have enough leisure time to develop talents and to take part in the life of their community.

Supporting Human Dignity

In addition, everything surrounding work should accommodate the worker's dignity:

- **A safe work environment.** Employers have a responsibility for the general safety of their workers, even in dangerous jobs. The Church asks employers not to give workers more work than they can do, not to give them work unsuited to their age, and to avoid harming their safety in any way.

- **Permission to join unions.** All workers should be allowed to join unions so that they have a voice in corporate decisions. A strike by employees is one of the methods used by unions in the struggle for justice. The strike is a legitimate tool, but one that should be used only as an extraordinary measure. Employees and employers should first strive to work together in solidarity to create justice in the workplace.

> **Church teaching urges that all workers should be treated equally.**

- **Equal treatment.** Church teaching urges that all workers should be treated equally. The working class are citizens by nature and right, the same as the rich. It would be a grave injustice to favor one portion of the population over another. Though workers may have varied jobs with different levels of responsibility and required skill sets, no occupation is superior to another. Regardless of the job, the work put forth is deserving of equal respect and treatment.

- **The right to private property and economic initiative.** Because all people have the right to work, all people also have the right to **economic initiative**—in other words, to be self-employed, to start a business, and to expand one's business. The structure of society should avoid limiting the right to economic initiative. The right to own private property is part of the right to economic intiative. Both of these rights are meant to serve the common good and are therefore limited by the need to respect human life and dignity as well as to care for God's creation.

> Think about how a work experience has helped you be more fully what you are meant to be. (Your example does not have to be paid work.) What did you do, and how did it affect you?

economic initiative The right to be self-employed, to start a business, and to expand one's business.

The Right to Education

To the list above, we can add one more right necessary for good work: the right to a good education. The lack of an adequate education prevents millions of people from developing their talents and finding work that is needed by their communities.

Among developing nations, many governments have directed most of their national budget to the military or to repaying debts. Little money may be left for education. When the quality of schools is low and the cost of attending them is high, parents send even their youngest children to work. These children are denied the education they deserve; later they cannot find skilled employment as adults. The long-term result is a population unfit for the kind of jobs necessary for their country's development: the people remain poor, and their government continues to borrow.

Solidarity in Work

Historically, discussions about work, workers, and justice have tended to divide people along ideological lines. The exploitation of workers that occurred during the Industrial Revolution led to a debate between those who favored unrestricted capitalism and those who favored forms of socialism.

The Church responded to this debate by rejecting the extremes of both systems. Catholic social teaching has always advocated that economic systems be based on love of God and neighbor. The key to creating good work for all is solidarity between employers and workers.

Cardinal Cupich:
Committed to Workers

When Pope Francis appointed Cardinal Blase J. Cupich to the Archdiocese of Chicago in 2014, one of Cardinal Cupich's first priorities was to express his commitment to supporting workers. Cardinal Cupich delivered a clear message about the position of the Catholic Church on the dignity of work and the rights of workers in his speech at the Plumber's Union Hall in 2015. "I have come today to tell Chicago's workers, the Catholic Church is with you; Pope Francis is with you; and I am with you," Cupich proclaimed. Though he acknowledged that the Church cannot weigh in on every issue, he insisted, "when the Church sees fundamental values being threatened or undermined, the Church will speak up—to offer basic moral principles, to defend the weak and vulnerable and to promote the common good."

When people heard this message, it gave them the courage to speak out regarding their working conditions and needs. The Catholic Church in the Archdiocese of Chicago, led by Cardinal Cupich, continues to take action to ensure union labor is used in construction projects, picket lines are honored, and a safety net for all workers is provided.

> **The key to creating good work for all is solidarity between employers and workers.**

The model for this solidarity is Christ. The Church teaches that when we approach our work with love, it can transform the world. Solidarity with others is not a feeling of vague compassion or shallow distress at the misfortunes of so many people, both near and far. Rather, it demands a "firm and persevering determination to commit oneself to the common good" (Pope Saint John Paul II, *Compendium of the Social Doctrine of the Church*, 193).

For Review

1. What does the parable of the laborers in the vineyard say about human work?
2. Explain the difference between the subjective and the objective aspects of work.
3. Does Catholic social teaching put more value on the subjective or objective aspects of work, and why?
4. List the rights of workers, including a brief explanation of each.
5. How does inadequate education affect work?

Restoring Work's Promise

Is the Church's vision of just work practical? Obviously, making just work available to all people would require broad changes in society and in workplaces. Those changes are practical only to the extent that we base our work on solidarity with one another.

The primary responsibility for the welfare of workers falls to employers. But the competitive nature of the marketplace makes it difficult for individual employers to make these changes alone. Making changes on a social level lays the foundation for changing the way we work.

Indirect Employers

An **indirect employer** is any policy-making institution that helps regulate what employers may or may not do. An indirect employer could be a labor union, a national government, or a worldwide organization. Although the employer is directly responsible for working conditions, the indirect employer needs to create a climate that encourages just labor practices. For example, the International Labour Organization (ILO) is the United Nations' agency that "helps advance the economic and working conditions that give all workers, employers and governments a stake in lasting peace, prosperity and progress." ("Mission and Impact of the ILO"). This organization draws up and oversees international labor standards. Creating fair economic structures for everyone would curb such concerns and help in the fight against working conditions that are dehumanizing.

Ask a few employed adults who the indirect employers are that regulate what they may or may not do.

indirect employer Any policy-making institution that helps regulate what employers may or may not do.

The Power of Cooperation

Acting alone, it may be difficult for us to imagine transforming the experience of workers. But the key to changing labor conditions is cooperating with others to influence direct and indirect employers.

Political Activism

In a democracy, citizens have not only the right but also the responsibility to influence the decisions made by government. Voting is not the only way to influence public policy. Students, even those who are not old enough to vote, can and should let their voices be heard by public policymakers. Which of the following are ways you would be willing to work to influence policy?

> The key to changing labor conditions is cooperating with others to influence direct and indirect employers.

- ☐ Organize a petition.
- ☐ Sign a petition.
- ☐ Speak at a local government meeting.
- ☐ Write letters to the newspaper.
- ☐ Put up posters about upcoming legislation or issues.
- ☐ Wear a t-shirt or pin supporting a cause
- ☐ Join in a public demonstration or march.
- ☐ Write letters to your congressional representatives or senators.
- ☐ Use social media to bring awareness to issues around work that are of community importance.
- ☐ Participate in social justice projects that focus on workers' rights through your school, and submit coverage of the events to local news media.

Purchasing Power

Another way young people can exercise their power for justice is through their purchasing practices. The power of consumers can be used in practices such as boycotts. Boycotts put pressure on companies, and even countries, to change their practices. Nationally, the Diocese of Columbus in Ohio has joined many individuals, organizations, and other faith leaders in a boycott, started by the Coalition of Immokalee Workers, of a popular fast-food chain. The goal is to encourage this chain to join other fast-food restaurants and small grocery companies to enroll in the Fair Food Program. Through this action, the Diocese of Columbus is holding true to Catholic social teaching by taking actions that support the dignity of work and the fair treatment of people who do the work. When restaurants and grocers refuse to participate in the Fair Food Program, they are profiting from farmworker abuse and poverty. Would you be willing to participate in a boycott to ensure the fair wage of the workers who provide your food?

Altogether, young people in the United States spend billions of dollars every year. Some have been very influential in boycotts of manufacturers whose labor practices are unfair. For example, colleges and

> **Young people can exercise their power for justice through their purchasing practices.**

Young people have influential purchasing power. Have you ever considered who produces the things you buy?

universities receive income from the sale of clothing, such as sweatshirts and caps, that display their logos. At campuses across the country, college students have asked school administrations to sign agreements only with those clothing manufacturers who can guarantee, through independent inspections, that their clothing is not manufactured under unjust working conditions.

A Voice in the Workplace

Finally, if you work, you may be able to have some input on policies at your workplace. Every employee can take responsibility to find out about working conditions where they work, and about the indirect impact the business has on other workers.

It can be difficult to picture ourselves questioning accepted practices, especially at work, but justice calls each of us to take a high degree of responsibility and to use whatever influence we do have. We are each called to demonstrate a commitment to solidarity, not just to approve of it abstractly.

> "We are each called to demonstrate a commitment to solidarity, not just to approve of it abstractly."

The Special Role of Business Leaders

Business leaders have a good deal of power to shape not only the working conditions of their employees but the structures of society as well. As a result, they have a special responsibility to work for justice in solidarity with workers, the rest of the human community, and God's creation.

What happens when business leaders base their practices on solidarity? The following three examples illustrate the good that can result:

Solidarity with Employees

Tom Colicchio is the chef and owner of Crafted Hospitality. He appeared in the documentary *A Place at the Table*, which examined the issue of hunger in America through the stories of people suffering from food insecurity. Colicchio knows what it's like at the bottom. He started work scooping ice cream, flipping burgers, and being a busboy at a seafood restaurant. To get work experience before culinary school, he worked in restaurants, sharpening his skills and moving on.

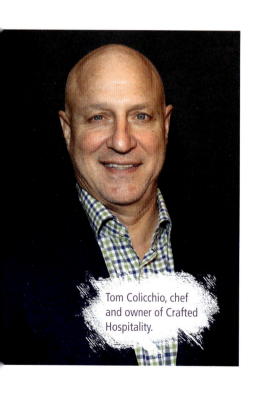

Tom Colicchio, chef and owner of Crafted Hospitality.

© lev radin / Shutterstock.com

Now Colicchio is flexing his power to help workers in the restaurant industry. He is an outspoken activist for the hospitality industry, cofounding Food Policy Action in 2012 and the Independent Restaurant Coalition in 2020. Colicchio has been recognized within the grassroots of the hospitality industry, as well as honored by the Restaurant Opportunities Center United for "high road" practices in his businesses. This means Colicchio and other honorees have raised their wages and provided benefits such as earned sick days. Colicchio ensures that his employees receive a fair wage by including tips in their paychecks. This protects the employees at tax time, and safeguards against wage theft that can occur if servers or bartenders have a slow or low-tipping shift. Restaurants are legally obligated to make up those lost tip wages in an employee's paycheck. But a common practice is to keep the employees' low hourly wage the same regardless of how much money is given in tips. Colicchio is spearheading an effort to create a policy that would guarantee a fair wage for all hospitality workers in order for them to support themselves and their families without the subsidy of government assistance programs such as Medicaid and food stamps.

How would you describe Tom Colicchio's actions as coming out of an understanding of solidarity?

Solidarity with the Marginalized

A special dimension of solidarity is choosing to help the poor and vulnerable. The story of Dave's Killer Bread and Dave Dahl's involvement in other vocational programs illustrates how doing so can transform lives.

Dave Dahl was born in Portland, Oregon. Growing up, he worked at the family bakery founded by his father. In his teen years, he fought with his father and turned to a life of drugs and petty crime. Dave spent the next fifteen years of his life in and out of prison for various crimes, including burglary. When he was finally released from prison, he worked for minimum wage for his brother at the family bakery. He developed an organic cornmeal loaf and sold it at farmer's markets.

When it became more popular, the team began selling the bread with the name "Dave's Killer Bread"

A special dimension of solidarity is choosing to help the poor and vulnerable.

Dave Dahl, creator of Dave's Killer Bread.

and printed Dave's rehabilitative story on the packaging. Rather than be turned off by the story of an ex-con baker, people were inspired. With the success of the bread, their company grew from twenty-five employees to over three hundred. Dave's Killer Bread went on to become the number 1 organic bread in the United States. Dave and his brother Glenn continued to make a practice of hiring felons, as finding employment after incarceration is incredibly difficult. After selling more than half of the company so it could continue to expand, Dave invested $250,000 in Nucleos, a program that provides credentialed education and training programs to incarcerated inmates.

But the work of solidarity does not stop there. The new management of Dave's Killer Bread sponsored the Second Chance Project, partnering with San Quentin State Prison. The program's purpose is to provide people with the training and resources needed to turn around and avoid relapsing into criminal behavior. Dave's Killer Bread doesn't avoid people with criminal records. In fact, they find them to be among their most loyal, dedicated, and trustworthy employees.

Dave's Killer Bread, Nucleos, and the Second Chance Project are all excellent examples of how human-centered work allows marginalized workers to become more fully all they are meant to be.

Solidarity amid Globalization

As with many efforts to eliminate labor abuses, activists run into the reality of **economic globalization**, which means that the economies of different nations are increasingly tied together by interdependent relationships. As a result, working conditions in one country are often influenced by business practices in another country. Catholic social teaching has emphasized the need for this globalization to be accompanied by solidarity.

economic globalization An interdependence of nations around the globe fostered through free trade.

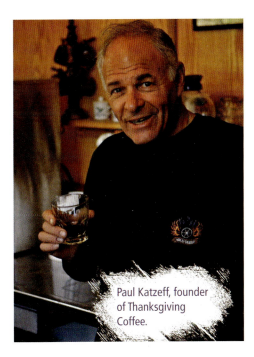

Paul Katzeff, founder of Thanksgiving Coffee.

Paul Katzeff, the owner of a company that sells expensive gourmet coffee nationwide, illustrates the importance of solidarity in a globalized economy: It was a spirit of solidarity that led Paul to accept an invitation to visit the fields of a Nicaraguan coffee grower. Paul wanted to become more aware of his relationship with the people who provided the beans for his coffee. He was shocked by the poverty that he saw among the coffee growers, and he learned that a coffee picker's family might earn only 30 to 50 cents for a pound of coffee that sold for $10–15 in the United States.

As a result of what he saw in Nicaragua, Paul developed the Coffee for Peace program. Through this program, Paul would buy coffee directly from the farmers, eliminating the middlemen. In addition, Thanksgiving Coffee, his coffee company, added a surcharge

From
Soup Kitchen
to Bakery Kitchen

A group of regular visitors to Haley House, a popular soup kitchen offering a variety of services for poor and homeless people in Boston, wanted to learn a trade so that they could find work. With financial help from the Catholic Campaign for Human Development, Haley House started training the people in bakery skills. The popular bakery training program offers six months of paid instruction in basic baking and food service skills. And while the trainees are learning the trade, the food and baked goods they create are sold at the Haley House café and catering business.

Dozens of the trainees have completed the bakery training program and have found work in the Boston area. According to Haley House's executive director, the food service industry typically pays a living wage and is one of the few industries open to people who may have a criminal record. Haley House's Bakery Training Program is an excellent example of a program that teaches the dignity of work and supports the rights of workers.

Find something in your house that was produced in another country—for instance, food, clothing, electronics. Then contact the manufacturer's customer service department by phone or online. Ask for any information the company can provide about the working conditions of the people who produced the product (use the list of workers' rights as a guide). If the company does not provide any information, consider your opinion about whether consumers have a responsibility to know how products are produced.

of fifty cents to each coffee bag's purchase price that would go directly back to the villages where the coffee came from, allowing villagers to buy livestock, plant gardens, or otherwise improve their situation.

As Paul learned more, however, he realized that protecting the environment was a related and important justice issue, so he enlisted the help of experts to develop a system that would encourage coffee-farming practices that protected the environment while earning more for the farmers. The coffee farmers who grow for Katzeff's company are monetarily rewarded for farming according to safe environmental practices: growing coffee in the shade, using natural fertilizers, and so on. But the reward of improved living conditions ensures their future. The invitation that Paul Katzeff accepted turned out to be an opportunity to recognize that his business in North America had a direct impact on working families around the world. In fact, the company motto came to Paul on his flight home from Nicaragua—"Not Just a Cup, but a Just Cup." The solidarity Katzeff strives for is necessary to end inhumane working conditions globally.

When work provides us with dignity and the ability to provide, as well as contribute to the community, the full value of work is experienced.

Toward More Human Work

What is the value of work? We have answered that question in many ways. Work has value when it provides good things for both the workers and those who use what the workers produce. But it also has value because through it we continue God's work of creation in the world. Work has value because it makes us "more fully human," that is, more like the images of God we were made to be.

Ultimately, the ability of work to help us really live—by what it provides for each of us and our community, as well as for what it helps us as workers to become—is its true value.

> With some classmates, prepare a skit that shows the value of good work. Be prepared to share how your skit illustrates the dignity of work and the rights of workers.

For Review

1. Explain the term *indirect employer*.
2. What are three ways people can cooperate to change the policies of employers?
3. Define *economic globalization,* and explain its implications for work.
4. Briefly explain the role solidarity should play in good business practices.

- When you are making job or career decisions, ask yourself: Will this work help me become who I am called to be? Will it help or harm the common good?

- Make your work a prayer by doing it as well as you can, for the good of yourself and others.

- If your employer's practices or workplace conditions seem to be harming workers, customers, or the environment, tell your supervisor. If possible, offer an alternative way of doing things that solves the problem. If the problem is serious and your employer doesn't do anything to stop it, notify the government agency that regulates your workplace. Confrontation and risk can be uncomfortable—especially if a job is at stake—but justice calls us to take such risks for the sake of the well-being of others.

- Use your purchasing power to practice solidarity with people working under unjust labor conditions. Find out whether the company that produces your school's uniforms, sweatshirts, or athletic wear can guarantee just working conditions at the clothing factories that make its products. If not, work to change the company that provides your school uniforms.

- Look for an organization that promotes work with dignity and plan a campaign at your school to raise money to support or build a school in an area of the world that needs one.

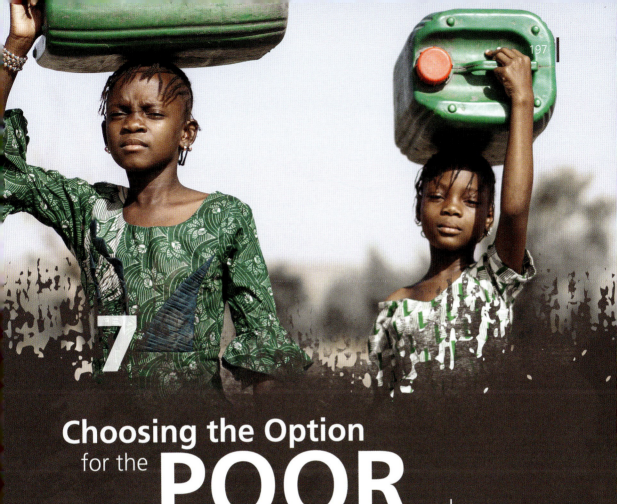

7

Choosing the Option for the POOR and VULNERABLE

Breaking the Cycle of Poverty

In This Chapter

Seeing the Face of Christ in Others

Poverty in One of the World's Wealthiest Nations

Poverty in the World's Poorest Nations

Seeing the Face of Christ in Others

What does the face of Christ look like in others? To Igor Bitencourt and his sister, Adriana, the face of Christ can be seen in the homeless community of Biddeford, Maine. Of course, homeless shelters and community services provide for some of the needs of these people, but for many, obtaining basic things such as food and clothing is a daily struggle. Igor was eager to help the homeless population in his city but was concerned with a specific group of this marginalized population—students who are homeless. He submitted his service project proposal to the principal at his middle school. The principal approved his request, and the challenge was on to collect snacks and basic items for children living in shelters, hotels, or the houses of friends. The project wasn't just about meeting an immediate need. The mission was to say to the homeless, "In spite of your situation, I am going to treat you with as much dignity and love as I can."

While Igor was collecting snacks for homeless kids, his sister started an initiative for the greater Portland, Maine, community. She collected food, toys, and grocery money to donate to the refugee community.

Each of their projects focuses on the needs of the individual in a personal way. When they deliver the food, toys, or money, the volunteers can visit and hear the stories and concerns of those being served. Many of the homeless people and refugees express that this is the first time they have felt "seen." Just the small action of offering a snack, a toy, and a listening ear can offer dignity that had disappeared long ago.

Where do you see the face of Christ in your community?

Living in survival mode means each person who has to scramble for necessities is not living with full dignity.

The thoughtfulness of Igor and Adriana has made their principals and parents proud. But the siblings aren't in it for the recognition. They notice a need and know that they can help meet that need by seeing Christ in the face of every person they serve.

> How do you think Igor and Adriana "see the face of Christ" in each person they serve?

Life on the Edge

Food, clothing, shelter, health care, and education are all basic requirements for a good life—things most of us take for granted. For the first time in the history of the world, humanity has enough resources to provide these things to all people. Yet billions of people around the world and millions of people in the United States are not able to live a good life—a life of dignity that allows them to thrive as God intended—because they lack one or more of these necessities. It may be impossible for them to even keep themselves and their loved ones alive. The experience of not having the basic things one needs to live a full and dignified life is called **poverty**. Poverty denies people their basic human rights.

> **Poverty denies people their basic human rights.**

Everyone should have the same chance with this

I agree with this statement

poverty The experience of not having the basic necessities for living a full and dignified life.

"Catholic social teaching does not require absolute equality in the distribution of income and wealth," the US Catholic bishops note in their pastoral letter "Economic Justice for All" (185). But extreme inequality that causes people to suffer as a result of poverty is contrary to God's will for creation. Catholic social teaching is concerned with poverty because poverty can prevent people from fully living out their God-given human dignity. The way poverty harms people differs from person to person. But we can note some common characteristics of poverty that most poor people experience.

The nearness of death. Poor people are always at greater risk of death than people who are not poor. The International Database of the US Census Bureau indicates that while the life expectancy of a person in Japan is approximately 85 years, it is only 58 for someone who lives in Somalia. For the poorest people in the United States and the world, survival is an everyday concern. Chronic hunger, health problems, and violence are some of the most common ways people living in poverty experience the **nearness of death**.

Marginalization. Poverty is both caused by and results in exclusion from the community. In "Economic Justice for All," the US Catholic bishops describe the marginalization of the poor this way:

> Poverty is not merely the lack of adequate financial resources. It entails a more profound kind of deprivation, a denial of full participation in the economic, social, and political life of society and an inability to influence decisions that affect one's life. (188)

nearness of death The conditions of chronic hunger, health problems, and violence that put those who live in extreme poverty at greater risk of death than people who are not poor.

Would car trouble be an inconvenience for your family, or would it have consequences beyond the challenge of having it repaired?

Living on the edge. As a result of marginalization, people who live in poverty live life "on the edge." Because they have so little, it does not take much to make life worse for them. For most families, an illness or an automobile breakdown is an inconvenience. For poor families living on the edge without medical insurance or money for car repairs, these things can mean the loss of a home or a job. *Is there an easier way*

The cycle of poverty. Poor people often become *to* trapped in a **cycle of poverty**, in which the lack of *escape* basic resources creates barriers that prevent people *this* from obtaining those resources. Without a car, for instance, job opportunities are limited; and without a job, it is difficult to get a car. In the cycle of poverty, interrelated problems cause and reinforce one another: homelessness and hunger lead to an inadequate education for homeless children, for instance. Inadequate education leads in turn to reduced job opportunities— and so the cycle continues.

Barriers to full development. Finally, poverty prevents people from developing their full potential— all the unique talents, self-confidence, and social skills that allow people to thrive.

> Where would a family of four with an income below the poverty level live in your community? Research rental listings to find housing that costs less than one-third of poverty-level income. Would you be willing to live in the housing you found? Based on your findings, are poor people marginalized in your community? Why or why not?

I believe that there should be a program to help people like this

cycle of poverty A situation in which the lack of basic resources prevents people from obtaining those resources. These interrelated problems cause and reinforce one another in a continuous manner.

Choosing the Option for the Poor and Vulnerable

Having your basic needs met is necessary for full development.

Poverty creates a **barrier to full development** in two ways. First, the experience of poverty can lead people, especially children, to develop a worldview in which a better lifestyle seems impossible. People learn how to live a good life through the example of others. When people live on the margins of society, where everyone they know is poor, it is difficult to see a way out.

Second, people who live in poverty are denied the resources necessary for their full development. Dr. Abraham Maslow, an American psychologist, proposed a theory of human motivation based on a hierarchy of human needs. According to him, individuals seek to fill their basic needs first—food, drink, sleep, health. Once these needs are met, people can move on to fill the higher-level needs of safety, love, self-esteem, and self-actualization (becoming who we are meant to be).

If basic needs go unmet, higher needs become more difficult to fill. It is hard for a child who has not eaten for a day to develop their curiosity, and it is difficult for someone who is unable to find a job to maintain self-esteem. People need personal resources like self-esteem and a sense of safety if they are to have the best chance of escaping the cycle of poverty.

An Option for the Poor

Because poverty can prevent people from fully living out their God-given human dignity, Catholic social teaching calls society to make the needs of its poorest and most vulnerable members a top concern. The choice to do so is called the option for the poor and

barrier to full development Something that holds people back from developing their full potential. For those in poverty, this includes denial of basic resources and the development of a worldview in which a better lifestyle seems impossible.

Maslow's Hierarchy of Needs

According to Dr. Abraham Maslow, people focus on meeting their most basic needs before moving on to meet higher needs that aid in their full development:

Self-actualization needs
fulfillment of potential, challenge, curiosity, creativity, aesthetic appreciation

Esteem needs
recognition and prestige, leadership, achievement, competence, strength, intelligence

Love and belonging needs
acceptance, belonging, love and affection, participation

Safety needs
security, protection, comfort, peace, order

Physical needs
food and drink, sleep, health, exercise, rest

---

vulnerable. Igor and Adriana made the option for the poor and vulnerable a focus by organizing their service to homeless people and refugees. Notice, though, that the purpose of their projects went beyond giving away food, clothes, or personal care items. The students went deeper, trying to create an environment and community where refugees and poor people would be treated with a respect that recognized the image of God in each of them. When that happened, the people they were serving were better able to recognize themselves as "real persons."

Igor and Adriana's projects reflect the true spirit of the option for the poor and vulnerable. It is about more than just giving people the basic resources necessary for living; it is about providing them with whatever they need to live out their dignity as images of God.

> Look at Maslow's hierarchy of needs, and choose the three that are most important to you. Why are they important, and how would your life be different if you were unable to fulfill them?

What are some disadvantages poor children experience that are taken for granted in every-day life by those who do not live in poverty?

The Church's call for society to make an option for the poor and vulnerable flows from this conviction: people deserve fair access to the earth's material resources, as well as the resources of the human community, so that they can fully develop their own unique ways of loving God and others (based on "On Social Concern," 27–34).

How do we develop a society in which everyone has what they need to live a full and dignified life? We need to raise our awareness of the reality of poverty by asking two other questions: How does poverty affect people? And why are so many people so poor?

For Review

1. What is the option for the poor and vulnerable?
2. What is poverty?
3. Briefly describe the following characteristics of poverty: nearness of death, living on the edge, the cycle of poverty.
4. What is the basic premise behind Dr. Abraham Maslow's theory of the hierarchy of needs?
5. Why does the Church say that people deserve fair access to the resources of the earth and the human community?

Poverty in One of the World's Wealthiest Nations

The United States is one of the world's richest countries in terms of overall **purchasing power**. According to the University of Michigan's Center for Sustainable Systems, the US constitutes less than 5 percent of the world's population yet consumes approximately 16 percent of the world's energy. Even with its wealth and purchasing power, more than forty-two million people still live in poverty within its borders.

When people talk about poverty in the United States, they are usually referring to an annual income level below the poverty threshold set by the US Census Bureau. The poverty level for a single adult is approximately $13,000; for a family of four, about $27,700. Because each family lives in unique economic circumstances, these numbers are not a perfect measurement of who really is poor. But they do provide a general picture of the extent of poverty in the United States:

- About 15 percent of the nation's youth are poor.

- There is a big difference in the poverty rate within different racial groups. People of color experience some of the highest poverty rates in the country. Children of color are 2.5 times more likely to be poor than their white, non-Latino peers.

- Contrary to the myth that people are poor because they are lazy, more than 70 percent of poor children live in a family in which at least one relative works.

> **purchasing power** The value of currency to purchase goods and services.

Why does poverty affect so many people in a prosperous country such as the United States?

Choosing the Option for the Poor and Vulnerable

> Why do you think so many people in the United States are poor? Find a reliable resource that provides evidence supporting your ideas.

Writer, poet, and teacher Pat Schneider (1934–2020) helped poor women develop their potential by teaching them to express themselves through creative writing. In doing so, she often found herself drawn into their struggles with the effects of poverty. Read this excerpt from a journal entry by Pat about her interactions with women living in poverty:

> This morning, I left home at 7:45 and returned at 3:00. Remembering where I have been, my heart is heavy. I want to know why, as a nation, we allow mothers and children to suffer.
>
> My day began at a community college where I helped a woman withdraw from a course that I had encouraged her to take and had raised money to send her to. I made a mistake. The course was too hard for her. . . . She needed a course to help her pass the GED exam, but all the others were offered in the evening. She has no childcare, no money for childcare, and no way to get to the course site. I've tried to set up tutoring, but she has no telephone, and it has been impossible to make arrangements between her and the tutor.
>
> Later today, I stood in another woman's bedroom where water seepage has corroded and crumbled half a wall, and pipes show through two yawning holes in the ceiling. Although she has complained repeatedly, she has been forced to live

> **I want to know why, as a nation, we allow mothers and children to suffer.**

Why do people continue to live in unsafe conditions if they know it is a danger to themselves and their children?

with water leaking into her bedroom for two and a half years. She threw her mattress away because it got waterlogged. Now her back hurts because she sleeps on a couch with no springs and her skin breaks out in allergic reaction to the moldy air.

I sat today in another woman's kitchen watching her prepare food. She cares for ten children in a very small space. She told me how the noise from the next apartment comes through the walls and how her bathtub needs caulking so badly that she can't wash her hair for fear the water will leak into the next apartment. She doesn't understand why she has a problem with depression.

I looked out of the window of another woman's living room, her child playing on the floor between us. She told me she wants to get a job. She worries about the thousands of dollars she owes for classes she's taken at the college. She is afraid to go on in school. I wonder whether her welfare payments will be cut if she gets part-time work. (Pat Schneider, "The Cost of Love")

Each of these situations is a good illustration of the sort of difficulties people face as a result of poverty. To deepen our understanding of how poverty affects people in the United States, we can look at three of its most harmful consequences: hunger, homelessness, and inadequate education.

How are the characteristics of poverty listed at the beginning of this chapter evident in these women's stories?

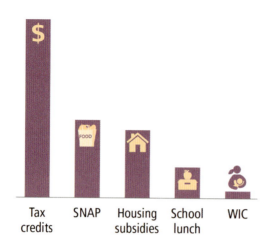
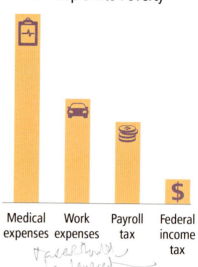

Hunger

Everyone has experienced ordinary hunger—a growling stomach, maybe some lightheadedness—at some point. But most people who are poor suffer from **chronic hunger**, meaning they never have enough food to give the body the nutrients needed to grow and maintain itself properly.

Chronic hunger takes two forms. Starvation occurs when the body does not receive enough calories to maintain itself. The metabolism slows down, and the body begins to feed on itself. In other words, lacking food, the body's own fat, muscle, and tissue become the body's fuel. The immune system breaks down, making victims of starvation susceptible to disease. Brain chemistry is also damaged, causing the victim's mental functions to deteriorate. Technically, starvation begins to occur when an individual has lost one-third of their normal body weight. Few people actually die of starvation in the United States.

More common, both in the United States and in the rest of the world, is malnutrition. A victim of **malnutrition** gets enough calories to prevent their body from feeding on itself, but the diet of a malnourished person is extremely limited, often consisting of just three or four foods. As a result, they do not receive all the vitamins and minerals needed for proper physical and mental development and maintenance. Nutritional deficiencies can cause diabetes, heart ailments, vision problems, obesity, skin diseases, and other problems.

chronic hunger The situation when a person is unable to consume enough food to maintain a normal, active lifestyle over an extended period.

malnutrition A physically dangerous situation caused by inadequate nutrition.

Even short periods of malnourishment can affect the long-term health and development of children.

Chronic hunger contributes to the cycle of poverty. It affects the health and development of children, and it seriously harms their ability to learn in school. When people are hungry, they have little energy or motivation to concentrate on other aspects of their lives, such as finding work or housing.

Although the number of hungry people throughout the world has dramatically decreased since the 1970s, the number of people requesting emergency food assistance from food shelves in the United States continues to rise. According to the US Department of Agriculture, about 19.5 million households, which is approximately 15 percent, are **food insecure**, meaning the household does not have consistent access to enough food for active, healthy lives for all household members at all times during the year.

> **Chronic hunger contributes to the cycle of poverty.**

Homelessness

The typical image of homelessness is one of people sleeping in cars or on the street—and, in fact, this is all too common. According to the National Law Center on Homelessness and Poverty, more than 580,000

---

food insecure The inability to obtain or afford nutritionally sufficient food on a regular basis.

Homeless shelters, like the one pictured here, often do not have facilities for families.

> **True homes are safe, stable places where human dignity is respected and each person is free to develop their potential.**

people are homeless in the United States on any given night. According to the Children's Defense Fund, children comprise about one in five of those who are homeless on any given night.

Clearly, shelter—someplace to eat, sleep, bathe, and be protected from the elements—is a minimum requirement of human dignity. But to be truly life-giving, homes must provide more than shelter. True homes are safe, stable places where human dignity is respected and each person is free to develop their potential. True homes also provide a place for people to participate in a community by building life-giving relationships with others who live nearby.

Although the housing crisis in our society most visibly affects those who are literally homeless—that is, without shelter—millions of people are the hidden homeless, people whose poverty prevents them from living in sufficient housing. The hidden homeless include the following:

- **Those whose housing costs consume too much of their income.** According to federal government guidelines, the cost of housing should not exceed more than a third of a family's income. Yet, low-income families typically spend half their income on rent. Such a situation makes it more likely that people will go hungry or lose their housing entirely.

Often, homeless camps are made out of scrap material and lack electricity, running water, and plumbing.

- **Those who live in inadequate housing.** Often, poor people can afford to live only in inadequate housing—housing that is unsafe or broken down in a way that degrades the life and dignity of the residents. *Every house should be stable to live in*

- **Those who live in others' housing.** Many people avoid being homeless by doubling up with other families who live in already crowded apartments.

- **Those who live in unsafe homes.** Violence, crime, and substance abuse are all factors that prevent a home from being a safe, nurturing place. *Can't they move to suburb areas?*

People who live in poverty often shift between each of these four kinds of homelessness. Consider the true story of Peter, Megan, and their five children, a family from New York City. Peter worked on construction projects as a carpenter, while Megan took care of the children. The family was able to get by on a low income, but one catastrophic event caused a chain reaction. While at the beach one Sunday, the family received word that their apartment was on fire. They rushed home, but the fire had already destroyed all their belongings:

> Peter could then not find work. "Not since the fire. I had tools. I can't replace those tools. It took me years of work." He explains he had accumulated

> Imagine this scenario: You lost your job two months ago, and with only a high school education, you are having trouble finding another job that pays enough to cover your expenses. Now your landlord is threatening to evict you. Based on the situation in your area, brainstorm a list of strategies for your immediate and long-term survival.

tools for different jobs, one tool at a time. Each job would enable him to add another tool to his collection. "Everything I had was in that fire." (Jonathan Kozol, *Rachel and Her Children*)

They were forced by these circumstances to apply for welfare and were placed in a run-down hotel contracted by the city to house homeless families. The conditions at the welfare hotel were quite poor:

> The city paid $3,000 monthly for the two connected rooms in which they lived. [Megan] showed me the bathroom. Crumbling walls. Broken tiles. The toilet didn't work. There was a pan to catch something dripping from the plaster. The smell was overpowering.
> "I don't see any way out," [Peter] said. "I want to go home. Where can I go?"

The accidental and tragic loss of their home and belongings, including the tools of Peter's trade, led to a cycle of poverty that the family was unable to break. After two years in the welfare hotel, the children were placed in various foster homes. Their family shattered, Peter and Megan had to live on the streets.

Inadequate Education

A good education is one of the best ways to break the cycle of poverty. This is true not only because a good education opens up good job opportunities but also because education—in and out of the classroom—is one of the ways we develop our full potential as

> **Successful learning helps build the self-confidence we need to continue developing our full potential as adults.**

Is this why the gov pays

The gov they pay to help the less rich kids

Where does the revenue come from to fund public schools? Why does this source of revenue help explain why schools in poor areas receive less funding than those in more prosperous areas?

human beings. And successful learning helps build the self-confidence we need to continue developing our full potential as adults.

Yet, as a group, children who live in poverty lag behind their better-off peers when it comes to academic achievement. This is so even when poor kids come from intact families and safe neighborhoods.

Education leaders debate the reasons students from poor families tend not to do as well at school as their better-off peers. Race-based stereotypes and discrimination are factors. Inequalities in school funding play a role too. Taxes that fund public school districts (or the tuition revenue that funds Catholic schools) often reflect the economic well-being of the area. Schools in poorer areas receive less funding for materials, facilities, and general maintenance.

But the reasons for the learning difficulties that poor children face can go beyond funding issues. Even where more money is allocated per student in low-income areas compared to suburban schools, the students in the suburban schools thrive while the students from low-income areas fall behind. This data is reflected not just on report cards but on standardized test scores as well. While suburban students tend to excel, students in low-income areas repeatedly receive poor scores on standardized tests. The problem can be

> What factors enable you to do your best work in school? Write a students' "bill of rights" based on the factors you identified.

having a safe school that cares about education

the teachers and lifestyle should be better

rooted in substandard housing, transportation issues, and educational policies that are not pertinent to economically stable students. Students show the stress of living in poor, unstable, or insufficient homes.

A Tangle of Causes

What causes these problems? To some extent, each problem causes and reinforces the others. Children whose families drift in and out of homelessness move frequently, interrupting their education. And the sheer stress of poverty poses other barriers to education. But we can find other reasons for these problems as well, some rooted in the characteristics of poverty, and some rooted in social structures.

Low Wages, High Costs

Two trends make it more difficult for people to afford basic resources like food and housing. First, real incomes— that is, incomes adjusted for inflation— have gone down in recent decades, so the average worker has less purchasing power. Second, the cost of basic necessities—especially housing—has increased. The result is more hungry and homeless people.

This is especially evident in the **affordable housing** shortage. As more people work for less money, the need for low-cost housing has increased. But the supply of low-cost housing has decreased significantly because developers are building mostly expensive rental units so they can make a higher profit. According to the National Low Income Housing Coalition, only thirty-seven affordable and available homes exist for every one hundred extremely low-income renter households. Seventy percent (7.5 million) of the nation's 10.8 million extremely low-income renter households are severely cost-burdened, spending

affordable housing Housing for which the occupant is paying no more than 30 percent of their income for total costs, including utilities.

Do you know of any government-subsidized housing in your area?

more than half of their income on rent and utilities. When households spend so much of their income on housing, they have insufficient funds left over for their other basic needs. Families then spend only two-thirds as much on food as they need and half as much on clothing.

Government Aid

The federal government spends some of its annual budget on aid to individuals and families facing hardship. The aid provides families with a small income (still below the poverty level) to provide temporary assistance until the head of the family is able to find work. For a majority of families, this assistance is a lifeline during a rough period. Others need more help than government aid provides, however. Take Mrs. Harrington, for instance. After much searching, she found a kind landlord who offered to rent her an apartment for $365 a month. But that was more than the government was willing to pay at that time:

"It's like a dream: This lady likes me and we're going to have a home! My worker denied me for $365. I was denied. $365. My social worker is a nice man but he said: 'I have to tell you, Mrs. Harrington. Your limit is $270.' Then I thought of this: The difference is only $95. I'll make it up out of my food allowance. We can lighten up on certain things. Not for the children, but ourselves. We'll eat less food at first. Then I can get a job. He'll finish his computer course. The house had a backyard. . . . They told me no. I was denied." (Jonathan Kozol, *Rachel and Her Children*)

Legislation has passed that sharply limits federal welfare benefits. Limiting government assistance to poor families was supposed to motivate more poor people to find work. Many did, although the jobs they found often did not pay enough to lift their families out of poverty. Others were unable to find work because they lacked the necessary training or resources to do so.

The working poor are often denied enough benefits to afford suitable housing.

> **Reductions in federal aid have contributed to both hunger and homelessness.**

Reductions in federal aid have contributed to both hunger and homelessness. People receiving aid feel any limits on funding even more because the supply of rental housing available to low-income renters is in extreme shortage.

Physical and Mental Health Issues

The poorer a person is, the less likely they are to have health insurance. Without health insurance, the financial strain of a major illness or injury can lead to the loss of housing. Homelessness, in turn, leads to poor emotional and physical health. Malnutrition, inadequate housing, and stress are among the reasons homeless children experience health problems at more than twice the rate of other children (National Law Center on Homelessness and Poverty).

Lack of health care is especially hard on those who are mentally ill. As many as 25 percent of the single-adult homeless population suffers from some sort of severe and persistent mental illness. While mental illness makes it difficult for people to obtain employment and housing, only a small portion of those who are mentally ill and homeless require long-term care in special institutions. Federal programs have demonstrated that the majority of mentally ill and homeless people are able to live in the community if they are provided with adequate support, including appropriate housing, counseling, and ongoing contact with social workers. Such services are not widely available, however.

> Choose one of the aspects of poverty mentioned so far in this chapter and research how it affects your local community. Conduct a web search or contact at least three government or nonprofit organizations that work with the poor in your area for information related to your topic.

How can social workers help those who are living in poverty improve their work and living situations?

Poverty in One of the World's Wealthiest Nations   217

Do you think depression contributes to preventing those who are living in poverty from changing their living situation?

Hopelessness

People trapped in the cycle of poverty—especially youth who are born into it—frequently lack hope for the future. Hopelessness may not seem like a "real" reason for the poverty that leads to homelessness, hunger, and poor academic performance. Nevertheless, it is a very real reason, and one of the most powerful. "We haven't even begun to consider how much depression there is among the very poor," says Richard Zorolla, a former San Antonio social worker. "We don't seem to think they have a right, or the ability, to feel deeply enough" (Peter Davis, "Who Are the Poor?").

Without hope, people tend to live for the moment, rather than working toward a better future. This may be one reason teen pregnancy rates and high school dropout rates are much higher among poor people.

Hopelessness drives others to look for an easy escape in drugs and alcohol. In some decaying housing projects, for instance, it is common for children to become addicted to mood-altering inhalants—paint, glue, antifreeze—by the time they are teens. Rather than providing an escape, substance abuse only reinforces the cycle of poverty. Often, poor people have little or no access to drug treatment programs.

> With a group of your classmates, brainstorm ways the Catholic Church can help people who are living in poverty find hope. Then plan a short liturgy around the theme of hope in the face of poverty. Write down the prayers, gestures, symbols, and music you would use.

For Review

1. Compare and contrast how the two forms of chronic hunger affect people.
2. Describe four types of hidden homelessness.
3. Why is education one of the best ways to break the cycle of poverty?
4. In your own words, summarize four factors that contribute to poverty.

Poverty in the World's Poorest Nations

All poverty limits the ability of people to develop their full potential. Unlike poverty in the United States, however, poverty in the world's poorest nations is more likely to result in death:

- According to the World Bank, almost half the world's population (3.4 billion people) struggles to meet basic needs.
- According to the World Health Organization (WHO), about 2.2 billion people do not have access to clean drinking water, and 2 billion people lack access to basic sanitation, which results in a greater risk of disease.
- WHO reports that in developing countries, 297,000 children under the age of five die annually as a result of diarrhea and other diseases caused by unclean water and poor sanitation.

Life for the World's Poorest Three Billion

The experience of Malekha Khatun, a Bangladeshi woman, illustrates some of the common ways poverty affects the world's poorest three billion people:

Born in the village of Dhemsha in Bangladesh, she lost her father, the family's wage-earner, when she was very young. Malekha, her younger brother and mother slept outside since they had no house. In this wet climate, they got soaked when it rained unless someone else offered shelter. Her childhood was spent helping her mother work to earn money, attending a few years of school and witnessing the death of her nine-year-old brother from fever.

At 14, Malekha was married off to a man from another village for a small dowry equaling about nine

U.S. dollars. She became pregnant right away and lived with her husband's family, while he left to work as a menial laborer so he could send money back to her and the baby. Upon his return, she became pregnant again. When Malekha's husband left a second time, she received no money or word from him. Left on her own with two small children and no means of income, her youngest child died of malnutrition and diarrhea.

Malekha worked at a variety of jobs in order to support herself, becoming skilled at knitting and making nets. She moved out of the home of her husband's family to live with her mother. Hard work and resourcefulness enabled her to run a small grocery store, but competition caused her business to suffer and she sometimes had to fall back on begging.

Malekha's constant hard work and industriousness could not overcome the poverty and hunger that shadow a woman alone at the bottom rung of an already poor nation. For all her struggling, Malekha ended up with no food to feed herself, no umbrella to protect her from the rain and only one sari to her name. (Scott A. Leckman, "Grameen Bank Borrowers")

> Imagine you wake up tomorrow in a place where you have to live on $5.50 a day, without access to safe drinking water, toilets, health care, transportation, or education. Brainstorm ways you would try to improve your situation.

How Much Do the World's People Live On?

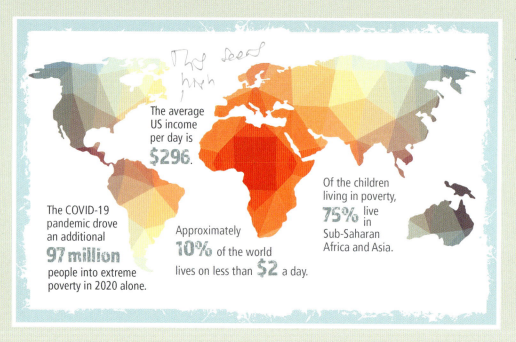

To see how poverty affects the world's poorest people, we can look at the same problems that poor people in the United States face: hunger, homelessness, and a lack of access to education.

Hunger

According to the World Health Organization, almost 700 million people do not have access to the food and water they need. Some are so lacking in daily nourishment that they barely have the energy to do even the simplest activities. Chronic hunger—mostly malnutrition—afflicts more than 815 million people worldwide each year (worldhunger.org).

Health issues in impoverished countries are completely connected with hunger and poverty. More than 2 million children die each year from the direct effects of chronic hunger and malnutrition that stunts growth and saps energy and potential (actionagainsthunger.org).

Unsafe drinking water is not an issue only in developing countries. Can you think of any places in the US where it is not safe to drink tap water?

Two other symptoms of poverty, unsanitary conditions and unhealthy drinking water, transmit these diseases to people already weakened by hunger. When human and animal waste is left out in the open or gets into drinking water, people die from cholera, typhoid, malaria, and diarrhea, as well as dehydration (Church World Services).

The quantity of available water is also important. Keeping the body properly hydrated requires six to eight glasses of water per day. Most of the world's poor people, however, must travel far distances to obtain safe water, or *any* water, and then they must carry it the same long distance back home, usually on foot.

> Look through the Bible for a passage in which Jesus talks about food or water. Reflect on how the plight of the world's hungry and thirsty people affects the way you understand Jesus' words.

Homelessness

Homelessness for the world's poorest people sometimes resembles the common perception of homelessness in the United States: people sleeping on the streets and in makeshift shelters. This is especially true in nations where changing economic or social conditions displace large numbers of rural people who have traditionally made a living off the land. Often, these people migrate to large cities to look for work. Those who are unable to find employment might end up being homeless. Others build makeshift shelters from scrap wood; whole "cities" of shanties can spring up on the edges of urban areas.

Fr. Pedro Opeka, a priest of the order of Saint Vincent de Paul, witnesses this kind of homelessness and poverty every day in his adopted home of Antananarivo, Madagascar:

> The city dump teems with men, women, and children who burrow in filth for their daily bread. They have excavated large tunnels through the compressed layers of waste in order to find things they can sell—bones, for example, are used for traditional medicine and animal feed.
>
> In the center of the city, at every junction, barefoot children approach cars and implore the drivers for change. At night, rows of homeless families sleep on the pavement. During the rainy season, competition is fierce to find a place in the road tunnels. As children grow older, begging becomes less lucrative, and so the boys often turn to stealing, while some girls, as young as 14, sell sex for less than the price of a soft drink. (Magnus MacFarlane, "Friends in Deed")

For more than thirty years, Father Opeka has served the people of Madagascar through the organization he founded—Akamasoa (which means "the faithful and good friends"). Approximately thirty thousand people in eighteen villages are fully sustained by Akamasoa, but over nine hundred thousand Malagasy people have been supported in the short term (anywhere from one day to three weeks) with rice, shelter, clothing, and necessities. But millions around the world do not receive such help.

Many of the world's homeless people are **refugees**—people displaced from their homes by wars or political persecution. Refugees differ from other migrants in that they cannot return home for fear of persecution. Sometimes, refugees are victims of intentional attempts by political factions to displace specific ethnic groups from their homes, a practice known as **ethnic cleansing**. The Church has long urged more stable, wealthy nations to welcome refugees. Today, there are approximately 26.6 million refugees worldwide (United Nations).

> **Many of the world's homeless people are refugees—people displaced from their homes by wars or political persecution.**

Where do these people stay?

Inadequate Education

Education plays a crucial role in lifting young people out of poverty. A few years of primary education can help those who work the land increase the yield of their crops. Education also opens the door to better employment. Access to even the most basic education is still denied to many.

---

refugee A person who flees to another country to escape danger in their home country.

ethnic cleansing The displacement or extermination of an unwanted ethnic group from society.

Doesn't this also involve killing

What do you consider to be the essentials for a sound basic education for all?

- Almost 258 million children, adolescents, and youth do not attend school (United Nations Educational, Scientific, and Cultural Organization).
- About 70% of ten-year-olds are unable to read and understand a simple text (World Bank).

Recognizing the value of education, many children are desperate to attend school but cannot, either because they are struggling to survive or because they lack access.

Global Poverty Is Not Inevitable

Injustice does not just happen. Unfortunately, many people view poverty in the United States and the world as inevitable. This attitude may be partly the result of myths about the causes of poverty.

Take, for instance, the myths about hunger: A common belief is that there is not enough food to feed the world's growing population, but this is false. According to the United Nations, enough food is produced to feed everyone on the planet, yet hunger is on the rise in some parts of the world. Over 800 million people are considered "chronically undernourished." The problem is not the amount of food, but the way it is distributed. Redistributing a small amount of each country's food supply would eliminate hunger.

Another myth is that most hunger is caused by

> **A common belief is that there is not enough food to feed the world's growing population, but this is false.**

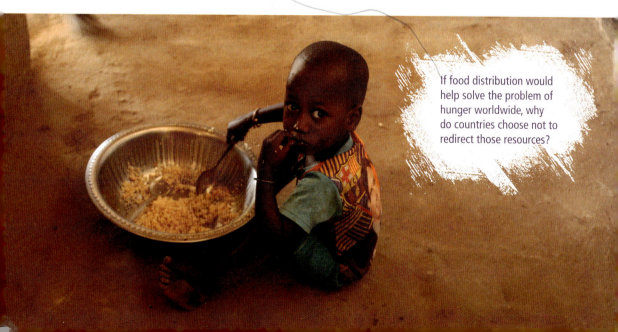

If food distribution would help solve the problem of hunger worldwide, why do countries choose not to redirect those resources?

droughts and natural disasters. But the people of the world have fed themselves for centuries despite droughts, floods, and other effects of weather. Strategies for coping with food loss due to natural disasters, such as collectively storing food and distributing it among themselves during periods of major crop failure, have been developed by various traditional cultures. Today, disruptions such as civil wars interfere with traditional life and the coping strategies that have been developed. In addition, many "natural" disasters are actually caused by human action, such as the droughts in Africa caused in large part by the elimination of forests.

Others suggest that the world's poor people just need to work harder to obtain the food they need. In fact, the world's poorest people work very hard every day just to survive. They are often unable to support themselves because they are losing access to the resources needed for self-reliance: land, water, tools, animals, credit, and markets for their crops.

> [The world's poorest people] are often unable to support themselves because they are losing access to the resources needed for self-reliance: land, water, tools, animals, credit, and markets for their crops.

The Legacy of Colonialism

Why, then, are so many of the world's people poor? To a significant extent, the pattern of poverty in the world today is rooted in European and United States history.

The most powerful European countries conquered Indigenous peoples and established colonies as they explored the world between 1500 and 1900. By 1914, Europe, its colonies, and its former colonies (including the United States) controlled 84 percent of the earth's land surface.

The main goal of colonization was to enrich the European powers. Wherever they established colonies, the European nations set up systems designed to extract the human and **natural resources** of the land for themselves while undermining local economies and peoples. For instance, Britain forbade the manufacture of goods that might compete with British-made goods. In the early nineteenth century, India had a thriving textile industry based in small shops. When

Contact an international emergency aid organization such as the Red Cross or Catholic Relief Services to find out about some recent food crises. Choose one crisis to focus on, answering these questions:
- What were the causes of the crisis?
- How did the organization respond?
- What obstacles did it face?

natural resources Materials that can be found in nature and harvested for use.

India's cheap cloth threatened to compete with the cloth being produced by British mills, steep export taxes were placed on all Indian goods. In Bengal, the British even broke the little fingers of thousands of Indian weavers to prevent them from making cloth. As a result, Indian-owned economic enterprises significantly decreased in number during British rule, causing the country to become underdeveloped.

In Africa, national borders were drawn by European powers, who divided the continent into zones of control at the Congress of Berlin in 1884. Nations were created with little regard to the reality of the people who lived there. Tribes that were traditional enemies were lumped together, while other tribes were split apart, causing ethnic tensions that continue to fuel conflict even today.

In many of the colonies, a handful of people came to control political power and the wealth of land and other natural resources. These powerful elites created plantations producing crops for export—coffee, tea, or sugar, for instance—that replaced the farming of crops meant to feed local populations, such as beans, corn, and rice. Such practices forced native peoples off the land, reducing their ability to feed themselves, and left the economies of the colonies dependent on just a few **cash crops** for income.

As a result of **colonialism**, Europe and the United States grew more powerful while the majority of the world's people who lived in their colonies grew weaker (J. Milburn Thompson, *Justice and Peace*).

cash crops Agricultural products produced for their commercial value.

colonialism The result of national expansion in which a people or a country is dominated by a foreign nation. This often results in the exploitation of the people and resources in the dominated country.

The areas in maroon represent the British empire at its height, including its colonized territories.

Barriers to Development

Although many former colonies gained their independence in the mid-twentieth century, power-over relationships between the world's richest and poorest countries continue to affect global patterns of poverty today:

- **Resource extraction.** Many poor countries attempt to support their weak economies by exporting the cash crops established when they were colonies. For example, the low price of coffee grown in Nicaragua and other countries impoverishes the people who produce it. At the same time, the coffee crops take away land that could be used to grow food for people locally. Moreover, multinational corporations based in developed countries extract resources from the poorest nations in the form of cash crops, natural resources, and cheap labor.

> **Multinational corporations based in developed countries extract resources from the poorest nations in the form of cash crops, natural resources, and cheap labor.**

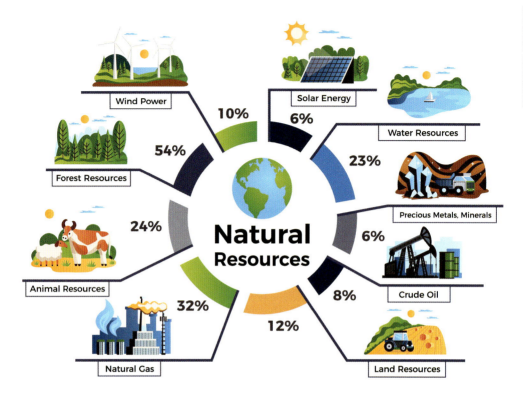

Choose a nation in Asia, Africa, or Latin America that is a former colony, and answer the following questions:
- What kind of society did the Indigenous population have before colonization?
- How did colonization change the society?
- What is the nation like today as a result of colonization?

- **Government by the elite.** Part of the legacy of colonialism is that a tiny number of people continue to control the majority of land, resources, and political power in the world's poorest nations. As a result, government policies tend to favor the interests of the wealthy rather than the poor.

- **Foreign aid problems.** Wealthy nations offer small amounts of aid to the world's poorest nations, although not as much as most people may think. Such aid is not always put to the best use, however. Donor countries may require that the aid be spent on projects or purchases that end up benefiting the interests of the donor nation and the ruling elite of the recipient nations more than the needs of poor people. Other times, aid is used for unwise development projects. Corruption is still another problem: government officials and the ruling elite of poor nations are capable of stealing billions of dollars meant for development.

- **Discrimination.** Ethnic, religious, and gender discrimination within poor countries also cause poverty. Religious and ethnic minorities are likely to be more impoverished than other groups. Indigenous peoples and women often suffer from prejudice, even if they are not in the minority.

- **Conflict fueled by arms sales.** Rich countries that make and sell weapons encourage military spending by poor countries. As a result, money that could fund programs to end hunger and poverty is spent on weapons. Military spending then fuels the intensity of regional conflicts, which, in turn, are a major cause of famine and a source of refugees.

The Debt Crisis

One of the greatest obstacles blocking the full development of poor nations is the **debt crisis**: poor countries owe billions in loan repayments to banks and wealthy nations, and paying interest on these loans takes money from social programs that could eliminate poverty.

The debt crisis began in the 1970s, when poor nations were able to get large loans at low interest rates. Although the money should have been used for social development programs, much of it was either stolen or invested in ways that would not strengthen economies. Some 20 percent of the

Living on One Dollar

Chris Temple and Zach Ingrasci are activists and award-winning filmmakers. They met in college as international development majors. But they are the first to admit that there are some things a textbook can't answer. So they planned to spend one summer living in a Guatemalan village on just $1 a day. Their mission was to experience the reality of extreme poverty firsthand. Their trip was eye-opening and inspired them to continue to explore people's stories. After the Guatemala trip, they lived and filmed in a Syrian refugee camp. To date, they have completed fifteen films and series that have raised over $91.5 million for the films' causes. After college, they started their own nonprofit called Optimist. They travel the United States as storytellers and champions for social justice. As public speakers, their expertise is in demand at the United Nations, the World Humanitarian Summit, TEDx, and is featured in numerous articles and publications. What started as a personal experiment became a mission to educate, inspire, and build empathy. At their appearances, Chris and Zach ask, "What can we do with what we have, where we are?" How would you answer those questions?

Chris Temple and Zach Ingrasci.

debt crisis A situation in which a country loses the ability to pay back the debt held by its government.

> After reading this chapter, how do you think you might be able to make an option for the poor? What specific actions might you be able to take? What would your motivation be?

borrowed money was used for military spending, for instance. Then, when interest rates soared in the 1980s, the interest on the debt soared too. Today, the debt-service burden in middle-income countries is at a thirty-year high. Oil prices are surging, and interest rates are on the rise worldwide. This trend indicates that a significant number of developing economies will be unable to service their debt. This is not the level of the debt crisis of the 1980s, but few of the poorest nations have any hope of ever repaying their debts, especially because debt repayments stifle their economic development.

Although poor people received little benefit from the international loans that caused the debt crisis, they bear the greatest burden of their nation's debt. The Catholic Church, along with other groups, has called on international lending institutions and the wealthiest nations to reduce or entirely cancel much of the poorest nations' debt. The call to forgive debts so that people might live more fully goes all the way back to ancient Jewish Law, but it is even more urgent for justice today.

For Review

1. Give two examples of the devastating effects of bad water and poor sanitation.
2. How does the Catholic Church say wealthier nations should treat refugees?
3. List three common myths about hunger.
4. What are three consequences of colonialism?
5. Briefly describe three modern barriers to development for poor nations.
6. Briefly describe how the debt crisis affects the world's poorest people.

- Recognize the dignity of those who suffer from poverty. This is the first step toward responding to poverty with compassion. Is compassion enough? It could be. The world contains enough resources to offer everyone a good life. If enough people respond to poverty with genuine compassion, it can be greatly reduced both in the United States and in the world.

- Challenge assumptions regarding poverty and homelessness so you do not unintentionally spread harmful biases. One misconception is that people experiencing homelessness choose not to work. This misconception is incredibly harmful because it negates the many uncontrollable and systemic conditions that can cause housing instability or poverty. In reality, people have to deal with many factors that make it hard to find employment, including loss of affordable housing, inequitable access to training and tools, and mental illness.

- Get informed! Poverty exists in every community. Ask questions about which organizations are assisting those who are living in poverty. Do some research about what resources are available and how you can help secure or distribute resources to those in need. Most certainly, you would be making sacrifices to volunteer, but nothing can change until we are all willing to go beyond our comfort zone.

- Follow Ballotpedia, a nonpartisan, nonprofit website that allows you to see who is running in your district and their track record with many of the key issues relating to poverty: foreign aid, climate change, hunger, gender equality, and education. When deciding who to vote for, resources such as Ballotpedia provide the data to keep you informed.

8

The Gift of SIMPLE LIVING

Focusing on the Essentials

In This Chapter

- The Wealth of Joy
- A Poverty of Riches
- A Eucharistic Response to Poverty
- Living Simply So Others Can Simply Li[ve]

The Wealth of Joy

After graduating from Cathedral High School in Saint Cloud, Minnesota, Julie Williams decided to spend a summer living in solidarity with a poor community in rural Mexico.

She wrote the following letter to her former high school justice teacher:

8 de Agosto

Dear Mr. LaNave:

How are things with you? I am doing well, although I am a little hot. It has been four days since the last rain and we are out of water. There are *pilas* about a mile away where we will go for water later when the sun is not too hot. I had gotten used to the late afternoon showers and nightly downpours. This summer I am living in the clouds—perched so high in the mountains that I feel like a bird in its nest. Home is a tin-roof schoolroom that I share with ten other young people aged 18 to 27 from Mexico, Colombia, Spain, Puerto Rico, and Canada (and many fleas, bedbugs, spiders, lice, etc.). We cook over a fire on an earthen stove—tortillas, beans, and rice, tortillas, beans, and rice. Just to live is physically difficult—it's an hour-and-a-half hike up the mountain to cut firewood, we must boil all of our water, wash our clothes with stones, and walk three hours to the nearest market. *I love it here.* Of course my family thinks I'm masochistic. . . .

I decided to come on this program because of its philosophy—it's different than most other programs I've participated in or heard about. It is a philosophy of respect for differences, and the reality that we are here to support the people and live with them and not [just] to help them. It's an interchange of experiences. Indeed, the people here are helping me more than I am helping them—I don't know which worms are venomous or anything about the land or way of life here.

The people here have nothing of material value—**campesinos** of indigenous origin, they work the land and receive almost nothing in return. The village is almost entirely made up of women and children. The youth and men of their families for the most part are in Mexico City, Monterey, Tampico, or the United States because that's where the money is. It's hard to understand why there is no "work" [for pay] here. It seems like where there are people, there is demand for goods and services, and Mexico is rich with resources, so there should be plenty of jobs and money to go around. There is not. . . .

Daily we do physical labor in the mornings from 8 a.m. to 1 p.m. We have assisted in building a wall for the school made of rocks we carried from all over (encountering four tarantulas and one viper), leveled a small hill in the schoolyard, planted a garden for the women's union, and now are helping them with a compost pile. . . . In the afternoons we have workshops Monday, Wednesday, and Friday—some we organize, like English class, embroidery, games for kids, . . . math, and sports; others the community and the union organize—like alternative medicine and cooking. Tuesday and Thursday we visit houses in the area. This is my favorite thing to do because you really get to know the people and their life—also because many women do not leave the house because they have too much work to do (lots of kids, cook, wash clothes, etc., etc.) and also because of **machismo**. The people here in

campesinos Latin American land or farm workers.

machismo A strong and often exaggerated emphasis on manhood, male pride, and the role of men in society.

Volunteers on mission trips level ground, build schools and clinics, and assist with agriculture projects.

general are very timid and shy, especially before they get to know us. . . .

I love to play with the children and chat with the women. I can experience some of what it feels like to be a campesina, but I will never completely understand their situation because I know that I will be leaving and have another world to go to. Even here, I don't worry about not having enough food or not being able to feed my children. . . .

Today is a big day for the community—as there is a basketball tournament and dance. What am I doing writing a letter? O.K., I'm out of here—

Sincerely,

Julie Williams

Which Way to True Happiness?

Julie's statement—"I love it here"—might be surprising, given that she lacked even the most basic comforts, like running water. Somehow, amid poverty and hardship, she managed to find joy. Julie's experience contradicts the message of the commercial culture that dominates life in North America, a message that says happiness is found in having what we want.

Material things are certainly necessary for human fulfillment, as we saw in the previous chapter. But Jesus announces a different message, one that says true happiness—what we might call joy—is found not in possessing material things but in loving relationships with God and one another.

Catholic HEART
Work Camp

Julie Williams traveled to Mexico to live simply in the service of others. But you don't have to leave the US to do the same. Catholic HEART Work Camp (CHWC) was established in 1993 by Steve and Lisa Walker from Orlando, Florida. Inspired by their participation in nondenominational work camps, the first CHWC experience was an extension of their parish youth group. CHWC grew exponentially in the years to follow, growing from one camp to fifty locations in the US and around the world. Teens put their faith into action as they live out Christ's commands to love and serve those around them. Throughout their week of service, they participate in the Sacraments of Reconciliation and the Eucharist, as well as prayer services.

The mission of CHWC is to share the love of Christ as they serve the neglected, brokenhearted, and the marginalized. The organizations who work in cooperation with CHWC in each city choose the work projects. These agencies exist to improve the lives of low-income families, children, and the elderly. At the selected sites, teens paint, clean, clear, build, and perform any assistance needed. You can volunteer with CHWC to "love, serve, and connect" by living simply with those who are most in need of your help. Just like Julie, this experience can also bring you joy.

> What have been the three happiest, or most joyful, times of your life? What qualities of the experiences made them joyful? What do these experiences have in common?

God wants this joy for all people. This is why we are called to live in solidarity with the world's poorest people, much as Julie did. The choice to do so makes it easier for both those who are poor and those who are not poor to better live out their dignity as beings made in the image of God.

Transforming the structures of society so that all people, rich and poor, are able to fulfill their human potential and live dignified lives is a process called **development**. When people talk about development, they usually focus on **economics**—the way societies produce, manage, and distribute material wealth. Though the Christian understanding of development focuses on economics too, it also goes beyond. True development considers all aspects of what it means to be human, including the spiritual dimension.

We do not need to travel to a poor community as Julie did in order to pursue development with those who are poor, but we do need to live in a way that values the sacredness of ourselves, others, and God's creation more than material possessions. This way of living, which we will call **living simply**, is about making choices that deepen our joy because they focus on the essentials of life, not on illusions of what brings happiness.

> "Living simply is about making choices that deepen our joy because they focus on the essentials of life, not on illusions of what brings happiness."

development The process by which the structures of society evolve so that all people, rich and poor, are able to fulfill their human potential and live dignified lives.

economics The way societies produce, manage, and distribute material wealth.

living simply Living in a way that values the sacredness of ourselves, others, and God's creation more than material possessions.

Living simply can mean many things, but most importantly, the focus is on the essentials of life.

For Review

1. What does Julie's story of finding joy amid poverty and hardship reveal to us about true happiness?
2. What was Jesus' message about where true happiness is found?
3. Define the terms *development* and *living simply*.

A Poverty of Riches

It is clear how material poverty prevents people from developing their full potential. This is the sort of poverty Julie encountered. But material poverty is not the only type of poverty that prevents human development.

The Wealth Gap

Extreme poverty of the type Julie encountered is very rare in the United States. In fact, a huge difference exists between the lifestyle of the world's richest people, which includes most of the people in the United States, and the world's poorest people:

- According to the United Nations, the richest 10 percent of the world's people own almost 80 percent of its wealth. Meanwhile, the poorest 50 percent of the world's people own barely 2 percent of its wealth. ("World Inequality Report 2022")

- Although the United States comprises less than 5 percent of the world's population, its people consume approximately 25 percent of the world's goods and services. (Associated Press)

- In recent years, the richest 1 percent of the US population received about 14 percent of all income. To be in this top 1 percent, you would need to earn about $3.25 million a year. About 90 percent of the working population of the US receives about 60 percent of the nation's income. (Economic Policy Institute)

The difference between the wealthiest and the poorest people is known as the **wealth gap**.

---

wealth gap The difference between the wealthiest and the poorest people in any given population.

> **Christianity rejects the illusion that people can find fulfillment through the possession of material wealth alone.**

Stuff: Necessary, but Not Sufficient

Our culture tends to view wealth as a good thing. Conventional wisdom says that the more we have, the happier we will be. Most political and business leaders make the decisions that shape our society based on the assumption that the way to improve society is primarily by increasing its ability to produce wealth. As a result, political leaders use economic growth—growth in the ability to produce wealth—as a primary indicator of the health of a society.

Christian justice views material resources as basically good; after all, God gave humanity the resources of the earth so that each of us can live a dignified life. But Christianity rejects the illusion that people can find fulfillment through the possession of material wealth alone. That's because living a fully human life involves nurturing our souls, not just our bodies.

Materialism

Though it is possible to be both wealthy and happy, material possessions are no guarantee of either a happy life or a healthy society. Consider, for instance, the experience of people in the San Francisco area who became suddenly rich from the growth of technology companies. Although some adjusted well to life with their newfound fortune, others found that having more made them *less* happy:

"For many people, part of them would just like to close their eyes and make [the wealth] go away," says Mark Levy, a psychiatrist who treats those suffering from what has been called sudden wealth syndrome. "Life would be simpler and more manageable."

When Karsten Weide became a multimillionaire, he quit his job—and then did nothing. "The first thing I did was spend two months crashing and burning," recalls Weide. "I found myself in this big black hole where there was nothing to do."

The one thing he did do was worry, a lot. Having a huge pile of cash didn't make his life a breeze. "For me, the opposite happened," he says. "I'm stressing more now than ever. You have to take care of money, invest it somewhere, keep track of it and create something for yourself to do."

Another internet executive works eighty hours a week. "I see a price paid for not being with my family more," Mark Walsh says. "My family is healthy, happy, and smart, but time is all we have on this planet, and money is meaningless. I'm spending the only asset that matters, my time, a lot of it, on the company and growth. I wish I could clone myself." (Adapted from Laura Fraser, "The Experience of Being Suddenly Rich")

Individuals and families are not the only ones who suffer when having money and the things it can buy become more important than becoming who we were made to be. Society suffers as well:

> The gold rush in the San Francisco Bay area, where many of the [internet] rich live, drove up the median price of a condo. . . . The middle class fled into the suburban netherlands to find a place they could afford, and the homeless population showed no signs of shrinking. Traffic congestion—as well as over-

Often, we sacrifice investing in our relationships to earn a more generous paycheck. But will we have the opportunity to enjoy the fruits of our labor with our friends and family?

> Do you think the dissatisfaction of the people in this story came primarily from being wealthy or from their attitude toward wealth?

> What are the three most important things you own? List them, and then think about how each contributes to the development of your full human potential.

crowded stores and restaurants and buses—only added to everyone's frustration at the deteriorating quality of life in San Francisco. "In the end, you end up with a much meaner society," says Cornell University economist Robert Frank. "It's ironically a society that the people at the top don't find attractive either."

Karsten Weide agrees. "A lot of people I know are moving away [from San Francisco]; they can't afford to live here with normal jobs. And the atmosphere has changed a lot, from easygoing, tolerant, laid-back, nonmaterially oriented to a money culture—pushy, aggressive—and they're sad about it." (Adapted from Fraser, "The Experience of Being Suddenly Rich")

If living simply leads to greater joy in life, we might call the way of life described by the people in this story **materialism**. Materialism results when we value having things more than being true to who we are as images of God. It is a lifestyle that emphasizes *having* over *being*.

> **Materialism results when we value having things more than being true to who we are as images of God.**

Poverty of Being

Anyone, rich or poor, is capable of materialism. In a way, materialism is another form of poverty. It is clearly not the same as material poverty, but because it prevents us from developing our full potential as images of God, we might say it is a **poverty of being**. This sort of poverty causes us to forget who we really are, to forget that we are called to community, and to forget that we live within the limits of God's creation.

Forgetting Our True Identity

When we start defining ourselves by what we have rather than who we are, we lose sight of our dignity—

---

materialism The belief that the acquisition of material possessions is a greater goal than other intellectual, spiritual, or communal goals.

poverty of being The state of being unable to reach one's full potential as an image of God because of misdirected values.

Material goods cannot fulfill our deepest needs like love, self-esteem, creativity, and spirituality.

our true identity as images of God. The belief that "we are what we have" creates the illusion that we can fill our deepest needs—things like love, self-esteem, and creativity—in the same way we fill our basic physical needs, such as food and shelter, through material possessions.

The reality is that the things we own are not sufficient to provide us with true happiness. If we do not realize this, though, we can end up buying one thing after another. A new purchase might make us happy for a while, but when that happiness fades, we start feeling the need to buy something better. The attempt to find happiness by buying what we do not really need is called **consumerism**. During his papacy, Saint John Paul II observed that consumerism "easily makes people slaves of 'possession' and of immediate gratification":

> This is the so-called civilization of "consumption" or "consumerism," which involves so much "throwing away" and "waste." An object already owned but now superseded by something better is discarded, with no thought of its possible lasting value in itself nor of some other human being who is poorer. . . .
>
> One quickly learns . . . that the more one possesses the more one wants, while deeper aspirations remain unsatisfied and perhaps even stifled. ("On Social Concern," 28)

> Take a critical inventory of products at a local mall or department store. Make three columns on a sheet of paper, titling the first "Harms True Happiness," the second "Depends," and the third "Promotes True Happiness." Make a list of twenty products, placing each under the appropriate column. Then choose one from each column and explain why you categorized it as you did.

consumerism The unbalanced focus on buying things to find happiness.

> *If we expect to find fulfillment in what we have, we risk losing sight of the spiritual and social side of who we are.*

In your opinion, when do the needs of others become more important than what an individual wants for themselves?

Forgetting Our Call to Community

Materialism also has consequences for the way we relate to others. As images of God, we find fulfillment in our relationship with the Holy Trinity and others. But if we expect to find fulfillment in what we have, we risk losing sight of the spiritual and social side of who we are. Getting more stuff can become a higher priority than the needs of others.

This can lead to individualism, a concept we discussed at the beginning of this course. In terms of economics, the basic assumption of individualism is this: The world is made up of separate individuals, each seeking their own good, indifferent to the success or failure of other individuals seeking their own good. Furthermore, society is simply the sum of individuals seeking their own good. Looking after the common good is unnecessary because a good society will emerge automatically as more and more individuals achieve their goals. In this individualistic view of economics, moral concerns are kept to a minimum. Genuine fairness and kindness, for example, are not required in economic dealings because social relationships are limited to the impersonal world of contracts, rules, and laws.

Forgetting the Limits of Creation

Finally, materialism affects the way we relate to creation because it causes us to view the resources of the earth as something we own rather than as a gift from

What can you do as an individual to address the strain on the world's resources?

© Patryk Kosmider / Shutterstock.com

God we are called to care for. If the primary way we find happiness is through consumption of the earth's resources, it becomes tempting to overlook the limits of those resources.

Lazarus at the Gate

Catholic social teaching has long seen the wealth gap as a glaring sign of injustice. The injustice lies in the fact that those who have more resources than they need or could ever use are often reluctant to share them with those who lack the basic necessities of life.

Pope Saint John Paul II often noted that the wealth gap dividing the world closely resembles the parable Jesus told about Lazarus and the rich man:

> There was a rich man who dressed in purple garments and fine linen and dined sumptuously each day. And lying at his door was a poor man named Lazarus, covered with sores, who would gladly have eaten his fill of the scraps that fell from the rich man's table. Dogs even used to come and lick his sores. When the poor man died, he was carried away by angels to the bosom of Abraham. The rich man also died and was buried, and from the netherworld, where he was in torment, he raised his eyes and saw Abraham far off and Lazarus at his side. And he cried out, "Father Abraham, have pity on me. Send Lazarus to dip the tip of his finger in water and cool my tongue, for I am suffering torment in these flames." Abraham replied, "My child, remember that you received what was good during your lifetime while Lazarus likewise received what was bad; but now he is comforted here, whereas you are tormented. Moreover, between us and you a great chasm is established to prevent anyone from crossing who might wish to go from our side to yours or from your side to ours." (Luke 16:19–26)

This parable sounds harsh, but its message is clear. By ignoring the suffering of Lazarus, the rich man hurt not only Lazarus but himself as well. It was not only Lazarus's poverty that separated the two men but also the rich man's failure to love.

> **Catholic social teaching has long seen the wealth gap as a glaring sign of injustice.**

React to this statement: *Those who have wealth ought to share what they have with those who are poor.* How might individuals, institutions, and countries respond to this statement?

The parable of Lazarus and the rich man calls us to reach out across the gap that separates those who "[feast] sumptuously every day" from those who are unable to satisfy their hunger. The way to bridge the gap—and bring true joy for the people on both sides—is through love.

Lazarus at the Gate

1. Find the rich man in the painting. What characteristics helped you identify him?
2. Find the food items in the foreground of the image. How does their placement help you understand how selfishly the rich man treats Lazarus?
3. Look at the faces of everyone in the picture. What do you think it means that no one is looking at Lazarus, or even in his direction?

For Review

1. What is the wealth gap? Provide a statistic that illustrates the gap.
2. What is our culture's dominant attitude toward material wealth? How does the Christian attitude toward material wealth differ?
3. Define the term *materialism*.
4. Name and briefly describe three aspects of poverty of being.
5. Why does Catholic social teaching regard the wealth gap as a sign of injustice?

A Eucharistic Response to Poverty

Overcoming poverty is about overcoming the forces of death. Because Christians believe that death can be overcome only in Christ, they turn to him as they strive to overcome poverty.

The Eucharist: A Source of Life

The central way Catholics turn to Christ is through the Eucharist. Those who celebrate the Eucharist enter into communion with Christ and share in his victory over death. For this reason, the Eucharist is the source and the high point of all Christian life, the root of all Christian ministries, and the heart of a Catholic response to poverty.

What does the Eucharist have to do with poverty? First, the Eucharist is a source of life. When we celebrate it, we participate in Jesus' death and Resurrection; when we receive it, we receive "food that makes us live for ever in Jesus Christ"[1] (*CCC*, 1405). As bread feeds physical hunger, the Eucharist feeds spiritual hunger.

> Listen carefully to the Eucharistic Prayer during Mass, or find a copy of one of the prayers. How might the words of the prayer apply to our response to poverty?

Second, the Eucharist strengthens the solidarity necessary to overcome poverty. By receiving the Body of Christ in the Eucharist, Catholic Christians *become* members of the Body of Christ—that is, they are united with one another through Christ to become Christ's physical presence in the world, the Church.

By uniting people with Christ, the Eucharist also unites them with all those who yearn for fullness of life, committing them in a special way to those who are poor and hungry. Saint Paul scolded the Christians of Corinth because at their celebrations of the Lord's Supper, some members were going hungry. Paul said that by receiving the Eucharist while ignoring those who were hungry, they "show contempt for the church of God and make those who have nothing feel ashamed" (1 Corinthians 11:22).

Sharing Loaves and Fishes

Breaking the Eucharistic bread recalls the story of the miraculous multiplication of the loaves and fishes, a story that is found in slightly different forms in all four Gospels. These accounts have an important lesson to teach about responding to poverty.

Give Them Something to Eat

Jesus had been teaching a crowd of about five thousand people. Late in the day, his disciples urged him to send the people away so they could buy food for themselves in the surrounding villages.

> Recall a time when you shared something you really wanted just for yourself.

He said to them in reply, "Give them some food yourselves." But they said to him, "Are we to buy two hundred days' wages worth of food and give it to them to eat?" He asked them, "How many loaves do you have? Go and see." (Mark 6:37–38)

The disciples returned with five loaves and two fish. In a foreshadowing of the Eucharist, Jesus blessed the food, broke the bread, and had the disciples distribute it to the crowds. When the disciples collected the leftovers, they filled twelve baskets.

Life Is a Banquet

Like the disciples, our first reaction to the crowds of poor and hungry people in the world might be to send them away to fend for themselves. Just as the disciples suggested it would cost too much to feed the crowds, many people today suggest it would cost too much to respond to poverty with compassion.

Yet, Jesus calls us to "give them something to eat." This call comes with the promise that if we respond to one another's needs with love, all people will have enough to live a full and abundant life.

Dorothy Day took that call and promise seriously enough to act on it. Dorothy is the Catholic convert mentioned at the beginning of chapter 2. Together with Peter Maurin, she started the *Catholic Worker* newspaper in 1933. At the same time, the two also founded a movement by the same name. The Catholic Worker movement, like Dorothy's life, is dedicated to works of mercy such as feeding the hungry, sheltering the homeless, and working to change the social structures that cause poverty and injustice. Catholic Workers choose a lifestyle of voluntary poverty to better serve God and those who have been forced into poverty. They follow the words of Peter Maurin, quoted in chapter 1: "Everybody would be rich / if nobody tried to become richer. / And nobody would be poor / if everybody tried to be the poorest."

In her autobiography, Dorothy describes how the Catholic Worker movement started and grew. The following passage reflects the spirit of the movement, which reflects a **Eucharistic response to poverty**:

> We were just sitting there talking when lines of people began to form, saying, "We need bread." We could not say, "Go, be thou filled." If there were six small loaves and a few fishes, we had to divide them. There was always bread.
>
> We were just sitting there talking and people moved in on us. Let those who can take it, take it. Some moved out and that made room for more. And somehow the walls expanded. . . .

Eucharistic response to poverty Actions taken to reduce poverty that are based on the understanding that the Eucharist is the source of life, that it strengthens solidarity, and that it reminds us that if we share, there will always be enough.

Dorothy Day.

I found myself, a barren woman, the joyful mother of children. It is not easy always to be joyful, to keep in mind the duty of delight. . . .

We cannot love God unless we love each other, and to love we must know each other. We know Him in the breaking of bread, and we know each other in the breaking of bread, and we are not alone any more. Heaven is a banquet and life is a banquet, too, even with a crust, where there is companionship. (*The Long Loneliness*)

At the heart of Dorothy's reflection, and at the heart of a Eucharistic response to poverty, is this conviction: *If we share, there will always be enough.*

> If someone came up to you on the street and said, "I'm hungry," how would you respond?

Learning to Share

Sharing the world's resources more equitably is key to the economic aspect of human development. Sharing might sound like a simple solution to poverty, but putting it into practice on the scale of whole economies has proven to be more complicated.

Recall that in chapter 2, we discussed the way two major economic systems, capitalism and socialism, approach the distribution of wealth. Catholic social teaching has criticized both of these systems, however, for failing to fully respect human dignity. In its communist form, socialism does not respect human freedom and basic human rights. And the Church has criticized capitalism for being too individualistic and ignoring the needs of society's poorest members.

Rather than endorse a specific economic system, Catholic social teaching offers principles that should guide economic decision-making. The following three principles suggest a way of living together that is the opposite of materialism.

> **Rather than endorse a specific economic system, Catholic social teaching offers principles that should guide economic decision-making.**

1. People, Especially the Poorest, Are More Important than Possessions

Although Catholic social teaching accepts the need for economic growth in order to create living-wage jobs for all people, it rejects the notion that economic growth in itself is the best measure of a society's health. Rather, it says that because people are more important than possessions, concern for human dignity should be the most important guide for all economic decisions. According to "Economic Justice for All":

> Our faith calls us to measure this economy, not only by what it produces, but also by how it touches human life and whether it protects or undermines the dignity of the human person. (1)

> Wherever our economic arrangements fail to conform to the demands of human dignity lived in community, they must be questioned and transformed. (28)

Our economic decisions are guided by concern for human dignity in three basic ways: respecting human rights, enabling participation in community, and making an option for the poor.

Human rights and participation. The extent to which human dignity is being respected can be measured by the extent to which human rights are respected, especially the right to participate in all aspects of the life of the community.

Option for the poor. When promoting human dignity rather than selfishness is the ultimate goal of all economic activity, then the needs of those who are poor become a top concern. The justice of a society is tested by how it treats its poorest members, the Church says.

People are more important than possessions.

Sister Miriam Theresa

Dorothy Day was not alone in working to lift up the marginalized. While she established the *Catholic Worker* and focused on serving the poor, Caroline Gleason (1886–1962) was shaping the social justice movement in the Northwest. Born into a politically active, Roman Catholic family, Caroline was encouraged to become educated and work for justice. As the field secretary for the Catholic Women's League, she organized a staff to survey women's working conditions in the factories, stores, and offices of Oregon. The findings of that survey would become the data used for Oregon to pass the nation's first minimum-wage and maximum-hour law in 1913. Caroline became Sister Miriam Theresa when she joined the Sisters of the Holy Names in 1916, and she continued to be a prominent figure in the labor rights movement. In fact, her doctoral dissertation on the Oregon labor movement was published by the US Department of Labor. During an era when women were outsiders to the formal structures of public and political life, including voting, serving on juries, and holding elective office, contemporaries Dorothy Day and Sister Miriam Theresa lived simply and worked tirelessly in the service of others.

School meal programs are a lifeline for children who are malnourished or food insecure.

Inventory everything you own. How much of what you own is surplus—more than you really need? How did you distinguish between what you need and what is surplus?

2. The Earth Is God's Gift for All People

The Genesis Creation story teaches us that everything we have comes from God. Therefore, we never really "own" the resources of the earth; God is the earth's only true owner. God calls us to be caretakers of the resources of the earth, to use them to promote our own good, the good of others, and the good of all creation.

The concept that all the resources of the earth are intended for all people is called the **universal destination of goods**. Though Catholic social teaching affirms the right of all people to own private property to develop their dignity as images of God, that right is limited by the basic needs of the larger community. We are called to manage our economic resources in a way that benefits the common good of the whole global household:

> From the patristic period to the present, the Church has affirmed that misuse of the world's resources or appropriation of them by a minority of the world's population betrays the gift of creation since "whatever belongs to God belongs to all.² " ("Economic Justice for All," 34)

universal destination of goods The concept that all the resources of the earth are intended for all people.

The concept that "whatever belongs to God belongs to all" guided the economic life of the ancient Jewish community as well as the first Christian communities. Jewish Law called people to ensure that those who were poor would have access to their share of the earth's wealth: "If one of your kindred is in need, . . . you shall not harden your heart nor close your hand against your kin who is in need. Instead, you shall freely open your hand and generously lend what suffices to meet that need" (Deuteronomy 15:7–8).

Catholic social teaching, as expressed by Pope Paul VI, echoes this demand for justice: "No one may appropriate surplus goods solely for his own private use when others lack the bare necessities of life" ("On the Development of Peoples," 23).

> How would living by each of these three economic principles, plus trust in God's providence, change your community?

3. We Are Called to Care for God's Creation

Recognizing that the earth belongs to God implies that we need to care for the earth's natural resources, not only to preserve them for future generations who have as much a right to use them as we do, but also simply because they are good in and of themselves.

Trusting in God, Not Possessions

Fear is a major obstacle to our willingness to share with one another. We fear that we may not be happy if we share our wealth with others, or we hoard resources out of fear that we will not have enough at some future time of crisis.

In the Christian worldview, sharing is made possible because of a deep trust in the providence of God. Jesus taught that loving God before possessions opens our hearts to receiving all God's gifts:

> "Therefore I tell you, do not worry about your life and what you will eat, or about your body and what you will wear. For life is more than food and the body more than clothing. . . . Notice how the flowers grow. They do not toil or spin. But I tell you, not even Solomon in all his splendor was not dressed like one of them. If God so clothes the

> **Fear is a major obstacle to our willingness to share with one another.**

When we share with others, it does not mean that we will not have enough. Sharing resources with others ensures that no one goes without.

grass in the field that grows today and is thrown in the oven tomorrow, will he not much more provide for you, O you of little faith? As for you, do not seek what you are to eat and what you are to drink. . . . All the nations of the world seek for these things, and your Father knows that you need them. Instead, seek his kingdom, and these other things will be given you besides." (Luke 12:22–31)

Jesus is not suggesting that we ignore our own material needs or the needs of others. But his words call us to imagine a new reality for our economic life together. What if trust in God freed us from fear and the accompanying urge to have more than we need? What if our economy was based on love rather than selfishness? What if we shared rather than hoarded? In an economy based on love, there would always be enough resources for everyone's full development, and enough joy to go around.

Such a vision of economics may seem impossible, and without God's transforming grace, it is. Love and sharing are only possible when people experience conversion, a change of heart in which they turn away

> **Love and sharing are only possible when people experience conversion, a change of heart in which they turn away from sin and selfishness.**

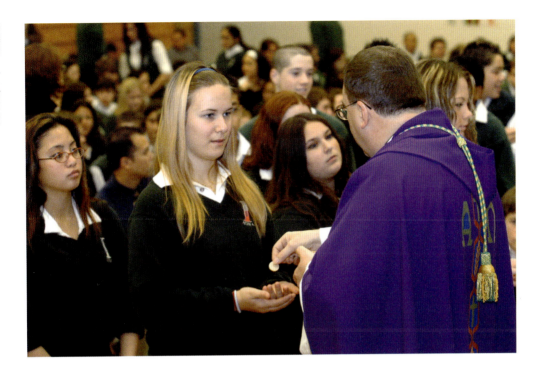

from sin and selfishness. For Catholics, celebrating the sacraments, especially the Eucharist, nurtures the ongoing conversion necessary to practice Eucharistic sharing in everyday life. If we live the power of the Eucharist, the words of the Gospel might be realized again: "They all ate and were satisfied" (Mark 6:42).

For Review

1. How does the Eucharist call us to commitment to those who are poor?
2. What conviction is at the heart of a Eucharistic response to poverty?
3. What does Catholic social teaching say should be the most important guide for making economic decisions?
4. What tests the justice of a society?
5. Briefly explain the universal destination of goods and its major implications for economic life.

Living Simply So Others Can Simply Live

When we apply the spirit of the Eucharist to the way we live together, we can begin to live more simply. Because living simply enables us to focus on the essentials of life, it promotes true human development, transforming the structures of society so that all people are able to fulfill their potential and live in dignity. The saying, "Live simply so others can simply live" is what this is all about.

A Different Kind of Wealth

When people hear the suggestion that they should live more simply, they often fear that they are being asked to live a deprived life. But living simply is not the same as poverty. Those who live in poverty lack sufficient resources to take care of their well-being. Simple living, on the other hand, enhances our well-being. It is not a state of destitution, but one of knowing what is enough and sufficient. It is an attitude of being, not having. When we live simply, we allow the spirit of the Eucharist to guide the choices we make in our everyday lives:

- **Human dignity.** We value people more than possessions. Our lifestyle decisions are primarily guided by how they affect our dignity and the dignity of others.

- **Relationships.** We look for joy in our relationships with others, rather than trying to find happiness only in what we possess. We

Our dignity is affected by how we treat others.

What are some small lifestyle changes you can make to positively impact the environment?

are aware that we live in a world of interdependent relationships, and so we try to be conscious of how our decisions affect others in the global community. Concern for the common good guides our decisions, not just our own interests.

- **Environment.** We include the well-being of the environment as an important factor in our lifestyle choices.
- **Trust.** We trust that when we live in love, God will provide us with what we need.

Simple living can influence all aspects of our lives: the quality and quantity of the goods we buy, the way we earn our money, our attitudes toward learning and recreation, and the way we relate to friends and family. Simple living can ease us of the burden of too many possessions and dispel false ideas about who we are. It can eliminate the distractions that prevent us from experiencing deep emotion. In short, simplifying our lives can make us more authentic human beings.

> **Living simply is also a way of living in solidarity with the poor.**

A Way of Living in Solidarity with the Poor

Living simply is also a way of living in solidarity with the poor. Material poverty and simple living are both economic conditions, but poverty is involuntary, and simple living is a choice. Because both of these economic conditions have to do with how resources are

We can make a difference by buying fair-trade products and supporting local merchants and small businesses.

> Most of us have lifestyles that fall in between living simply and materialism. Reflect on aspects of materialism and simplicity in your life. How does each affect your personal development? How does each affect your relationship with those who are poor?

distributed in society, the choice for a simple lifestyle rather than an excessive one can indirectly affect those who live in poverty. Each time we spend a dollar on a certain product, we support the whole system that produced and delivered that product.

So, for example, when the Christmas shopping season comes around, many people who want to live a simple lifestyle decide to buy crafts made by people living in poverty in remote areas of poor nations. In doing so, the purchaser supports economic opportunities for people who have been marginalized in the global economy.

Sharing to Overcome Poverty

By helping us to live out our human dignity more fully, giving us more free time, reducing our dependence on material goods, and deepening our solidarity with others, living simply makes it easier for us to share ourselves and our resources with those who are poor. The principles of living simply must be applied on a

> Brainstorm a list of ways you could simplify your life today, two years from now, and ten years from now.

social level as well as a personal level if the gap between rich people and poor people is to be bridged.

How can living simply be applied to society? The following people and communities show the way.

Direct Action: Feeding the Hungry

Catholic Charities works in tandem with the Diocese of Joliet to provide services to the homeless and hungry at the Daybreak Center. Daybreak Center operates twenty-four hours a day, 365 days a year, providing emergency housing and support services to their clients who are homeless. It is also used as a warming and cooling center during extreme weather. Daybreak Center offers homelessness prevention services for individuals and families who are at risk of losing their homes. Daybreak Center is a safe and clean environment with comprehensive case management services to assist with access to community resources, as well as educational assessments and services (including GED and ESL courses). In addition, the volunteers at Daybreak Center administer employment assistance, healthy living workshops, and group support meetings. Daybreak Center also runs Shepherd's Table, which is a service by which members of the community who need a midday meal are fed.

Promoting Self-Sufficiency

Direct aid is a necessary response to poverty. Without such action, people die. The ideal, though, is direct assistance that respects human dignity by

What Can Living Simply Look Like?

Living simply can take a variety of meanings, but it entails engaging in practices to simplify one's lifestyle. Here are some different approaches:

- **Minimalism:** Simplifying life by reducing one's possessions and consumption.
- **Self-sufficiency:** Simplifying life by providing for oneself as much as possible without modern systems or appliances. For example, some people choose to live off the grid, grow their own food, use solar power, and make their own self-care products.
- **Digital minimalism:** Simplifying life by reducing or eliminating access to certain technologies like cell phones, social media, television, or the internet.
- **Connection with nature:** Spending more time outside, camping, or in wilderness environments, all while leaving as small a carbon footprint as possible.
- **Slower pace:** Simplifying life by reducing a sense of urgency or the need to be busy.

It can be challenging to live simply when you are not yet independent. However, you can introduce some practices into your personal routine, and perhaps your friends and family would also be willing to do the same. Implementing one thing at a time allows you to see what best fits your life and goals, as well as giving you an appreciation for those who must live simply out of necessity rather than choice.

> Investigate a state, national, or international policy that prevents poor people from living self-sufficiently (for example, welfare limits that prevent people from going to school, or international trade rules that hurt poor nations). Explore the policy, its effects, and the views of people for and against it. Analyze it from the perspective of Catholic social teaching. What ways might the policy be improved?

enabling greater freedom to participate in the economic life of the community.

One such organization that promotes this kind of aid is **Catholic Relief Services** (CRS), an international poverty-fighting organization founded by the US Catholic bishops in 1943. Besides its emergency relief work in war-torn and famine-stricken countries, CRS helps people provide for themselves. The organization's work in Cambodia is a typical example. After two decades of civil strife, the Cambodians' average annual income was just $285, and most had no access to bank loans they needed to increase their income.

In response, CRS helped create village banks run by groups of thirty to fifty low-income women. The women are trained in reading, basic math, organizing, and record-keeping. They meet once a month to conduct bank business. Ngean Sarem, a single mother of three, used village bank loans to invest in her small grocery stand and her pig-raising business. The profits allowed her to repair her house, expand her business, and save $10. Over five years, 390 village banks provided $3.2 million in loans to nearly 25,000 Cambodians. With continued support and training, CRS sees a time when the banks will become self-sufficient.

Catholic Relief Services An international poverty-fighting organization founded by the US Catholic bishops in 1943.

Sharing by Changing Social Structures

Of course, **grassroots** efforts can go only so far to eliminate poverty. Many poor people are prevented from becoming self-sufficient by the larger political, social, and economic structures under which they live. Changes in national and international policies are a critical part of worldwide efforts to provide economic well-being for all people.

Changing the structures of society is the best way to alleviate poverty in the long run. However, it is often easier said than done. Fear and selfishness are powerful forces that cause many people to resist such changes. But it is something that Catholic social teaching calls us to address and continue working toward, trusting that God is with us, and knowing that the well-being of others and the community as a whole is at stake.

Catholic Relief Services
in Action

Catholic Relief Services supports hundreds of transformative projects in more than one hundred countries around the world. As the official international agency of the Catholic Church in the United States, this organization works with the local Church and other partners to create a world in which people live as one human family. The relief and development work Catholic Relief Services provides is accomplished through programs of emergency response, HIV education, health, agriculture, water, education, microfinance, peacebuilding, and partnership.

For Review

1. Name four principles that guide simple living, and briefly explain each.
2. How does living simply better enable us to work to overcome poverty?
3. What are some examples of direct action that can be taken to address the issue of poverty?

grassroots Foundational or fundamental.

- [ ] Start living a simple lifestyle: Avoid prepackaged or processed foods and junk food. Use fewer electrical appliances when hand-operated appliances are available. Buy more locally grown food and locally made products. Use fewer disposable products. Plant home and community gardens. Place more value on family ties and friendships than on making money.

- [ ] Practice sharing your possessions with others who might need them more than you do.

- [ ] Volunteer to tutor kids who need help in school.

- [ ] Start a food distribution program. Ask for help from a respected adult and some of your friends. Start by volunteering with a local program that helps the homeless so you can get to know the people you want to serve. Then ask local restaurants and stores to donate food that is too old to be sold but still good enough to eat.

- [ ] Work for more affordable housing in your community by getting involved with local housing advocacy organizations such as Habitat for Humanity.

- [ ] Support the political lobbying efforts of your state's conference of Catholic bishops. Contact your diocese to find out what poverty-related issues the Church is asking politicians to address, and then write or call your representatives.

- [ ] Pray for the Holy Spirit to help you and others in your community bridge the gap between those who are rich and those who are poor.

9
RESPECT for the EARTH
Caring for God's Creation

In This Chapter

Our Common Home | Creation as Gift | Our Environmental Responsibility | Make a Difference

Our Common Home

Molly Burhans never imagined meeting the pope. In fact, when she was growing up, she wanted to be a ballerina. After years of training, Molly was sidelined by a debilitating foot injury and returned home. During this time, she began to take classes at Canisius University, where her mother was a professor. It was at Canisius that she experienced a spiritual awakening. Eventually, Molly spent a week on a service retreat at a monastery in northwestern Pennsylvania. Molly realized that the resident religious sisters could be doing much more with the monastery property, which was located on a vast amount of land.

> "There were many acres of forest, but, at that time, there was no forest plan, no erosion plan, no invasive-species plan," she said. "And I thought, wow, this could be done better. They could be doing sustainable forest management and earning revenue, or they could implement a permaculture farming system and actually feed people." (David Owen, "How a Young Activist Is Helping Pope Francis Battle Climate Change")

This revelation was the beginning of Molly's mission to document the global landholdings of the Catholic Church. Molly understood that the Church has the means to address climate issues directly through strong land management and, by doing so, can contribute to the protection of populations that are vulnerable to the consequences of global warming. Molly believes the Catholic Church must proactively engage with its own lands and property if climate change is to be addressed in any sort of timely manner.

Molly is creating land-use maps like this one to help the Catholic Church record their global landholdings and usage.

Molly began the work of painstakingly documenting and mapping the Church's landholdings by starting in her own state of Connecticut. In making calls, she discovered that many parishes in her area weren't necessarily aware of what exactly they owned, and a great number didn't have paper records. If this was true locally, she thought, the situation was likely similar on a global level. Molly traveled to the Vatican in hopes of finding someone who could give her access to the records to fill in the gaps. Once there, she was disappointed to discover that the Vatican had no **cartography** department. The only records of Church landholding they possessed were frescoes painted on the walls.

Molly Burhans.

Molly went on to found GoodLands, an organization whose mission is "mobilizing the Catholic Church to use her land for good"(good-lands.org). After several years, Molly was invited back to the Vatican to take part in two conferences, one of which related to Pope Francis's groundbreaking encyclical "On Care for Our Common Home." Molly became known by cardinals from all over the world as "the Map Lady." Interest in her project was evident, as many of the cardinals had never seen a map of the global Church. On that trip, Molly saw the pope in passing, but two years later she would find herself in a face-to-face meeting. The pope was very interested in Molly's proposal, though funding and the COVID pandemic created obstacles to beginning the work. While Molly waited for the situation to resolve, she continued to pursue the mission of GoodLands:

> We are working towards a future where (1) Catholic conservation and sustainability operate at the same scale as Catholic healthcare, aid, and education, (2) the Catholic Church re-invigorates its rich history of cartography and knowledge stewardship, (3) the Catholic Church integrates sciences, art, and technology to promote its mission, (4) the Catholic Church works to ensure their land-use and land management is aligned with their values to care for

> If you could champion one area of social action within the Church, what would it be? What are some of the steps you might take toward accomplishing your goals?

cartography The science of making and using maps.

> What is the purpose of Molly Burhans's work of attempting to document the global landholdings of the Catholic Church?

the poor and steward creation, (5) the Catholic Church becomes a role model for and engages more deeply with conversations concerning the ethical applications of IT. (good-lands.org)

GoodLands provides information, insights, and implementation tools for the Catholic Church to leverage its landholdings to address pressing issues from environmental destruction to mass human migration. Under Molly's direction, GoodLands combines community involvement, design, and mapping technology to reveal land-use strategies that help transform the attitude of land ownership into a sense of caring for our common home.

Pope Francis: Champion of Creation

Many people think of creation as a product of God's love that activates and sustains life. Earth is a vast network of **ecosystems** providing oxygen, food, water, and shelter to support millions of life forms. This living planet is our common home.

> "This living planet is our common home."

From humans to invisible organisms, we are all interconnected and interdependent. Even when we aren't fully aware of this, each of us depends on others to survive and thrive. Being interconnected means that our interactions with nature truly matter because they have consequences. We are provided with sustenance, enjoyment, and inspiration in nature, and we put these benefits at risk when we fail to care for our common home.

Consider the ways you interact with nature. Have you ever thought about how all our lives depend on nature? How often have you felt in awe of the beauty and power of the natural world? These reflection questions remind us that humans are only one part of the vast natural world in which everything was created out of love and with its own purpose. In his encyclical "On Care for Our Common Home" ("Laudato Sí") Pope Francis reminds us of this fact: "Our insistence

---

ecosystems A community of living organisms that interact, and the environment they share.

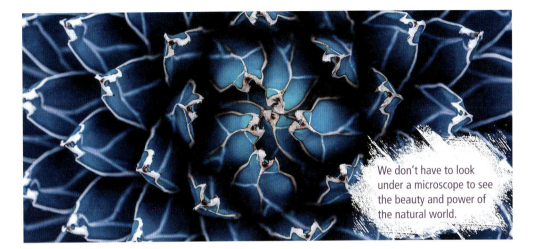

We don't have to look under a microscope to see the beauty and power of the natural world.

that each human being is an image of God should not make us overlook the fact that each creature has its own purpose. None is superfluous. The entire material universe speaks of God's love, his boundless affection for us" (84).

Pope Francis's encyclical expresses great concern for our planet in distress. He sounds the alarm for everyone in the world to look closely at how humanity is shaping our planet. But when we become more aware of the many environmental problems endangering livelihoods, health, and human survival, it can be overwhelming. One might even feel that the situation is hopeless. But Pope Francis guides us in the other direction as he wholeheartedly embraces the Gospel message of hope: "Hope would have us recognize that there is always a way out, that we can always redirect our steps, that we can always do something to solve our problems" ("On Care for Our Common Home," 61).

Even though years of human choices and activities have contributed to a complicated environmental crisis, there is still time and opportunities to turn things around. Redirecting our steps means envisioning and working together toward a more just and **sustainable** future.

> **Even though years of human choices and activities have caused a complicated environmental crisis, there is still time and opportunities to turn things around.**

sustainable A method of harvesting or using a resource so that it can be created and maintained without depleting or destroying other things in the process.

Vertical gardens and rooftop gardens are innovative ways to work toward a sustainable future.

What is something you intentionally do or avoid doing on a regular basis that impacts the environment in a positive way?

Themes in "On Care for Our Common Home"

Catholic theology teaches that creation is a gift from God and that we cannot survive without the natural world. Unfortunately, it is possible for humanity to take God's gift of creation for granted. In doing so, we can easily find ourselves facing the tragic effects of **environmental degradation** as we do now. Recognizing the gravity of this global crisis, Pope Francis speaks with urgency in "On Care for Our Common Home." Here are some important themes explored in this encyclical:

1. Be thankful for the gift of creation by cultivating and caring for nature.

2. By treating the earth as if it has an unlimited supply of resources, humanity is damaging our common home.

environmental degradation The deterioration of the natural environment caused by human activities, such as exploiting and polluting natural resources, destroying habitats, disrupting ecosystems, or depleting biodiversity.

3. Everything is interconnected.
4. Science can inform faith, and faith should also inform science.
5. Apathy and selfishness make environmental problems worse.
6. When creation suffers, people in poverty or vulnerable populations are most at risk of being adversely affected.
7. Less is more.
8. Being created in God's image with dominion over the earth does not justify human activities that destroy nature.
9. Young people demand and deserve a sustainable future.
10. Each person can make a difference given their culture, experience, involvements, and talents.

The environmental crisis is not just a challenge for science, economics, and politics. In "On Care for Our Common Home," Pope Francis helps us understand why care for this planet is also an urgent moral and spiritual concern. Human ingenuity exerts enormous power over creation through science and technology. The dangers of human beings abusing power and harming nature are real. The encyclical urges humanity to take seriously the responsibility for caring for the environment.

> **Young people demand and deserve a sustainable future.**

Think of places in your school or community where there is space for an urban garden. What tools and supplies would be needed to set up and sustain this type of project? Who would benefit from an urban garden in your area? Can you think of any negative aspects of establishing an urban garden? If so, what might they be and how could they be addressed?

> **Stewardship is most authentic when we see ourselves intimately connected to nature.**

Everything Is Connected

When we consider all the ways nature sustains human life, we begin to understand our role as **stewards**, or caretakers, of God's creation. Stewardship is most authentic when we see ourselves intimately connected to nature. Creation needs our care to survive, and humanity cannot survive without creation. Solidarity acknowledges this interdependent relationship. We rely on nature for both sustenance and leisure. Organisms in the earth's ecosystems work hard every day to provide services we depend on. These are called **ecosystem services**.

Here is a list of living things and the ecosystem services they provide:

- Microorganisms in the water and soil of wetlands, streams, rivers, and forests filter and improve water quality for wildlife **habitats** and for our recreation.

- Green plants absorb carbon dioxide and produce the oxygen we need to breathe.

- Animals, birds, and insects transfer pollen grains to fertilize crops that produce the nuts, fruits, and vegetables we eat.

- Plants and animals provide the fibers we use to make textiles, food, clothing, and shelter.

- Beautiful, scenic places like natural landmarks and nature trails inspire us to pray, reflect, or meditate to maintain our spiritual well-being.

stewards Those responsible for managing or caring for something else.

ecosystem services The benefits people obtain from natural environments, including provisioning services, such as food and water; regulating services, such as flood and disease control; cultural services, such as spiritual, recreational, and cultural benefits; and supporting services, such as those necessary for the production of all other ecosystem services.

habitats The natural environments of living things. Habitats are made up of physical factors, such as soil, moisture, range of temperature, and availability of light, as well as biotic factors, such as the availability of food and the presence of predators.

- Earthworms decompose animal waste, dead organisms, and plant matter to unlock nutrients that enrich the soil for growing crops we depend on for food.
- Trees and forests minimize soil erosion and control flooding to protect our farmlands and communities.
- Green spaces are open areas of grass, trees, and vegetation in urban environments that we depend on for recreation, education, public art, history, beauty, and health improvement.
- Coral reefs are crucial fish nursery habitats that also protect shorelines from erosion and provide tourism and recreational opportunities.

It's clear that ecosystem services are essential to life. Oxygen, food, and water are vital resources provided by the earth's ecosystems. However, other important provisions like medicines, fuels, and fibers also come from the earth. Additionally, services like climate regulation, pollination, recreation, and soil fermentation benefit us all. We depend on these systems operating throughout the natural world. But the health and vitality of our planet's numerous ecosystems also depend on us. Therefore, humans must embrace the role of steward to safeguard these important systems.

Urban Farming:
Feeding Families and Helping the Planet

Urban farming is becoming more popular as an eco-friendly way to address sustainability, food affordability, health, and convenience. Urban agriculture exists in many forms, including community and backyard gardens, rooftop and balcony gardens, as well as growth patches in vacant lots and parks.

On the top of a dorm building at the University of California at Berkeley, Bluma Farm grows vegetables, herbs, and edible flowers on just a quarter of an acre of rooftop space. Bluma demonstrates that when ground space is limited, green spaces can still be created to absorb city heat, produce more oxygen, reduce transportation costs, and feed more people. Urban farms play an important role in supporting low-income families, immigrants, and the elderly. With the cost of food steadily climbing, and the availability of some products becoming scarce, urban gardening provides free or low-cost fresh fruits and vegetables, which are often lacking in the diets of those who are food insecure.

Urban farming benefits not only society but also the environment. The Church can be an example in caring for and cultivating the earth by using portions of its properties as urban gardens.

For Review

1. Define *ecosystem*.
2. Give an example from the text of how to be a good steward of creation.
3. What are two important themes in Pope Francis's encyclical on caring for creation?
4. According to "On Care for Our Common Home," who is most at risk of being adversely impacted when creation suffers?
5. Name three ecosystem services that are essential for life.

Creation as Gift

Phil is a high school senior, an amateur photographer, and an outdoor enthusiast. After high school, he wants to pursue a career as a nature photographer. Phil has always believed that creation is a precious gift. He wants to ensure the natural world is cared for and treated respectfully. Through his photography, Phil wants to show what it looks like when people live in harmony with creation, and what happens to creation when that harmony is absent.

Recently, Phil won first place in a photo contest sponsored by a nature conservation society in the "People and Nature" category. The judges said that Phil's photo powerfully illustrated how people and nature depend on each

other for survival. "This is exactly what I want to convey in my photographs," Phil told the audience at the award ceremony. "If people take nature for granted and don't see it as a gift, it won't survive, and neither will we. We have to take care of nature for nature to take care of us."

Phil's photography articulates how nature brings sustenance, enjoyment, and meaning to our lives. The sacred balance between humans and nature must be respected. Creation is an incredible gift that requires our care.

Pope Francis teaches the same message in "On Care for Our Common Home":

> Once we start to think about the kind of world we are leaving to future generations, we look at things differently; we realize that the world is a gift which we have freely received and must share with others. . . . The world we have received also belongs to those who will follow us. (159)

Pope Francis begins his encyclical by describing the natural world as "our Sister, Mother Earth, who sustains and governs us" (1) but who also suffers from sickness. He describes the root causes of our planet's environmental problems as a result of years of irresponsible use and abuse of nature. That can change, but only if everyone works together.

Threats to the Environment Are Threats to Humankind

Unfortunately, we are realizing that humanity has taken the natural world for granted. Our lifestyles and our methods of production and consumption have disrupted, impaired, and severely threatened our planet's ecosystems. Nature can be plentiful and provide everything we need to survive, but we must find ways to live more harmoniously with God's creation by using and sharing the goods of the earth more responsibly in order to pass on a more sustainable legacy to future generations. The chart on the following page identifies some of the threats jeopardizing our common home.

> *The sacred balance between humans and nature must be respected.*

> *We must find ways to live more harmoniously with God's creation by using and sharing the goods of the earth more responsibly in order to pass on a more sustainable legacy to future generations.*

Environmental Problem	Impact on Humans
Climate change	Seventeen of the nineteen warmest years in the 136-year record have occurred since 2000. Global warming affects people's ability to grow sufficient crops.
Deforestation	**Rainforests** once covered 14 percent of the earth's surface. Now they cover approximately 6 percent. The loss of rainforests and their **biodiversity** disrupts the natural systems needed to create essential resources, such as food and medicine.
Dying coral reefs	Pollution and warming oceans have destroyed 27 percent of the world's coral reefs. Coral reefs are considered the medicine cabinets of the twenty-first century. As coral reefs die, humanity loses possibilities of treating diseases.
Melting glaciers and ice caps	In 1910, there were 150 glaciers in Glacier National Park. As of 2017, just 37 remained. As temperatures rise, glaciers and ice caps melt, and the oceans expand. Compared to the average rate of the past two to three thousand years, global sea level is rising more rapidly and putting the world's coastline communities at risk.
Declining biodiversity	Researchers predict a significant decline in marine biodiversity before 2050. An estimated one billion people, largely in low-income countries, rely on seafood that is disappearing.
Endangered species	The Great Pacific Garbage Patch has formed from bits of plastic bags, bottle caps, water bottles, and foam cups. Sea life ingests the plastic or gets tangled in the ocean debris. The improper disposal and accumulation of plastics causes the deaths of hundreds of thousands of animals in the food web, making seafood less available.
Water stress	In many parts of the world, undertreated sewage flows into the ocean. The waste from inadequate or nonexistent sewage systems endangers the lives of people who swim and fish in the ocean or consume the tainted seafood.
Air pollution	**Fossil fuels** are the primary source of energy in the United States. Burning fossil fuels releases toxic gases into the atmosphere, leading to serious health problems.

rainforests The earth's oldest living ecosystem, which consists of dense forests rich in biodiversity.

biodiversity The existence of many different forms of life in an environment.

fossil fuels Fuels (such as coal, oil, or natural gas) formed from dead plants or animals by natural processes.

Even though years of human choices and activities have caused this complicated environmental crisis, there is still time and opportunities to turn things around. It will require us to come together to work in unity toward those solutions, policies, and actions that will build a more sustainable future.

Nature Can't Wait

Did you know we are in the midst of a mass **extinction** of plants and animals? In fact, it has been estimated that there are some one million plant and animal species currently threatened ("UN Report: Dangerous Decline 'Unprecedented'; Species Extinction Rates 'Accelerating'"). The International Union for Conservation of Nature (IUCN) established a Red List, which is the world's most comprehensive assessment of the **conservation** status of animal and plant species. The main purpose of the Red List is to catalog and highlight plants and animals that face a higher risk of global extinction. An important reason to be concerned about **endangered species** is that the loss of species reduces biodiversity. Ecosystems depend on biodiversity to ensure that all the necessary functions sustaining ecosystem health are carried out. The loss of biodiversity risks the collapse of an ecosystem.

For example, in 2017, the red-legged fire millipede entered the Red

The Great Pacific
Garbage Patch

The Great Pacific Garbage Patch is a vortex of debris in the North Pacific Ocean estimated to be twice the size of Texas. It consists of billions of pieces of plastic, from large to microscopic in size, which are carriers of toxic pollutants that endanger marine life. About 80 percent of the debris comes from plastic waste thrown away on land that ends up in waterways. The remaining 20 percent is waste from oil rigs, fishing boats, and cargo ships.

Boyan Slat was just a teenager when he discovered that there was more plastic than fish in the water where he was diving in Greece. Boyan was so inspired that he came up with a plan to clean up half the garbage patch in the Pacific Ocean within ten years. He designed and built a system called Ocean Cleanup. It is a 1.2-mile-long system that uses the ocean's natural current to trap plastic trash. It doesn't use nets, so sea life can go underneath the barrier. Plastics lighter than water get caught in the top and are trapped by the barrier. Boyan's method doesn't generate any carbon dioxide pollutants and works 7,900 times faster than any previous methods! All the collected garbage is recycled to use as an alternative energy source.

Boyan turned his one-time diving experience into a lifelong mission to clean up the ocean. How might Boyan's commitment inspire you to be a better steward of creation?

---

extinction The dying out or permanent loss of a species.

conservation The act of preserving, protecting, or restoring the natural environment, ecosystems, vegetation, and wildlife.

endangered species Any species that is in serious danger of extinction.

> What if you were no longer able to benefit from the natural world due to damage caused by human activities? How would your life be affected?

List as critically endangered. Its forest habitat continues to decline due to logging for timber and clear-cutting to convert forests into rice fields. This millipede provides supporting ecosystem services in the Madagascar rainforest. Madagascar is among the world's poorest countries. Many people's survival depends on the biodiversity of the rainforests, and the survival of this species depends on habitat protection.

The good news is that we have proof that conservation works. For example, the status of the Rodrigues flying fox (a fruit bat) moved from critically endangered to endangered thanks to conservation efforts. It is vital to protect these bats as they are important pollinators. To do this, we must step up efforts to prevent the **deforestation** of mature fruit trees and root trees. Another example of the success of conservation efforts is the status of loggerhead sea turtles. They were moved from an endangered species to a **vulnerable species** in 2015 due to steps taken to protect their habitats. These highly migratory turtles rely on a variety of separated habitats during their lifetimes. When

> **The good news is that we have proof that conservation works.**

deforestation The intentional removal of an area of trees to convert the land to non-forest use, such as farming, industry, or housing.

vulnerable species Any species on the path to becoming an endangered species in the near future.

Loggerhead sea turtles are on the list of vulnerable species.

supported by healthy ecosystems, they have a life expectancy of fifty years or more. The main threat to loggerhead turtles is accidental capture in fishing nets. They can become entangled in fishing line, and pieces of net can become wrapped around their flippers. Development of beaches where they nest is also a threat, not just from the disturbance of their nests in the sand, but because artificial lights can direct the hatchlings to migrate toward the light instead of the ocean. Conservation efforts, such as designating habitat areas to protect nests, as well as researching and developing changes to fishing gear and practices to minimize the accidental trapping of the turtles have made a difference.

For Review

1. How does the loss of rainforests negatively impact humans?
2. How has the pollution of oceans with undertreated sewage affected humans?
3. What is the primary source of energy in the United States, and how does this affect the environment?
4. In what way do ecosystems depend on biodiversity?

Our Environmental Responsibility

The Book of Genesis emphasizes not one, but two tasks that God entrusts to humankind in relationship to the environment: cultivation and caring. "The Lord God then took the man and settled him in the garden of Eden, to cultivate and care for it" (Genesis 2:15). Our right to cultivate the earth comes with the responsibility to care for the earth.

From the day of his inauguration, Pope Francis has called all humanity to work toward a sustainable future in which the earth and all its inhabitants live in harmony, where cultivation and caring for the earth are seen in balance. In the homily at his inauguration in 2013, he addressed the importance of care for creation by reminding us that being a protector is not something

involving Christians alone. He explained that caring for God's creation involves everyone:

> Please, I would like to ask all those who have positions of responsibility in economic, political and social life, and all men and women of goodwill: let us be "protectors" of creation, protectors of God's plan inscribed in nature, protectors of one another and of the environment.

Pope Francis furthered his call to action in an address in Africa in November 2015:

> The grave environmental crisis facing our world demands an ever greater sensitivity to the relationship between human beings and nature. We have a responsibility to pass on the beauty of nature in its integrity to future generations, and an obligation to exercise a just stewardship of the gifts we have received.

We can look to many individuals as examples of good stewardship of creation. One of those people was Gaylord Nelson. He served as governor and senator of Wisconsin for nearly thirty years, where he created national hiking trails and helped author crucial environmental protection laws, such as the Wilderness Act.

However, his greatest contribution was the establishment of **Earth Day**. Nelson envisioned Earth Day as a **teach-in** that would create a national movement to raise awareness of environmental issues. Over one

---

Earth Day A worldwide event started in 1970 that supports environmental protection. It is celebrated every year on April 22.

teach-in An informal gathering in which a topic is introduced and discussed to raise awareness. It is usually centered on a current social or political issue.

million people participated in the first Earth Day on April 22, 1970. By the end of the year, Nelson's efforts led to the creation of the United States Environmental Protection Agency and the Clean Air, Clean Water, and Endangered Species Acts. Earth Day has since grown to include over 170 countries with over one billion participants. Nelson reminded us to consider what kind of world we leave for future generations when he challenged participants at Earth Day's twentieth anniversary:

> I don't want to have to come limping back here twenty years from now on the 40th anniversary of Earth Day . . . and have the embarrassing responsibility of telling your sons and daughters that you didn't do your duty—that you didn't become the conservation generation that we hoped for.

What do you think Nelson would think were he alive today? Did we fulfill his great hope, or do we still have more work to do? Are we doing a sufficient job as stewards of creation, leaving the world in a better condition for future generations? Gaylord Nelson committed his life to preserving the wonders of nature and the sacredness of the earth for generations to come. We are called to do the same. The call of stewardship is to provide for the common good in a way that preserves creation's integrity and the many

> Do some research to investigate positive changes that have come about since the creation of the United States Environmental Protection Agency or the Clean Air, Water, and Endangered Species Acts.

interdependent relationships that sustain the community of life and make it whole. To do this, we must simply begin with respect for the natural world.

Our Choices Matter

The struggle for environmental justice is both a moral and a spiritual task. We are in a battle against personal sin and social sin for the common good. We come up against the effects of personal sin when we see such things as recyclables that are simply thrown away, water that is used with no concern for conservation, or electronics that are not disposed of in environmentally friendly ways. We face social sin when we see how the collective effect of sin over time has led to social structures that allow for the abuse of the gift of creation.

We know we are called to live a moral life and work for the common good because we see ourselves in relationship with God, with one another, and with creation. When the common good is our focus, we become more willing to sacrifice our personal comfort for the good of another. We are then able to combine our creative energies to find solutions that will heal the earth.

> **When the common good is our focus, we become more willing to sacrifice our personal comfort for the good of another.**

What does it mean to you to love your neighbor?

God desires that we all live as one family and treat one another as brothers and sisters. We are called to love our neighbor. How we treat ourselves, others, and our planet really matters.

The environmental crisis is both an ecological and social crisis. When we are out of touch with the gift of nature or the people whose health and livelihoods are threatened by environmental degradation, we can become unaware, even apathetic, about prevailing concerns, needs, and sufferings. The love of neighbor we are called to is inclusive of all created things—the environment as well as the people who rely on the environment for life.

> Reflect on a time when you became aware of an environmental crisis, suffering, or need. What was your initial reaction? What type of action were you compelled to take?

New Habits

Because nature is vast and incredible, our choices about how we interact with nature can seem limitless. And yet, we are learning from history that this is not our reality. Humanity can no longer think and act as if the natural environment is unlimited with an infinite pool of resources. Nor can we continue to assume that the ecosystem services we depend on will indefinitely support lifestyle choices that harm the ecosystems providing these services. When we open our eyes to the realities of waste, pollution, climate change, and the loss of biodiversity, we can see that our planet can't recover as quickly as we produce, consume, and dispose of materials.

Composted waste turns into composted, nutrient-rich soil.

Saint Kateri Tekakwitha:
Champion of Conservation

Saint Kateri Tekakwitha was the first Native American canonized as a saint. Kateri encountered God through the gifts of creation. She often retreated to natural spaces as holy places to pray and be open to God's guidance in her heart. Today, people of faith who love nature and work for conservation look to Saint Kateri as their patroness for the protection of our planet.

Tekakwitha means "one who places things in order." One way Saint Kateri Tekakwitha placed things in proper order was by not taking nature for granted. As a champion of creation, Kateri viewed God's gifts in nature with eyes of appreciation. For Kateri, the diversity and interconnectedness of nature were reflections of God's sacramental or spiritual presence in this world.

Saint Kateri was known as the Lily of the Mohawks. In the Christian tradition, the Easter lily blooms, dies, and reblooms, making it a powerful symbol of hope and new life through Jesus' Resurrection. Saint Kateri Tekakwitha experienced many Christlike dyings and risings throughout her short life. Her name reminds us that the path to healing and protecting the earth is about placing things in their proper order. Because the environmental crisis is driven by a culture of convenience, consumption, and waste, we must choose to create alternative, countercultural ways of thinking and living. Kateri's Christ-centered life can be our inspiration for change. The motto that guided her life was, "Who can tell me what is most pleasing to God that I may do it?"

Think of something that took you time to learn, like how to tie your shoes or how to ride a bike. At first, this was difficult and required a lot of mental energy. Eventually, this activity became much easier because it became a routine . . . habitual. Now you no longer concentrate as much because the process has become hardwired in your brain. In this way, habits are very efficient.

It takes time, patience, and a lot of willpower to replace an old bad habit with a new healthy one. This is why it is illogical to think that we can solve the earth's environmental crisis in a short amount of time with the same detrimental habits, attitudes, and behaviors that have brought us to where we are today.

Learning from the Past

Before we choose to develop new habits, we must first identify our attitudes and actions that are problematic. To do that, we must look to the past. For example, one reason the environment suffers is because the things we purchase eventually get thrown away. All this unwanted material ends up in a landfill, incinerated, or exported to offshore barges. These waste disposal methods pollute the earth, air, and water, and change the climate. Consider the number of paper products that end up in a landfill. As that paper slowly decomposes with all the other materials in the landfill, this **biodegradation** generates high levels of methane, a

---

biodegradation The process of decomposition by bacteria, fungi, worms, and other living organisms.

Have you ever wondered how landfill material breaks down?

powerful **greenhouse gas** that contributes to climate change. This rotting and decaying also leach toxic liquid, or **leachate**, that can contaminate soil and groundwater.

Our planet can't recover as quickly as we produce, consume, and dispose of materials. In a throwaway culture, landfills are the norm. This doesn't have to be our reality. We can make better lifestyle choices that move our society toward a more sustainable future.

> Brainstorm a list of attitudes, actions, products, and practices that were commonplace in the past, and the new habits, attitudes, and products that have replaced them as we strive toward responsible stewardship.

For Review

1. What is considered Gaylord Nelson's greatest contribution as a steward of the environment?
2. Name at least one law that was a result of Gaylord Nelson's effort to raise awareness of environmental issues.
3. When the common good is our focus, what might we be willing to do to protect the earth and one another?
4. What are greenhouse gases?
5. According to the text, who is the patron saint for the protection of our planet?
6. Where can we find the teachings about the two tasks God has entrusted to humankind regarding the earth, and what are those two tasks?

greenhouse gas A gas such as carbon dioxide, water vapor, methane, and nitrous oxide that pollutes the air and causes the warming of the earth's atmosphere.

leachate A toxic liquid that drains or leaches from a landfill and can contaminate soil and groundwater.

Make a Difference

Real actions make real progress. In higher-income nations, renewable energy is meant to reduce dependence on fossil fuels that damage the environment. In lower-income countries, however, renewable energy may also provide electricity to people who currently have no access.

William Kamkwamba, a teenager from Malawi, in southeastern Africa, saw an image of a wind turbine in a library book. Thinking that free electricity could help his village irrigate crops, William used scraps from a junkyard and built a working turbine modeled after the picture in his library book. His family now enjoys lights and radio powered by his makeshift wind turbine. In fact, William's entire village benefits from his ingenuity. His original windmill was extended to catch wind from above the trees. Another windmill pumps gray water for irrigation.

William earned a scholarship to Dartmouth College. Since his graduation, he has continued to work on projects to benefit his village, as well as his home country. The story of how William's persistence and creativity saved his village became a film called *The Boy Who Harnessed the Wind*, based on William's memoir. William is proof that anyone can harness sustainable energy.

You Have the Power

You can make a real difference in the struggle against **environmental injustices** by sharing your God-given interests and talents. These diverse interests and talents can also be described as charisms. Here are some examples of charisms that serve the common good. Consider which charisms you possess.

- writing
- teaching
- speaking
- making music
- leading
- sharing knowledge
- being hospitable
- healing
- creating art
- encouraging others
- planning and organizing
- being generous
- sharing faith
- being compassionate
- peacemaking

Personal power is a gift every human being possesses. Each of us has the ability to make a difference when it comes to the environment. When we combine our passions, talents, knowledge, and actions in solidarity with other people, we amplify everyone's ability to make a difference.

See, Judge, Act

The environmental crisis is a moral and spiritual crisis of conscience. Fortunately, Catholic social teaching gives us a decision-making process to help us in-form our conscience and make good, moral decisions. This process is called the **See, Judge, Act** method of decision-making. It is both practical and spiritual and can be thought of as a way of listening to the voice of God.

In the See, Judge, Act process, we are called first to *see*. We must recognize a situation and understand what is involved to the degree possible. We can evaluate such things as what is happening, who is involved, and what the effects of this situation may be. Second, we must *judge*. This is a time to reflect on how we think and feel about the situation. What do we think should happen? What does our faith say about this situation? Third, we must *act*. In this stage, we are called to assess what we are going to do and who we might involve, and then proceed with action. Let's walk through the See, Judge, Act process by analyzing a real-life situation that involves the environment.

---

environmental injustices Actions that degrade the natural environment, harming ecosystems and living things, including human beings.

See, Judge, Act A decision-making process introduced in Catholic social teaching that is both practical and spiritual in nature. It can be thought of as a way of listening to God.

Meet the Kellers

Warren and Tish Keller had always dreamed of living close to the beach. Now that they were retired, they could. Their realtor found the perfect condo, which was under construction. When the Kellers visited the site, they could see that workers had dredged up a large amount of sand to lay the foundation. It concerned them that the condos were being built so close to the ocean. They also discovered that the area of construction was in a nesting habitat for the leatherback sea turtle. When they asked the realtor and contractor about beach erosion and the sea turtles, they seemed to not know or care about these situations. It was clear that the developer was going to go ahead with the building project whether the Kellers bought a unit or not.

Using the See, Judge, Act decision-making process, the Kellers were called to first *see* the situation for what it was—the condo they were looking at was being constructed in a place where the environment was being affected. In this case, it appeared as if the developers cared more about making money from

> Imagine yourself as a champion of creation. Which environmental injustice would you choose to act on to create a better future, and why?

the lucrative beach condos than beach erosion or habitat protection. The Kellers then needed to use their hearts and conscience to *judge* how they felt about the situation and whether their actions might contribute to the injustice. The developer would build regardless of the Keller's decision to purchase, but the Kellers could judge whether they would be contributing to harming the environment by purchasing this retirement home. They determined that their care for the environment would be at odds with purchasing this property. Now the Kellers had to *act*. They committed to rejecting the condo purchase, finding other properties that wouldn't endanger species, habitat, or biodiversity, and educating other potential buyers about the situation. If other prospective buyers were aware of the dangers to the environment, perhaps they would also refuse to purchase. Difficulty in selling units and bad press could influence the builder to consider making some changes to protect the beach and sea turtle habitat.

For Review

1. What different effects can renewable energy have in higher-income versus lower-income nations?
2. Explain each step of the See, Judge, Act method of decision-making.
3. What is a charism, and how might it be used to support the common good?

Dr. Jane Goodall.

Quotable Stewards

Review the following quotes from stewards of the environment. Consider which one speaks to you.

- "Earth has enough to satisfy every man's need, but not every man's greed." (Mahatma Gandhi)
- "The greatest danger to our future is apathy." (Dr. Jane Goodall, "The Power of One")
- "One who loves does not sit in an easy chair looking on, waiting for the advent of a better world, but gets up and goes with enthusiasm and simplicity." (Pope Francis, "Address to the Vincentian Family")
- "Creation is a gift from God. We're asked to steward it. The Book of Genesis asks us to keep and till the natural world. And sadly, we've done a very good job of tilling it, but not such a great job keeping it." (Fr. James Martin, *America*)
- "Everyone needs beauty as well as bread, places to play in and pray in, where nature may heal and give strength to the body and soul alike." (John Muir, *The Yosemite*)
- "Humankind is placed in the Garden by the Creator to 'till it and keep it' (Genesis 2:15). These concepts of 'tilling' and 'keeping' involve a vital and reciprocal relationship between humanity and the created world. They involve humankind . . . a sacred duty to draw from the goodness of the earth, and at the same time to care for the earth in a way that ensures its continued fruitfulness for future generations." (Cardinal Peter Turkson, "Trócaire Lenten Lecture")

- Replace incandescent light bulbs with more energy-efficient and money-saving LED bulbs. Conserve energy by turning off and unplugging lights, electronics, and appliances when not in use. Use rechargeable batteries.

- Buy used instead of new, and save lots of money in the process. Used-clothing stores, for instance, often have like-new clothes. Rather than throwing away an old computer or couch, try selling it or giving it to someone who could use it.

- Educate yourself about what can and cannot be recycled. If your community does not have a recycling program, lobby your city or county government for one. Buy recycled products so that companies have an incentive to reuse recycled waste.

- Get together with friends, neighbors, or siblings and see what you can share so that each person doesn't have to buy the same thing. Lawn mowers, cars, clothes, and tools are all possibilities.

- Limit driving by carpooling, using public transportation, biking, and walking.

- Designate a week to record food that gets thrown away to become more aware of which types tend to be wasted. Participate in a food-composting program or start a kitchen compost system in your home.

- Volunteer to pick up trash on a beach, in a park, or on the roadside.

10
WORKING toward PEACE
The Christian Path of Peacemaking

In This Chapter

| Solidarity in the Face of Violence | Violence, Nonviolence, and Peace | Following Jesus to Peace | The Christian Response to War | Peace through Love |

Solidarity in the Face of Violence

In northern Algeria, French Trappist **monks** established an **abbey** in 1947. During World War II, the Muslim inhabitants of a nearby town settled around the monastery for protection. This spurred the development of a village called Tibhirine. The nine monks that remained at the monastery continued their peaceful coexistence with their Muslim neighbors in the village. The monks followed the Rule of Saint Benedict, spending much of their time in silence and prayer. But they also contributed to the local community by teaching French, providing employment at the monastery's farm, and dispensing medicine to villagers and clothes to the poor. The monks tended the land adjacent to the abbey along with the villagers in an agricultural cooperative, which cemented their bond.

But in 1991, Algeria erupted into a civil war. The monks had the opportunity to leave and return to France, but they chose to stay. They put their own lives at risk in a tangible demonstration of solidarity with the local Muslim villagers who had nowhere to flee. In March 1996, twenty armed military men stormed the monastery and kidnapped seven of the nine monks. The remaining two monks were unable to contact the police because the telephone lines had been cut. They were finally able to report the kidnapping to the police the next morning.

The extremist military group wanted to negotiate an exchange of the monks for one of their leaders who had been arrested three years earlier. They provided voice recordings of the monks to the French Embassy in Algiers to verify

> **monk** A male member of a religious community who lives a life of prayer and work according to a specific rule of life, such as the Rule of Saint Benedict.
>
> **abbey** A building or group of buildings where monks or nuns live, work, and pray.

Algeria is located in northern Africa.

Community Peacemaker Teams

Community Peacemaker Teams (formerly Christian Peacemaker Teams) is a group dedicated to reducing violence through nonviolent means. The Community Peacemaker Teams (CPT) organization started by asking this simple question: What would happen if Christians devoted the same discipline and self-sacrifice to nonviolent peacemaking that armies devoted to war? Individuals who participate in Community Peacemaker Teams undergo extensive training in nonviolent conflict resolution. Then they are sent in teams to locations where there is ongoing violence. They attempt to reduce the violence by befriending local people, being in solidarity with them, praying for peace, and witnessing to nonviolent love and reconciliation. Sometimes, they even put themselves in the middle of tense situations to try to prevent violence from starting. CPT has served in Iraqi Kurdistan, Palestine, Colombia, Greece, Canada and the United States (known as Turtle Island), and other countries.

Community Peacemaker Teams is a small organization with a diverse membership working in coalition with other peacemakers. These efforts have made a difference in the lives of many people suffering injustice. This group is one example of the peacemaking praised by the Church: "Motivated by this same spirit, we cannot fail to praise those who renounce the use of violence in the vindication of their rights and who resort to methods of defense which are otherwise available to weaker parties too, provided this can be done without injury to the rights and duties of others or of the community itself" (*The Church in the Modern World*, 78).

that the monks were alive. Yet, before any negotiations could take place, the group announced that they had executed the seven monks. The Algerian government soon discovered the heads of the monks, but their bodies were never found. The remains were buried at the Tibhirine monastery, where they would always be with the community they had loved so deeply.

The brave monks who would not abandon their Muslim neighbors in a time of war and danger would not be forgotten. Their story was adapted into the movie *Of Gods and Men*. The film focuses on the chain of events that led to that fateful day, the decay of the government, the growth of terrorism, and the monks' confrontation with the terrorists and government authorities before their kidnapping and death. Though they encountered danger many times, the monks had agreed on the moral importance of remaining committed to their lives with, and ministry to, the local population—even in the face of violence and death.

When the story of the monks of Tibhirine became well known, many people praised them as brave for their willingness to stay with their neighbors. But Fr. Jean-Pierre Schumacher, the last surviving member of the monastery who died in November 2021, said their commitment was not unique. "All the Christian communities opted to stay in Algeria with the suffering people to help them," he said. "The entire Church has this attitude."

community peacemaker teams

A sit-in is a form of nonviolent protest.

Which Way to Peace?

Like the monks of Tibhirine, millions of people around the world live under the threat of some type of violence. Most people would agree that the world would be a better place if there were less violence. But what is less clear is how to achieve a more peaceful world. How should we respond to the world's violence? Conventional wisdom tells us that the party with the most strength or weapons will be the one to win a fight. For most people, then, the answer to a violent world is more violence: "Fight fire with fire," they say; violence can only be stopped on its own terms.

But Christianity claims that love, not violence, brings true order and peace to the world. It bases this claim on the belief that although Jesus was crucified and died, the life-giving power of his Father's love overcame that violence in his Resurrection. The Trappist monks bravely followed Jesus' example by challenging violence with love. And by doing so, they experienced a "resurrection" of their own, defying conventional wisdom. This is the paradox of the cross: love is stronger than violence, even the violence of death.

> Do a brief search of the story of the monks of Tibhirine. How did their insistence on staying with the people and their ultimate death demonstrate that love is stronger than violence?

> **Christianity claims that love, not violence, brings true order and peace to the world.**

Of course, it is easier to make that claim in church or religion class than it is to actually rely on it in daily life, especially under the threat of real violence. It's reasonable to ask, How can Jesus' way of love really work in a violent world? That is the question considered in this chapter.

For Review

1. Cite at least two examples from the text of the monks' commitment to the community of Tibhirine.
2. How does conventional wisdom suggest we respond to violence, and why?
3. How does Christianity suggest we respond to violence, and why?

Violence, Nonviolence, and Peace

To understand how love overcomes violence, we need to understand the basic nature of violence itself—specifically, what it is and why it happens. Once we understand this, we can see more clearly the role nonviolence plays in the world and how it can be instrumental in peacemaking.

What Is Violence?

What is violence? The answer might seem obvious: most often, we think of violence as any action that physically injures or kills a person or damages property. But in the understanding of Catholic social teaching, **violence** is *any* human action that causes harm to the life or dignity of another person. Because this definition of violence includes harm to human dignity, any action that harms a person's psychological, social, or spiritual well-being can also be considered a type of violence.

When violence is defined to include harm to human dignity, it becomes apparent that we have been examining

> **violence** Any human action that causes harm to the life or dignity of another person.

Racially motivated hate crimes are on the rise in recent years.

issues of violence throughout this course. Injustice itself is a form of violence. The sort of violence that occurs as a result of unjust social structures rather than as a direct result of one person's actions is often called **institutional violence**. Racism and poverty are some general forms of institutional violence, as are many of the situations we have examined throughout this book.

Injustice itself is a form of violence.

The Spiral of Violence

The **spiral of violence** is a concept used by Brazilian Archbishop Dom Hélder Câmara. Archbishop Câmara was known for his solidarity with the poor people in his country, and he wanted to explain to others how violence and injustice are related to each other. His concept was rooted in an understanding of the human tendency toward retaliation and revenge. He explained that when one person is harmed by someone else, the typical response of the person who was harmed is to retaliate and hurt the other person in return. Now the original attacker has become a victim, and they respond by attacking the original victim with an even

> **institutional violence** Violence that occurs as a result of unjust social structures rather than as a direct result of one person's actions.
>
> **spiral of violence** The tendency of violent acts to escalate as each party in a conflict responds to violence with even greater acts of violence.

The Spiral of Violence

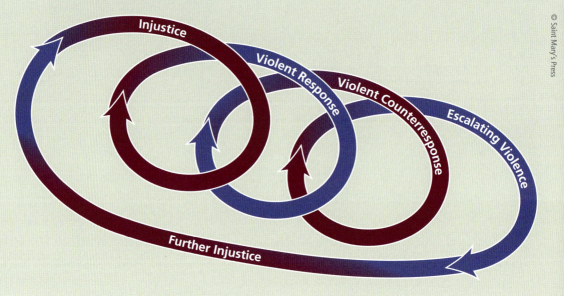

greater act of violence. Left unchecked, this spiral of violence can escalate in intensity and may grow to involve more people. Here are the steps involved in the spiral of violence, along with an example of how it might look in a real-life experience.

1. **Injustice.** The spiral begins when people resolve a conflict selfishly, seeking only their own interests at the expense of the good of others. This results in some type of injustice. For example, let's say a freshman is being bullied by other students in gym class. The freshman wears glasses, is small in size, and doesn't participate in any team sports. This makes them a target in some other students' eyes. Day after day, the freshman is teased, called names, and belittled.

2. **Violent response.** If the injustice is severe enough, it can prompt a response from those affected by it. People frustrated by injustice often see no other solution than the use of violence against their opponent. To continue the example, the freshman is tired of being picked on in gym class, so the next time they are taunted by the bullies, they lose their temper. Screaming insults, the freshman picks up a chair and throws it toward the group of bullies.

Have you ever been bullied? Have you ever bullied someone else?

3. **Violent counterresponse.** Once violence is used to solve a conflict, the other side might see no other choice but to respond with even greater violence. In the example, how do you think the bullies might react to the freshman's outburst? The truth is, now feeling violated themselves, their threats and taunting may increase, and they might physically harm the freshman.

4. **Escalating violence.** The level of violence escalates as each side attempts to overcome the other with the use of greater force. Each side feels justified in its response because of the harm that has already been inflicted. The freshman may search for other ways to get back at the bullies, and the bullies may intensify their reaction.

5. **Further injustice.** When one side finally uses enough force to overwhelm the other side, the conflict may appear to end. In reality, the spiral often returns to the first level, where the "winner" imposes their will on the "loser" in an unjust way. In that case, the spiral begins all over again. For example, school administrators might get involved to break up a physical fight between the bullies and the freshman. It may seem like the situation has been resolved. But the bullies are angry, and the freshman still feels vulnerable. The injustice may continue and, if so, the cycle will repeat itself.

Situations like this happen every day, all across the world. And this example takes place among only a small group of students. The same process is often at work in conflicts between

Thomas Merton
and Nonviolence

Thomas Merton was a Catholic convert and a Trappist monk. As a monk, he was a prolific author and is often thought of as the most influential Catholic writer of the last century. Yet, it was his writings about civil rights and his criticism of the Vietnam War that brought controversy. Many viewed his outspokenness on these issues as being inappropriate for a monk. Some people, angry with his position on the Vietnam War, burned his books near to the abbey where he lived. He was also silenced from writing for a few years by his own order.

Merton wrote about the problem of violence coming not only from individuals but also emanating from within the whole social structure, "which is outwardly ordered and respectable, and inwardly ridden by psychopathic obsessions and delusions" (*Faith and Violence*). You can imagine how attacking social structures and institutions as the source of hatred and violence was not a popular tactic with those in power. However, through his writings, Merton became an inspiration for the anti-war, nonviolence movement. Even though pointing toward social structures as the source of energy for the war machine was a startling idea in his time, it is an idea that is now popularly accepted.

Thomas Merton, 1915–1968.

> **The spiral of violence teaches us that the best way to confront violence is to address the issues that led to violence as early as possible.**

people of different cultures, tribes, and nations. How do we stop the escalation of violence?

The spiral of violence teaches us that the best way to confront violence is to address the issues that led to violence as early as possible. Jesus calls us to refuse to participate in the spiral by choosing not to return violence for violence, hate for hate, and evil for evil. He taught his disciples, "But to you who hear I say, love your enemies, do good to those who hate you, bless those who curse you, pray for those who mistreat you" (Luke 6:27–28).

To those who ask why we have war and other forms of violence in the world, Hélder Câmara might suggest looking at how those acts of violence are preceded by other forms of violence. Often, institutional violence lies at the root of more intense forms of violence. Unfortunately, it doesn't take long to find the spiral of violence at work in our world, at both an individual level and a global level.

> Drawing on history books, the news, or your own experience, find an example in which the use of violence led to a more violent response. Consider how and why violence escalated, using the spiral of violence as a guide.

Peace and Nonviolence

Nonviolence is not the same as **peace**. Nonviolence is a response. Peace is the outcome we hope for when responding to conflict with nonviolence. Peace exists when everything and everyone in creation are in right relationship with God and one another. Peace enables all to reach their God-given potential. It implies action and requires us to see all humanity as our brothers and sisters. Peace involves a commitment to justice.

For Review

1. How does Catholic social teaching understand the term *violence?* How might this be different from most people's definition of the word?
2. List the steps in the spiral of violence, and state how understanding this can contribute to peacemaking.
3. Explain the difference between nonviolence and peace.

---

peace The harmony that results when people resolve conflicts by working in love for the good of all.

Following Jesus to Peace

Christianity claims that the way of Christ is the way to true peace for the world. Often, when people refer to "world peace," what they have in mind is the absence of war and physical violence. But the peace to which Jesus calls us goes deeper than that.

Peace: The Fruit of Justice and Love

If we accept the claim that all injustice is a form of violence, then it follows that peace is more than the absence of war or physical violence. Really, true peace cannot be achieved until there is justice for all. This is what Pope Paul VI meant when he said, "If you want peace, work for justice" (quoted in *Peacemaking,* volume 1).

Here is how the Church defines peace in *The Church in the Modern World:*

> Peace is not merely the absence of war; nor can it be reduced solely to the maintenance of a balance of power between enemies; nor is it brought about by dictatorship. Instead, it is rightly and appropriately called an enterprise of justice. Peace results from that order structured into human society by its divine founder, and actualized [i.e., brought about] by [people] as they thirst after ever greater justice. . . . Since the human will is unsteady and wounded by sin, the achievement of peace requires the constant mastering of passions and the vigilance of lawful authority.

If true peace is more than the absence of war, how can celebrating a "day of peace" be a catalyst toward change in the world?

But this is not enough. This peace on earth cannot be obtained unless personal well-being is safeguarded and [people] freely and trustingly share with one another the riches of their inner spirits and their talents. A firm determination to respect other [persons] and their dignity, as well as the studied practice of brotherhood are absolutely necessary for the establishment of peace. Hence peace is likewise the fruit of love, which goes beyond what justice can provide. (78)

Working for justice transforms social structures that cause physical forms of violence, such as war, to erupt in the first place. But peace is even more than the fulfillment of justice. It is also the fullness of love.

Jesus Provides the Answer to Peace

Many people view peace as a far-off goal or even an impossible dream. But the Church says peace is a real possibility for those who are open to it, and Jesus is our greatest example of the path to peace.

As we learned in the spiral of violence, when people are hurt by violence, they tend to retaliate with violence. However, the logic of retaliation fuels the spiral of violence and separates us from one another and from God.

But Jesus refused to follow the logic of retaliation. Because he was totally committed to following the Father's will, he chose to act only in truth and love—even if it meant giving up his life. He responded to those who crucified him not with more violence but with

> **Peace is even more than the fulfillment of justice. It is also the fullness of love.**

What does peace look like for you? Choose a photo, painting, song, poem, or story that is an image of peace for you. Be prepared to share it in class.

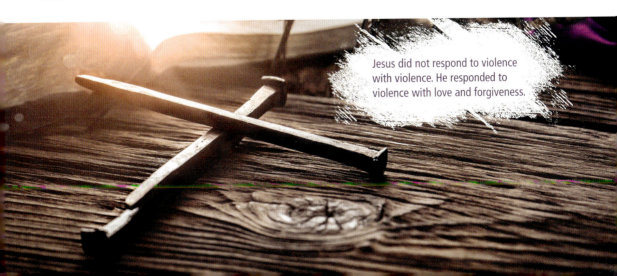

Jesus did not respond to violence with violence. He responded to violence with love and forgiveness.

> Few of us will ever be called to sacrifice our lives for the sake of peace. But what small, daily sacrifices can people make to contribute to peace? Name some ways you have observed people around you make sacrifices for peace.

forgiveness (see Luke 23:34). By refusing to retaliate, he broke the spiral of violence. And by following God's way of love even in the face of death, he liberated humanity from sin, the root cause of all violence. We too are called to act in love and proclaim the truth, even though we might suffer as a result.

Blessed Are the Peacemakers

Jesus was raised in the Jewish tradition with an intimate understanding of the concept of **shalom**. *Shalom* is a Hebrew word for *peace* that also means "wholeness, wellness, or perfection." Shalom is not just about the absence of war or conflict. It is the presence of love, harmony, safety, and healing. Shalom requires action. It invites people to make amends, to resolve conflicts, to build or rebuild trust, and to sacrifice for the good of another.

Shalom begins in our hearts and minds and expands to include our family, friends, communities, nation, and world. As peacemakers, we feel whole when we are at peace with ourselves and with one another. Therefore, shalom is not a solitary endeavor. It is meant to be shared.

During his ministry, Jesus challenged injustice, but he also encouraged shalom, or peacemaking. We see here just a few examples of Jesus' teachings from the Gospels:

- "Blessed are the peacemakers, / for they will be called children of God" (Matthew 5:9).
- Forgive one who sins against you "not seven times but seventy-seven times" (Matthew 18:22).
- "Love your enemies, do good to those who hate you, bless those who curse you, pray for those who mistreat you" (Luke 6:27–28).

> **"Shalom begins in our hearts and minds and expands to include our family, friends, communities, nation, and world."**

---

shalom A Hebrew word for *peace* that invites action to establish the presence of love, harmony, safety, and healing for all.

- When one of his disciples attempts to prevent Jesus' arrest by attacking with a sword, Jesus admonishes him, "Put your sword back into its sheath, for all who take the sword will perish by the sword" (Matthew 26:52).

Jesus calls his followers to live in a way that promotes peace and breaks the spiral of violence.

Jesus' Third Way

Jesus also taught his disciples, "You have heard that it was said, 'An eye for an eye and a tooth for a tooth'" (see Exodus 21:23–25, Leviticus 24:19–20, Deuteronomy 19:21). "But I say to you, offer no resistance to one who is evil. When someone strikes you on [your] right cheek, turn the other one to him as well" (Matthew 5:38–39). The Old Testament commandment was meant to moderate vengeance, teaching that the punishment should not exceed the injury done. But what did Jesus mean by "turn the other cheek"?

To gain understanding, let's learn about Jesus' cultural context. He lived in a society ruled by honor and shame. He was speaking to people who were members of out-groups that were used to being oppressed. The first blow from the oppressor would not be to injure, but to insult, humiliate, and degrade the target as inferior. It would be a backhand to the right cheek to force someone who was out of line back into

Envision how you would respond with the "third way" in an everyday scenario of violence you might encounter.

Nonviolence is the third way.

Pope Francis
Appeals for Nonviolence

In recent years, violent conflicts and protests have become more and more commonplace. Expressing concern about the tone of demonstrations, Pope Francis made an appeal for nonviolence, dialogue, and a guarantee of civil rights:

> While I urge the demonstrators to present their demands peacefully, without giving in to the temptation of aggression and violence, I appeal to all those with public and governmental responsibilities to listen to the voice of their fellow citizens and to meet their just aspirations, ensuring full respect for human rights and civil liberties. ("Angelus")

In areas of conflict and protest, the pope asks Catholic communities "to work for dialogue—always in favor of dialogue—and in favor of reconciliation."

These teachings are not new. Pope Francis has pointed out on numerous occasions that Jesus taught and modeled nonviolence. And, like Jesus, our nonviolent stance must be an active rather than passive role. It is not enough to accept the situation as "out of our hands" or wring our hands in distress, saying, "What can be done?" We must examine what it is that we can do to address violence with truth and love, and then do it.

their place in society. Turning the other cheek would be taking a brave stand against the oppressor. The oppressor would not use the left hand to backhand. So, turning the other cheek is a bold move that makes it impossible for the oppressor to strike again to assert dominance. The nonviolent act of turning the other cheek says: "I am human like you. I have dignity. I refuse to be degraded. I refuse flight and I refuse to fight." Turning the other cheek, or nonviolence, is Jesus' **third way**.

Jesus doesn't advocate nonviolence as a technique for outwitting an enemy. Nonviolent resistance is a just means of opposing an enemy that holds open the possibility of the enemy's transformation. Not flight. Not fight. Jesus' third way teaches us: Do not ignore or run from evil. Do not react violently to evil. Do not counter evil in kind. Do not allow evil to dictate the terms of opposition to violence.

Practicing Peace

Putting Jesus' way of love into action in our world takes practice and can be started on a personal level. Peacemaking takes awareness and intentional effort. Consider this: If you're six years old, playing with a sibling or a friend, it wouldn't be hard to imagine fighting over toys or games. If your babysitter forces you to apologize to each other and play apart until you forget you are angry, is this peacemaking? A forced apology and separation may reduce the

---

third way The alternative to flight or fight when responding to conflict or violence. Jesus teaches nonviolence as the third way.

Is trying to defuse a potentially violent situation part of peacemaking?

immediate conflict and lessen the frustration of the babysitter, but this approach doesn't teach reconciliation. Even young children can learn that peacemaking requires reconciliation and true forgiveness.

Many people are uncomfortable with conflict. When we witness it, we may become anxious or engage in our flight reflex to get away from it. When Matt saw two of his classmates arguing in the cafeteria, he wanted to turn around and walk out. But he decided to try to defuse the situation by asking, "Hey! What's going on?" When his interruption didn't create a break in the tension, and the argument continued to escalate, Matt signaled to the teacher on lunch duty. Trying to defuse a conflict and asking for help put Matt on the road to peacemaking.

Eve is concerned with how certain groups in her community are often a target of harassment and violence. She isn't able to vote or attend rallies, but she has a variety of social media accounts. In addition to posting selfies and updates, Eve has started using her social media to invite and inspire respectful dialogue about social justice issues that are important to

> Name a few everyday situations that might require you to act as a peacemaker.

Have you ever used your social media accounts to bring attention to an issue that is important to you?

her. In this scenario, social media is a powerful tool for peacemaking. Think about how many issues have been brought to your attention or have sparked your interest from your social media alone. Our online presence is another way we can practice peacemaking.

Grace: The Help We Need

"Peace is both a gift of God and a human work," the US Catholic bishops say in "The Challenge of Peace" (68). In other words, peace can be fully achieved only in the Kingdom of God, which we are called to prepare for by following the way of Christ. If we stop to consider seriously what the way of Christ requires, we might not be so quick to answer when he asks us to take up our cross and follow him.

How does peacemaking invite us to overcome fear, hesitation, or apathy?

The choice for peace can be daunting; to choose that way rather than the way of violent retaliation, we need God's help. But if we are open to the grace provided by the Holy Spirit, we might find that we are able to go beyond ourselves to accomplish what we thought was impossible. "No man can stop violence," Gandhi said. "God alone can do so. . . . The deciding factor is God's grace."

> Write a prayer, poem, or song for the grace to love enemies, or create a symbolic artistic image of God's grace restoring peace between enemies.

For Review

1. Define *peace*. What are two prerequisites of peace?
2. Explain why shalom requires action.
3. Define Jesus' "third way."
4. What role does grace play in the Christian response to violence?

The Christian Response to War

Over the centuries, how Christians have attempted to apply Jesus' teachings on peace and violence to their lives has depended on how they understood those teachings. For about the first three centuries of the Church, most Christians opposed the use of violence under any circumstances. Even though they faced sporadic persecution by the Romans, the early Christians refused to fight back. They also would not serve in the Roman military, which led to charges of being disloyal citizens.

The early Christians had various reasons for refusing to serve in the military, but most important was their belief that military service was inconsistent with the teaching and example of Jesus: "For we no longer take up 'sword against nation,' nor do we 'learn war any more,' having become children of peace, for the sake of Jesus," wrote Origen, a second-century Christian leader (Walter Wink, *Engaging the Powers*). Soldiers who converted to Christianity were encouraged to leave the military. "I am a soldier of Christ," declared Martin of Tours, a fourth-century Roman soldier, after his conversion. "It is not lawful for me to fight" (quoted in "The Challenge of Peace," 114).

> **The Church has always taught that violence should be used only as a last resort.**

Today, such opposition to using violence to resolve conflict is called **pacifism**. The Church strongly defends pacifism as a legitimate moral choice for individuals, as long as it does not harm the rights or duties of others. On the other hand, the Church also affirms the right of individuals and the duty of governments to self-defense and the defense of the innocent—even by the use of armed force.

But the Church has always taught that violence should be used only as a last resort. Even in the case of self-defense, the Church teaches that there are strict moral limits on the use of violence. Beginning in the fourth century, the Church began developing criteria for determining when the use of violence could be justified, and how it should be limited in those cases.

The Just-War Theory

The nonviolent practice of the early Church changed after Christianity was made the official religion of the Roman Empire in 380. Before, it had been illegal for a Roman soldier to be a Christian; not long after, however, all Roman soldiers were *required* to be Christians.

---

pacifism Opposition to the use of war or violence to solve conflicts and a commitment to nonparticipation in violence in any way.

The United Nations is an intergovernmental organization created to maintain international peace and security.

As members of the new majority religion, many Christians felt a responsibility to protect the community.

Saint Augustine of Hippo (354–430), a bishop who became one of the most influential theologians in Church history, argued that war could be morally justified in certain cases. Although he viewed war and other forms of violence as tragic and to be avoided, he believed they could be necessary to protect the innocent. Borrowing from Roman ethics, Augustine developed principles for determining the conditions under which war could be justified. Those principles, known as the **just-war theory**, were later refined by others, particularly Saint Thomas Aquinas (1225–1274).

The just-war theory rests on two assumptions. It begins by presuming that war and violence are always to be avoided and that we should not harm anyone, even our enemy. On the other hand, it also presumes that love calls Christians to restrain an enemy who would harm innocent people. The just-war theory attempts to balance these presumptions by suggesting that when it is necessary, limited violence may be used to protect the innocent—but it can only be justified after other peaceful options have been exhausted, and then only the minimum amount of violence necessary may be used. The purpose of the just-war theory is not to encourage war, but first to prevent it and then to limit it as much as possible.

> **The purpose of the just-war theory is not to encourage war, but first to prevent it and then to limit it as much as possible.**

just-war theory The premise that considers the use of military force morally acceptable when specific criteria have been met.

Just-War Criteria

In "The Challenge of Peace" (85–99), the US bishops restated the criteria for determining why and when going to war is justified. *All* the following criteria must be met for a war to be considered just.

Criteria for a Just War	Criteria Explained
Just cause	War is permissible only to confront "a real and certain danger," to protect innocent life, to preserve conditions necessary for decent human existence, and to secure basic human rights. Wars of vengeance are not permissible.
Competent authority	War must be declared by those with responsibility for public order, not by private groups or individuals.
Comparative justice	The party considering war must ask: Are the rights or values at stake consistent with Christian justice, and are they important enough to justify killing? In choosing war, the nation must be aware that its "just cause" for war is limited, and that its actions should therefore also be limited.
Right intention	The intention must be to use the least amount of force necessary to achieve the goal of justice; for example, soldiers should prefer capturing the enemy over wounding him, or wounding the enemy over killing him. Once war has begun, sincere efforts at peace must continue to be pursued.
Last resort	War must be the last resort for resolving a conflict. All other reasonable possibilities for a peaceful resolution must have been attempted in the time available.
Probability of success	To avoid causing even greater damage than would result otherwise, war should only be attempted if it is likely to succeed in achieving justice. For example, a weak country should not attempt to fight the invasion of a much stronger aggressor if doing so will only result in its greater destruction.
Proportionality	The good to be gained by a war should outweigh the damage and the costs, both material and spiritual, to be caused by it. For example, during the Vietnam War, the US bishops concluded that the damage being done to each side could not justify the continuation of the war.

In addition to these criteria for determining whether it is just to go to war, two criteria apply throughout the war itself. The **principle of proportionality** just mentioned applies not only to the decision to go to war but also to each decision to use violence during the war. The **principle of discrimination** also applies throughout the war: lethal force may be directed only at those who are threatening to do violence. Noncombatants, such as children, prisoners of war, and other civilians, may not be targeted.

> Find a short description of a war online or in a history book. Make some notes as to whether you think the war met the just-war criteria.

Is a Just War Possible Today?

As you can see, the criteria for a just war are difficult to meet. They were originally designed to limit and reduce violence at a time when wars were fought with swords and arrows, and some have argued that modern weapons make it impossible to meet all the

> **principle of proportionality** A rule of the just-war theory stating that the good to be gained by war must outweigh the damage and costs caused by it.
>
> **principle of discrimination** A rule of the just-war theory stating that if parties engage in war, lethal force is only directed toward those threatening to do violence.

The irony of United Nations peacekeeping troops is that they carry weapons while trying to keep peace. The challenge for all armed agencies is to decide if a violent response is necessary and justified.

> Do you believe a just war is possible today? Why or why not? Be prepared to discuss your position in class.

criteria today. As the US bishops put it, the decision to go to war "requires extraordinarily strong reasons for overriding the presumption *in favor of peace* and *against* war" ("The Challenge of Peace," 83).

In recent years, Pope Francis has suggested that a "just war" might not even be possible. In his 2020 encyclical "All Brothers," Pope Francis declared "it is very difficult nowadays to invoke the rational criteria elaborated in earlier centuries to speak of the possibility of a just war."

In fact, Pope Francis has gone beyond any previous Church authorities and teachings regarding a just war:

> There was a time, even in our Church, when people spoke of a holy war or a just war. Today we cannot speak in this manner. A Christian awareness of the importance of peace has developed. Wars are always unjust since it is the people of God who pay. Our hearts cannot but weep before the children and women killed, along with all the victims of war. War is never the way. ("Pope to Russian Patriarch: 'Church used language of Jesus, not of politics'")

Though there has been no official change to the Church's teaching on the just-war theory, it is clear that the requirements to meet these conditions, along with the pope's strong stance, direct our focus toward nonviolent means of settling conflicts.

Pacifism or Just War?

Although the Church accepts both the just-war and the pacifist response to violence, it reminds those who follow each approach of their obligation to meet the concerns of those who take the other way. Those who refuse to fight for the sake of peace are still obliged to seek justice, and those who wage just wars are obligated to always seek peace.

In "The Challenge of Peace," the US bishops empha-size the right of individuals to refuse to fight—not for reasons of cowardice, but for reasons of conscience. If an individual, in good conscience, sees all wars as immoral, they may object to being forced to serve, or drafted, in the military. The legal term for

> "Those who refuse to fight for the sake of peace are still obliged to seek justice, and those who wage just wars are obligated to always seek peace."

such opposition is **conscientious objection**, and someone who applies for this status under US law is called a conscientious objector.

The bishops also teach that individuals may practice selective conscientious objection, or "objection to participation in a *particular* war, either because of the ends being pursued or the means being used" (233, emphasis added). Current US law does not allow for selective conscientious objection. Nonetheless, the Church insists that Christians, even enlisted soldiers, may refuse to participate in a given war or follow certain orders if they view them as immoral.

To sum up the Church's teaching, we can say that resorting to limited violence, including war, may be better than doing nothing in the face of extreme injustice. But the Church also insists that resolving conflict through peace is always better than resolving it through violence. The history of modern warfare attests that even limited wars cause injury, death, and destruction. As such, any war is a failure of humanity to live up to its full potential.

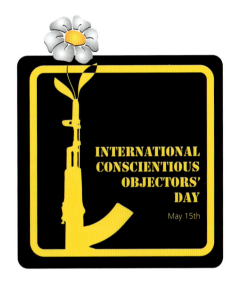

For Review

1. Describe pacifism and the just-war theory. How are they similar, and how are they different?
2. List the seven criteria for a just war.
3. Why does Pope Francis say that a just war is no longer a possibility?

conscientious objection Opposition on moral or religious grounds to serving in the armed forces or to bearing arms.

Peace through Love

While defending the validity of the just-war approach, the US bishops point to nonviolent tactics as the best way to challenge aggression:

> We believe work to develop nonviolent means of fending off aggression and resolving conflict best reflects the call of Jesus both to love and to justice. Indeed, each increase in the potential destructiveness of weapons and therefore of war serves to underline the rightness of the way that Jesus mandated to his followers. ("The Challenge of Peace," 78)

How can the principles of nonviolence be used to promote peace in a violent world?

Working toward Peace One Person at a Time

The spiral of violence teaches us that small-scale violence often leads to large-scale violence. But this principle also applies to peace: peace between individuals can lead to peace between nations. Here are some specific steps involved in promoting peace.

Correct Injustice

The title of Pope Paul VI's World Day of Peace message in 1972 was "If You Want Peace, Work for Justice." Because people saw the truth in this statement, the phrase became popular and spread throughout the world. When people have their freedoms

taken away by an authoritarian government, they will fight back. When the majority of a population lives in poverty and a small minority live in excessive luxury, it takes only a spark for violence to emerge. By working to end such injustices, we can help avoid the outbreak of violent conflict.

Work for Solidarity

Solidarity is an essential ingredient of peace. After all, people are less likely to use violence against their friends than against strangers. Programs that help people of different races, cultures, or nations know and appreciate one another build the solidarity needed for a peaceful society. It can be a challenge for us to leave our comfort zone and enter someone else's world, but the potential benefits make it an important act of love.

> After all, people are less likely to use violence against their friends than against strangers.

My Brother's Keeper

After murdering his brother Abel and trying to cover up his crime with a lie, Cain asks God, "Am I my brother's keeper?" (Genesis 4:9). Jesus' deep commitment to love is God's answer to this question. When we carefully examine Jesus' teachings and actions, we discover that the Son of God embodied an inspiring countercultural ethic of life.

When our mindset mirrors that of Jesus, we experience an intimate connection with all human beings. We hear and respond to the cries of those in need: the weak and vulnerable, the sick and dying, the poor and homeless, the targets of hate, and society's outcasts. Our hearts and minds yearn to do what we can to protect life and human rights. We take actions to ensure each person freedom and opportunities so they can fulfill their God-given dignity. We are called by God to be our sisters' and brothers' keepers because "God entrusts us to one another" (Pope Saint John Paul II, "The Gospel of Life," 19).

Support Economic Development

Someone once said that when fast-food restaurants are as prevalent in every country as they are in the United States, there will be fewer wars in the world. The person did not mean that fast food prevents violence, but that these restaurants are a sign that a society has a growing middle class and fewer people in poverty. And countries without widespread poverty are less likely to go to war, because their citizens have too much to lose and little to gain. When we help countries with widespread poverty develop their economies, we help promote peaceful societies.

Promote Forgiveness and Reconciliation

The pain and loss caused by past injustices and violence cannot simply be ignored. This does not bring peace to either the victim or the perpetrator. The guilty party must seek forgiveness, and the wounded party must be willing to extend forgiveness for reconciliation to occur. "The weight of the past, which cannot be forgotten, can be accepted only when mutual forgiveness is offered and received; this is a long and difficult process, but one that is not impossible" (*Compendium of the Social Doctrine of the Church,* 517). A good example of this long and difficult process is found in the work of the **Truth and Reconciliation Commission** that

---

Truth and Reconciliation Commission An official agency formed in South Africa after the end of apartheid to uncover the truth about injustices committed and to promote reconciliation as a way to resolve conflict.

was formed after the end of apartheid in South Africa. The commission provided a forum in which those who had violated human rights during apartheid could testify about their crimes and request **amnesty** from prosecution.

Make Time for Prayer

Prayer is one of our most powerful peacemaking practices. In prayer, we align ourselves with God's will, we are strengthened to persevere in the trials that come with working toward peace, and we are given the courage to make the sacrifices required. We ask for the intercession of Mary and the saints in healing wounded hearts and converting sinful social structures. We also nourish ourselves in the liturgy and strengthen our commitment to solidarity through prayer and receiving the Eucharist at Mass.

> In prayer, we align ourselves with God's will, we are strengthened to persevere in the trials that come with working toward peace, and we are given the courage to make the sacrifices required.

An Option for the Brave

Working toward peace requires all the courage, willpower, and perseverance needed to wage war, but it also requires imagination, patience, humility, and the grace of God. Peace may be a challenging path, but in the long run, the benefits for all humanity seem to be worth its challenges.

amnesty A pardon offered for past wrongdoings.

> Choose one of the ways of working toward peace one person at a time, and explain how it could be applied in your school or community.

Whether we are resolving conflicts in our own lives to experience more peace or are seeking to bring peace to our communities and to the world, being a peacemaker takes courage. Courage gives us the strength and wisdom to transform the world into a place where peace prevails. Like shalom, courage is not passive. It is an active commitment to creating peace. Courage is a gift from God that enables us to become disrupters, peacemakers, and even heroes for justice.

Each of us is called to create a culture of peace. To be peacemakers, we must disrupt the cycles of violence in our world. We can respond to injustice wherever we happen to encounter it on our life journey. We have the power to effect change in our own way. And we each have been given unique talents, passions, and life experiences that only we can contribute to the world. If we do that, our dream for a better world will come closer to becoming a reality.

For Review

1. List the specific examples from the text of how individuals are promoting peace. Explain one of them in detail.
2. What did Pope Paul VI say we should do if we want peace?
3. Why is solidarity an essential ingredient of peace?
4. What are some of the qualities we need in order to work toward peace?

- Practice the principles of nonviolence in arguments and disputes by trying to focus on the humanity of your opponent. Say a prayer: "Give me the wisdom and courage to settle this fight in a way that respects the dignity of both of us."

- Avoid media that promote a culture of violence.

- Speak up whenever you see violence—whether it is physical or verbal—being used against someone. If you're afraid to speak up against the violence, get the help of others who might speak up with you, or tell a responsible adult.

- Practice solidarity by reaching out to people outside your social group.

- Start a mediation program for peacefully resolving fights and conflicts at your school.

- Find out what organizations in your community are doing to stop violence, and then get involved.

Glossary

A

abbey A building or group of buildings where monks or nuns live, work, and pray.

ableism Discrimination that oppresses, discriminates against, and stigmatizes those who are not "able-bodied."

abolition The action of terminating a system, practice, or institution.

affordable housing Housing for which the occupant is paying no more than 30 percent of their income for total costs, including utilities.

Age of Enlightenment A movement that began in the nineteenth century that considered human reason as supreme in the acquisition and development of knowledge and so questioned both the possibility of Revelation and the teachings of the Church.

amnesty A pardon offered for past wrongdoings.

apathy The state of showing little concern or interest.

B

barriers to full development Something that holds people back from developing their full potential. For those in poverty, this includes denial of basic resources and the development of a worldview in which a better lifestyle seems impossible.

Beatitudes Blessings spoken by Jesus as part of the Sermon on the Mount and the sermon on the plain that reveal the path to happiness and holiness. The Beatitudes are often considered to represent the heart of the preaching of Jesus.

biodegradation The process of decomposition by bacteria, fungi, worms, and other living organisms.

biodiversity The existence of many different forms of life in an environment.

boycott The practice of refusing to support something, such as a person, a store, or an organization, to express disapproval and create pressure for change.

C

campesinos Latin American land or farm workers.

capitalism An economic system based on the private ownership of goods and the distribution of goods determined mainly by competition in a free market.

capital punishment The practice of killing people as punishment for serious crimes.

cartography The science of making and using maps.

cash crops Agricultural products produced for their commercial value.

Catholic Relief Services An international poverty-fighting organization founded by the US Catholic bishops in 1943.

Catholic social teaching The teaching of the Church that examines human society in light of the Gospel and Church Tradition for the purpose of guiding Christians as they carry on the mission of Jesus in the world.

chronic hunger The situation when a person is unable to consume enough food to maintain a normal, active lifestyle over an extended period.

circle of faith-in-action The approach to working toward justice that involves three steps: awareness, analysis, and action.

civil disobedience Intentionally breaking laws that are unjust.

Cold War The period between about 1945 and 1990, when the United States and the Soviet Union competed to dominate the world through military power.

colonialism The result of national expansion in which a people or a country is dominated by a foreign nation. This often results in the exploitation of the people and resources in the dominated country.

common good The social condition that allows all people in a community to reach their full human potential and fulfill their human dignity.

communism An economic and governmental system where goods are owned in common and are available to all as needed.

communities Groups of people who relate to one another based on common characteristics, circumstances, or interests.

compassion Concern for the suffering of others and the desire to relieve it.

conscience The "interior voice" of a person, a God-given internal sense of what is morally wrong or right.

conscientious objection Opposition on moral or religious grounds to serving in the armed forces or to bearing arms.

conservation The act of preserving, protecting, or restoring the natural environment, ecosystems, vegetation, and wildlife.

consistent ethic of life A system of pro-life principles claiming that protecting the life and dignity of any person or group requires that we protect the life and dignity of all people.

consumerism The unbalanced focus on buying things to find happiness.

conversion A profound change of heart; a turning away from sin and toward God.

culture The shared values, beliefs, and ways of relating and living together that characterize a particular group of people.

culture of death A worldview that fails to respect and protect human life in all its stages.

culture of life A worldview that recognizes that all human life comes from God and is meant to return to God; it respects and protects human life in all its stages, from conception to natural death.

cycle of poverty A situation in which the lack of basic resources prevents people from obtaining those resources. These interrelated problems cause and reinforce one another in a continuous manner.

D

debt crisis A situation in which a country loses the ability to pay back the debt held by its government.

deforestation The intentional removal of an area of trees to convert the land to nonforest use, such as farming, industry, or housing.

development The process by which the structures of society evolve so that all people, rich and poor, are able to fulfill their human potential and live dignified lives.

dignity of work The value work has because it supports human life and contributes to human dignity.

direct action Action that occurs on the level of individual relationships and is usually aimed at meeting an immediate need.

discrimination The act or practice of treating others as less than or unequal and using power to deny individuals or groups the right to fully participate in community.

diversity The inclusion of people of different races and cultures in a group or organization.

E

Earth Day A worldwide event started in 1970 that supports environmental protection. It is celebrated every year on April 22.

economic globalization An interdependence of nations around the globe fostered through free trade.

economic initiative The right to be self-employed, to start a business, and to expand one's business.

economics The way societies produce, manage, and distribute material wealth.

ecosystem A community of living organisms that interact, and the environment they share.

ecosystem services The benefits people obtain from natural environments, including provisioning services, such as food and water; regulating services, such as flood and disease control; cultural services, such as spiritual, recreational, and cultural benefits; and supporting services, such as those necessary for the production of all other ecosystem services.

encyclical A teaching letter from the pope to the members of the Church on topics of social justice, human rights, and peace.

endangered species Any species that is in serious danger of extinction.

enlightened self-interest The realization that by helping others we are, in the end, really helping ourselves.

environmental degradation The deterioration of the natural environment caused by human activities, such as exploiting and polluting natural resources, destroying habitats, disrupting ecosystems, or depleting biodiversity.

environmental injustices Actions that degrade the natural environment, harming ecosystems and living things, including human beings.

ethnic cleansing The displacement or extermination of an unwanted ethnic group from society.

Eucharistic response to poverty Actions taken to reduce poverty that are based on the understanding that the Eucharist is the source of life, that it strengthens solidarity, and that it reminds us that if we share, there will always be enough.

euthanasia A direct action, or a deliberate lack of action, that causes the death of a person who is disabled, sick, or dying.

exclusion The act of determining who does and does not belong to a community by focusing on the differences that separate people from one another.

extinction The dying out or permanent loss of a species.

F

food insecure The inability to obtain or afford nutritionally sufficient food on a regular basis.

fossil fuels Fuels (such as coal, oil, or natural gas) formed from dead plants or animals by natural processes.

free will The ability of a person to choose among options and to make decisions with freedom. Free will or self-determination is the grounds for an authentic relationship with God.

G

grassroots Foundational or fundamental.

greenhouse gas A gas such as carbon dioxide, water vapor, methane, and nitrous oxide that pollutes the air and causes the warming of the earth's atmosphere.

H

habitat The natural environments of living things. Habitats are made up of physical factors, such as soil, moisture, range of temperature, and availability of light, as well as biotic factors, such as the availability of food and the presence of predators.

human dignity The basic goodness and equal worth of human beings that comes from being created in God's image and being loved by God.

humanity The quality or state of being human and being created in God's image with shared dignity; all human beings collectively.

human rights The fundamental rights that belong to all humans.

I

Incarnation The central Christian belief that the Son of God assumed human nature and became flesh and lived among us.

inclusion The act of recognizing that the differences that make each person unique are small compared to the dignity people share as images of God.

indigenous A name given to the first known peoples who inhabited a place

indirect employer Any policy-making institution that helps regulate what employers may or may not do.

individualism A belief that each person should take responsibility for their own life, and that others should not be expected to help them if they fail to take responsibility for themselves.

injustice A condition in which people have put obstacles in the way of loving relationships, thus preventing life from flourishing as God intends.

institutional violence Violence that occurs as a result of unjust social structures rather than as a direct result of one person's actions.

interdependent The state of things or people depending on one another.

J

justice The establishment of loving relationships among human beings, God, and creation so life can flourish in the way God intends.

just wage A salary that recognizes the value of the work being performed and that is high enough to allow the laborer and their immediate family to live a life of human dignity. Minimally, this means a wage above the poverty line.

just-war theory The premise that considers the use of military force morally acceptable when specific criteria have been met.

K

Kingdom of God The center of the preaching of Jesus and the way things are when love is more important than anything else in people's lives. It is both initiated and fulfilled in Jesus Christ.

L

leachate A toxic liquid that drains or leaches from a landfill and can contaminate soil and groundwater.

livelihood Work that provides the basic necessities of life.

living simply Living in a way that values the sacredness of ourselves, others, and God's creation more than material possessions.

living wage A wage that enables workers to support a decent life for themselves and their families.

M

machismo A strong and often exaggerated emphasis on manhood, male pride, and the role of men in society.

malnutrition A physically dangerous situation caused by inadequate nutrition.

marginalized Those who have been relegated to an unimportant or powerless position within a society or group.

materialism The belief that the acquisition of material possessions is a greater goal than other intellectual, spiritual, or communal goals.

monks A male member of a religious community who lives a life of prayer and work according to a specific rule of life, such as the Rule of Saint Benedict.

N

natural law The expression of the original moral sense that God gave us that enables us to discern by our intellect and reason what is good and what is evil. It is rooted in our desire for God, and it is our participation in his wisdom and goodness because we are created in his divine likeness.

natural resources Materials that can be found in nature and harvested for use.

nearness of death The conditions of chronic hunger, health problems, and violence that put those who live in extreme poverty at greater risk of death than people who are not poor.

nonviolent noncooperation A way to respect life and dignity by refusing to cooperate with anything that harms it.

O

objective aspect of work What the worker produces as a result of their work.

oppressed Those who are subjected to another's abuse of power or authority.

option for the poor and vulnerable The choice to put the needs of society's most poor and vulnerable members first among all social concerns.

P

pacifism Opposition to the use of war or violence to solve conflicts and a commitment to nonparticipation in violence in any way.

participation The right and responsibility of all people to take an active part in all aspects of human society.

peace The harmony that results when people resolve conflicts by working in love for the good of all.

poverty The experience of not having the basic necessities for living a full and dignified life.

poverty of being The state of being unable to reach one's full potential as an image of God because of misdirected values.

power The God-given ability everyone has to affect their own life, the lives of others, and the world around them—including its social structures—in either positive or negative ways.

power-over worldview An outlook in which power is seen as something acquired to be used for any purpose, even at the expense of others.

power-with worldview An outlook in which power is seen as something to be used with and for others to bring about the good of everyone.

praxis Living according to one's beliefs, not just in private, but in a way that affects the world.

prejudice An attitude of hostility directed at whole groups of people. Prejudice involves judging someone or something before knowing all the facts or without considering the facts.

principle of discrimination A rule of the just-war theory stating that if parties engage in war, lethal force is only directed toward those threatening to do violence.

principle of proportionality A rule of the just-war theory stating that the good to be gained by war must outweigh the damage and costs caused by it.

purchasing power The value of currency to purchase goods and services.

R

racism The belief that one race is better than another, which is based in prejudicial thinking and often leads to discrimination.

rainforests The earth's oldest living ecosystem, which consists of dense forests rich in biodiversity.

refugee A person who flees to another country to escape danger in their home country.

relationship map A map showing the connections between people that shape our society.

responsibilities Those things a person is obligated to do.

restorative justice An approach to dealing with convicted criminals in which they are urged to accept responsibility for their offenses through meeting victims or their families and making amends to victims or the community.

Resurrection The bodily rising of Jesus from the dead on the third day after his death on the cross and his burial in the tomb.

retributive justice The approach to those who have committed crimes that is concerned with punishing or rewarding an individual.

rights Those conditions or things any person needs to be fully what God created them to be.

rights of workers The items necessary for dignified work, including fair pay, a safe workplace, and anything else necessary for the basic life and health of workers.

S

Sabbath The weekly day of rest to remember God's work through private prayer and communal worship.

sacred A place, object, or person that is considered holy because it is dedicated to God or set aside for religious purposes.

Sacred Tradition Refers to the process of passing on the Gospel message. Tradition, which began with the oral communication of the Gospel by the Apostles, was written down in Scripture, is handed down and lived out in the life of the Church, and is interpreted by the bishops of the Church in union with the pope under the guidance of the Holy Spirit.

seamless garment Another name for the consistent ethic of life, taken from the image of Jesus' tunic in the Gospel of John, which refers to the ethical, religious, and political threads of moral issues that are unified in one vision.

See, Judge, Act A decision-making process introduced in Catholic social teaching that is both practical and spiritual in nature. It can be thought of as a way of listening to God.

shalom A Hebrew word for *peace* that invites action to establish the presence of love, harmony, safety, and healing for all.

Shema A Jewish confession of faith, which Jews recite daily.

social A characteristic of human beings that recognizes they are made to live in relationship with one another.

social action Action that attempts to change the behavior of society and its institutions in a way that promotes justice.

social analysis The process of understanding how people's lives are affected by the relationships that shape the society in which they live.

socialism An economic system in which there is no private ownership of goods, and the creation and distribution of goods and services is determined by the whole community or by the government.

social justice The defense of human dignity by ensuring that essential human needs are met and that essential human rights are protected for all people.

social structures The patterns of relationships that shape any society.

solidarity The union of one's heart and mind with all people. It leads to the just distribution of material goods, creates bonds between opposing groups and nations, and leads to the spread of spiritual goods such as friendship and prayer.

spiral of violence The tendency of violent acts to escalate as each party in a conflict responds to violence with even greater acts of violence.

stereotype A positive or negative characterization applied to a group of people that is developed by assumptions, lack of direct experience, or biased thinking.

steward Those responsible for managing or caring for something else.

strike An organized work stoppage whereby workers refuse to work in order to gain public support and to pressure their employer to address their rights.

structures of sin The effects of personal sin over time, which can affect social structures and institutions.

subjective aspect of work What the worker experiences in the action of working.

subsidiarity The moral principle that large organizations and governments should not take over responsibilities and decisions that can be handled by individuals and local organizations, and that large corporations and governments have the responsibility to support the good of human beings, families, and local communities, which are the center and purpose of social life.

survival rights The rights necessary for people to be able to live.

sustainable A method of harvesting or using a resource so that it can be created and maintained without depleting or destroying other things in the process.

T

teach-in An informal gathering in which a topic is introduced and discussed to raise awareness. It is usually centered on a current social or political issue.

third way The alternative to flight or fight when responding to conflict or violence. Jesus teaches nonviolence as the third way.

thrival rights The rights necessary for people to fully recognize their God-given dignity, such as education, employment, a safe environment, and enough material goods to support a family.

Truth and Reconciliation Commission An official agency formed in South Africa after the end of apartheid to uncover the truth about injustices committed and to promote reconciliation as a way to resolve conflict.

U

unions Organizations of workers formed to protect the rights and interests of their members.

universal destination of goods The concept that all the resources of the earth are intended for all people.

V

violence Any human action that causes harm to the life or dignity of another person.

vulnerable species Any species on the path to becoming an endangered species in the near future.

W

wage gap The difference between the amount paid to different groups of people for their work.

wage theft The denial of wages or employee benefits rightfully owed to employees. It can occur in various ways, such as failing to pay overtime, violating minimum-wage laws, forcing employees to work "off the clock," and misclassifying employees as independent contractors to avoid paying benefits.

wealth gap The difference between the wealthiest and the poorest people in any given population.

work Any sustained effort expended for a purpose that makes a difference in the world.

worldview The basic beliefs that guide the way someone relates to the world.

Index

A

abbeys, 289
Abel, 314
ableism, 159–160
abolition, 130
abortion, 7, 108, 113, 119–121, 123
action
    categories of, 100–101
    as circle of faith-in-action step, 73, 99
    as decision-making step, 283, 285
    goals of, 102
    for justice, 71–72, 101
    opportunities for, 99–100
    in solidarity, 102–103
activism, 37, 165, 188, 302
ADA (Americans with Disabilities Act), 159
"Address to the Diplomatic Corps" (Francis), 116
"Address to the Vincentian Family" (Francis), 286
Africa, 225, 226, 282, 289–290
African Americans, 51–53, 148, 149, 150–151, 166
age discrimination, 50, 148, 166
Age of Enlightenment, 40
air pollution, 272
Akamasoa, 222
"All Brothers" (Francis), 47, 116, 130, 310
America (Martin), 286
Americans with Disabilities Act (ADA), 159
amnesty, 315
Amos, 23
analysis, 73, 88–95, 99
"Angelus" (Francis), 302
anti-war movements, 296
apartheid, 148, 314–315
apathy, 155, 267, 279, 286
Apostles, 37, 38

Aquinas, Thomas, 307
Archdiocese of Chicago, 185
Archdiocese of New York, 113
arms sales, 229
artificial conception, 122
Augustine of Hippo, 307
awareness
    of business practices, 168, 188, 190
    as circle of faith-in-action step, 72, 99
    environmental, 265, 276–277
    of food wasting, 287
    global poverty, 229
    impact of, 75
    information interpretation for, 76–77
    for peacemaking, 302
    political, 231
    worldviews impacting, 77–87

B

Ballotpedia, 231
Bangladesh, 165, 218–219
banking programs, 258
barriers to full development, 201–202, 227–229
bats, 274
Beatitudes, 31
beginning-of-life issues, 119–123
Begtrup, Bodil, 59
Benedict XVI, Pope, 47
Bengal, 226
Bernadino, Minerva, 59
Bernanos, Georges, 42
Bernardin, Cardinal Joseph, 111, 112–113
biodegradation, 280–281
biodiversity, 272, 273–275, 279
Bitencourt, Adriana, 198
Bitencourt, Igor, 198
Bluma Farm, 269

Board of Education, Brown v., 51–52
Body and Blood of Christ, 34
Body of Christ, 137–138, 246
boycotts, 97, 105, 189–190
Boy Who Harnessed the Wind, The (film), 282
Bravly, Michael, 156–157
"Brothers and Sisters to Us" (USCCB), 151, 153
Brown v. Board of Education, 51–52
bullying, 7, 53, 143, 294–295
Burhans, Molly, 262–264
businesses
  employer responsibilities, 186–194
  ethics of, 51, 89, 190
  power structures of, 97
  programs for development of, 258
  stereotypes promoted by, 145–146

C

Cain, 314
"Call to Action, A" (Paul VI), 72
Câmara, Archbishop Hélder, 293–297
Cambodia, 258
campesinos, 234
capitalism, 39, 42, 185, 248
capital punishment, 108, 113, 127–130
Carmelite NGO, 67–68
cartography, 263
cash crops, 226, 227
Catechism of the Catholic Church (CCC), 14, 17, 130
Catholic Campaign for Human Development, 193
Catholic Charities USA, 86, 113, 257
Catholic Church landholdings, 262–264, 269
Catholic Guardian Services (CGS), 113
Catholic HEART Work Camp (CHWC), 235
Catholic Mobilizing Network (CMN), 129
Catholic Relief Services (CRS), 258, 259
Catholic social teaching. *See also* Catholic social teaching themes
  community life, 139
  decision-making processes of, 283
  definition, 36
  documents of, 41–48
  economic systems, 248
  historical context and development of, 38–40
  on living together, 248–251
  mission descriptions, 36–38
  on poverty, 44–45, 200
  resource management, 250–251
  violence definitions, 292–293
  wealth gap, 243
Catholic social teaching themes
  human dignity, 48–51
  interdependence of, 48
  list of, 49
  option for the poor and vulnerable, 43, 62–63, 113, 202–204
  participation, 53–56
  rights and responsibilities, 56–59
  solidarity, 67
  work, 43, 65–66, 168–169, 178, 185–186, 192
  workers' rights, 65, 66, 182–185
Catholic Women's League, 249
Catholic Worker movement, 36, 37, 247
Catholic Worker (newspaper), 31, 36, 247, 249
CCC (*Catechism of the Catholic Church*), 14, 17, 130
CGS (Catholic Guardian Services), 113
"Challenge of Peace, The" (USCCB), 304, 305, 308–311, 312
charisms, 283
charity. *See* service
childbirth, 15
child labor, 6, 164, 165
children
  education, 51–53, 185, 224
  homeless, 198–199, 216
  hunger, 220
  poverty, 205, 220
  substance abuse, 217
  working, 6, 164, 165
Children of Labaneth, 156–157
Christian Peacemaker Teams, 290
chronic hunger, 208, 220

Church in the Modern World, The. See *Pastoral Constitution on the Church in the Modern World*
CHWC (Catholic HEART Work Camp), 235
circle of faith-in-action, 72–73, 99
civil disobedience, 105
civil rights
  advocacy of, 296
  approaches to, 302
  desegregation for, 51–53
  as human right, 116, 141
  leadership influences, 21, 105
  legislation for, 65, 159
  slavery and, 81–82
Civil Rights Act, 65
civil wars, 225, 289–290
CIW (Coalition of Immokalee Farm Workers), 167–168, 189
class cooperation, 42
Clean Air Act, 277
Clean Water Act, 277
climate change, 262, 272, 281
Climbing the Walls (Ortega), 177
cliques, 134–135
CMN (Catholic Mobilizing Network), 129
Coalition of Immokalee Farm Workers (CIW), 167–168, 189
Coffee for Peace, 193–194
Cold War, 45
Colicchio, Tom, 190–191
colonialism, 225–226, 228
Commission of Human Rights (United Nations), 59
common good
  as community requirement, 140
  environmental justice for, 278–279
  individual gifts for, 139, 283
  individualism *vs.*, 242
  as participation aspect, 54–55
  resource management for, 250–251
  work as contributing to, 172–173
communism, 39
community
  approaches to, 135–136
  benefits of, 138–139
  definition, 135
  exclusion from, 135–136, 142–151
  inclusion in, 136, 141, 151–161
  materialism impact on, 242
  models of, 137–138
  participation in, 53, 135, 137, 141
  personal responses to, 162
  poverty impacting, 200
  requirements of, 139–141
  school campaigns for promoting, 134–136
Community Peacemaker Teams (CPTs), 290
comparative justice, 308
compassion
  as Church's mission, 37–38
  definition, 12
  euthanasia rejection as, 126
  as love-based worldview component, 83, 86–87
  for poverty, 231
  as response to suffering, 10–12, 13
Compendium of the Social Doctrine of the Church (John Paul II), 186, 314
composting, 234, 287
conception, 122–123
conflict resolution, 290, 317
Congress of Berlin, 226
conscience, 57, 58, 283, 285, 310–311
conservation, 273–275, 284–285
consistent ethic of life, 111–113
consumerism, 235, 238–240, 241
consumption, 241, 243, 257, 271, 279–281
conversion, 153
coral reefs, 269, 272
Corinthians, First Letter to, 137–138
courage, 34, 73, 315–316
COVID-19, 220
CPTs (Community Peacemaker Teams), 290
Crafted Hospitality, 190–191
creation. *See also* environment; stewardship
  biblical stories on, 14–15
  as gift, 16, 118, 242–243, 266, 271
  human responsibility toward, 16–17, 275
  of humans, 15–17
  work as value in, 173

CRS (Catholic Relief Services), 258, 259
Crucifixion, 33, 153, 291
culture, 79–81, 114–118, 124, 145–146
"Culture of Life and the Penalty of Death, A" (USCCB), 127, 128
Cupich, Cardinal Blase J., 185

D

Dahl, Dave, 191–192
Dahl, Glenn, 192
Dave's Killer Bread, 191–192
Day, Dorothy, 36, 37, 247
Daybreak Center, 257
death, 114–117, 124, 125, 200, 391
death penalty, 108, 113, 127–130
debt bondage, 6, 164
debt crisis, 229–230
deforestation, 272, 274
depression, 10, 177, 207, 217
desegregation, 51–52
development
 barriers to full, 201–202, 227–229
 definition, 236
 economic, 47, 230, 314
dialogue, 156–157, 302
Diary of a Country Priest, The (Bernanos), 42
dignity
 as Catholic social teaching theme, 48–51, 111
 community participation for, 135, 137
 culture of death and lack of, 116
 definition, 16
 equality of, 111, 128
 as justice foundation, 102
 loss of, 240–243
 possessions *vs.*, 248–249
 protection of, 141
 respect for, 105
 threats to, 125, 147, 166, 198, 199, 200, 292
 as wealth, 254
 of work, 43, 65–66, 168, 171–172, 183–184
Diocese of Columbus, 189

Diocese of Joliet, 257
direct action, 100, 101
direct assistance, 257–258
disabilities, 135, 159
discrimination. *See also* prejudice; racism
 age and, 166
 definition and descriptions, 147–148
 disabilities and, 159–160
 in education, 51–53, 135, 150, 157, 159–160, 213
 employment, 65, 177
 as exclusion, 142, 143
 as global poverty cause, 229
 just-war theory and principle of, 309
 social structures of, 148–151
 stereotypes and, 147–148
 of women, 59, 148, 149, 166, 177, 229
 workplace, 65, 165, 166, 184
diversity, 138–139, 154
dominion, 16, 267
Down syndrome, children with, 135

E

Earth, 264–265, 280. *See also* environment; environmental degradation; stewardship
Earth Day, 276
economic development, 314
economic globalization, 192–194
economic initiative, 184
"Economic Justice for All" (USCCB)
 community, 135, 137, 139–141, 161
 economic growth measurements, 249
 global inclusion, 160
 option for the poor and vulnerable, 63
 poverty, 200
 unemployment, 176–177
economic rights, 57
economics
 consumerism, 235, 238–240, 241
 definition, 236
 materialism, 235, 238–243
 priorities, 249
 systems of, 39, 42, 45, 185, 248
 trust in God, 251–252
ecosystems, 264, 268–269, 273–275

ecosystem services, 268–269
education
  benefits of, 212–213
  charitable programs for, 193, 257
  discrimination impacting, 51–53, 135, 150, 157, 159–160, 213
  dropout risks, 217
  employment barriers due to lack of, 177, 215
  inadequate, 212–214, 223–224
  inclusion efforts in, 51–53, 135, 157–160
  poverty impacting, 201, 202, 206, 207, 213–214
  right to, 185
electric energy, 282, 287
Emerson, Ralph Waldo, 81
employers, 186–194
employment. *See* work; workers' rights
employment discrimination, 65, 177
encyclicals, 41, 45–47. *See also specific titles*
endangered species, 272, 273–275, 277
Endangered Species Act, 277
enemy relations, 33, 105–106, 296
enlightened self-interest, 9–10
environment. *See also* environmental degradation; natural resources; stewardship
  agricultural sustainability practices supporting, 194
  choices for, 278–281
  high school projects supporting, 67–68
  injustices, 283–284, 287
  interconnection and interdependence of, 69, 89, 264–265, 267, 268–269
  materialism impact on, 242–243
  papal encyclicals addressing, 67–68, 263, 264–265, 266–267, 271
  patron saints for protection of, 280
  simple living supporting, 255
  and sustainability, 67–68, 263, 265, 267, 269, 282
  threats to, 271–275
  worldwide events for awareness of, 276–277
environmental degradation
  causes of, 265, 267, 271, 273
  conservation efforts addressing, 273–275
  definition, 266
  papal encyclicals addressing, 67–68, 263, 264–265, 266–267, 271
  personal responses to, 278–285, 287
  types of, 271–273
environmental injustices, 283–285, 287
equality, 69, 111–113, 138–139
Equal Pay Act, 64
ethnic cleansing, 223
Eucharist, 34, 245–253
Eucharistic response to poverty, 247–248
euthanasia, 116, 124, 125–126
"Everyday Christianity" (USCCB), 170
exclusion
  cycle of, 151
  definition and descriptions, 135–136, 141
  excuses for, 143
  factors contributing to, 143–151, 200
  scenarios of, 142–143
  school campaigns for addressing, 134–136
Exodus, 20–21
experience, as worldview influence, 79
extinction, 273
"eye for an eye" (slogan), 129, 301

F

Fair Food Program, 167, 189
Fair Labor Standards Act, 64
Faith and Violence (Merton), 296
Fall, 24
family, 54, 113, 171, 182–183
farming, 269
farmworkers, 165–166, 167–168, 234–235
fear, 147, 149, 154, 251, 259
food distribution programs, 260
food insecurity, 209
Food Policy Action, 191
Foraker, Beth, 135
foreign aid, 228
forests, 269
forgiveness, 153, 300, 303, 314–315
fossil fuels, 272, 282

Francis, Pope
 charity, 11
 Church land management projects, 263
 culture of death, 116
 death penalty, 130
 environmental justice, 67–68, 263, 264–265, 266–267, 271
 just-war theory, 310
 nonviolence, 302
 papal encyclicals of, 47
 stewardship and sustainability, 275–276, 286
 work, 172, 173, 180
Frank, Robert, 240
Free the Children, 164, 165
free will, 18, 19
friendships, 66–67, 82–87, 102
Fugitive Slave Law, 81

G
Gandhi, Mahatma, 285
Gandhi, Mohandas Karamchand, 105
gay students, 7, 143
gender discrimination, 59, 148, 149, 166, 177, 229
Genesis, Book of
 brother's keeper, 314
 creation, 14–18, 68, 250, 275, 286
 work, 173
genetic engineering, 51, 123
Gibbons, Cardinal James, 41
glacier melt, 272
Glacier National Park, 272
Gleason, Caroline, 249
globalization, economic, 192–194
global poverty
 causes of, 225–230
 consequences of, 220–224
 income comparisons, 220
 myths about, 224–225
 public education for awareness of, 229
 statistics, 218
 stories of, 218–219
global warming, 272

God. *See also* image of God
 creation, 14–18, 118, 242–243, 266
 Incarnation, 26
 as love, 13
 nature of, 16
 peace through, 304–305
 as power source, 98
 relationship with, 17, 235–236
 salvation plans, 29
 suffering responses, 20
 trust in, 251–253, 255
 work reflecting work of, 173
Goodall, Jane, 286
GoodLands, 263–264
goodness
 of creation, 14, 15
 Jesus' teachings on, 31
 justice to reestablish, 24
 of work, 169–170
 worldviews based on belief in, 76, 77, 78
"Gospel of Life, The" (John Paul II), 114, 124, 314
Gospels
 blindness to injustice, 81
 equality and right to life, 111–112
 inclusion, 151, 152–153
 Jesus' natures, 26
 justice, 26–27
 love, 22, 28–29, 33, 105–106, 296
 option for poor and vulnerable, 31
 peace, 300–302
 service, 31
 sharing, 252
 violence responses, 300
 wealth gap, 243
 work parables, 178–179
government
 Catholic social teaching and roles of, 43, 44, 55–56, 58–59
 colonialism impact on, 228
 disability inclusion legislation, 159–160
 welfare assistance limitations, 177, 207, 212, 215–216
 workers' rights protections, 64–65, 159, 167, 168
grace, 34, 304–305

grassroots, 259
Great Depression, 36, 79, 86
Great Pacific Garbage Patch, 272, 273
greenhouse gasses, 281
green spaces, 269
Griffin, John Howard, 149

H

habitats, 268, 274–275, 284–285
habits, 279–280
Haley House, 193
happiness, 235–236, 238–243, 254–255
health insurance, 10, 64, 177, 216
health issues, 177, 208, 215, 218, 221
heaven, 17
"Heritage and Hope" (USCCB), 158
Hispanics, 157–158
homelessness
    action opportunities for, 99–100, 101
    assumptions and myths about, 231
    awareness of, 75, 79, 83–84, 85–86, 87
    of children, 198–199
    factors contributing to, 89
    hunger relationship to, 100
    invisibility of, 198
    service and assistance, 198–199, 203, 247, 257
    social analysis of, 88–89, 93–95, 98
    in United States, 209–212
    worldwide, 221–223
homosexuality, 7, 143
hopefulness, 21, 29
hopelessness, 7–8, 217
Hous, Rafael, 77
housing. *See also* homelessness
    affordability challenges, 100, 210, 214–215, 260
    charitable organizations assisting with, 257
    cost guidelines for, 210–211
    discrimination in, 147, 150–151
    education challenges due to inadequate, 214
    fire catastrophes, 211–212
    homeless situations in, 210–211

humanity, 153
human rights
    as Catholic social teaching theme, 56–59
    community and participation rights as, 141
    definition, 151
    factors denying, 199
    minimum requirements for, 141
    participation as, 141, 249
humans
    creation and responsibility of, 16–17, 275, 278–281
    culture of death and value of, 114–117
    culture of life and value of, 117–118
    dignity of, 16, 49–51, 102
    environmental degradation caused by, 265, 267, 271, 273
    equality of, 111–113, 138–139
    free will of, 18
    gifts of, 137–138, 139, 283
    as image of God, 11, 15, 16–17, 53, 117–118
    needs of, 202, 203
    possessions *vs.* value of, 248–249, 254
    power of, 95–98
    relationships of, 16–17, 53, 135, 137
hunger
    action opportunity assessments for, 99–100, 101
    awareness of, 75, 79, 83–84, 85–86, 87
    charitable organizations for, 257
    consequences of, 208–209
    definitions, 208
    documentaries addressing, 190
    factors contributing to, 89
    homelessness relationship to, 100
    Jesus' miracles addressing, 246–247
    myths about, 224–225
    social analysis of, 88–89, 93–95, 98
    in United States, 208–209
    worldwide, 220–221
Hussein, Forsan, 156–157

I

Ikramullah, Begum, 59
ILO (International Labour Organization), 187

image of God
  description, 15
  equality due to, 111
  free will as attribute of, 18
  human dignity due to, 16
  humans created as, 11, 15, 16–17, 53, 117–118
  love, 16–17
  poverty of being as loss of, 240–243
  relationships as, 16, 53, 135
  work as, 65, 168, 173
immigrants and immigration, 58, 86, 113, 165–166, 175, 176
Incarnation, 26, 153
inclusion
  change for, 153–155
  definition, 136
  descriptions, 136, 141, 157–158
  Jesus' teachings on, 151–153
  school campaigns for promoting, 134–136
  steps for creating, 156–160
independence, 9, 90
Independent Restaurant Coalition, 191
India, 59, 105, 175, 225–226
Indigenous peoples
  Church apologies to, 158
  colonialism and, 225, 226
  definition, 158
  discrimination against, 148, 158, 229
  Mexican villages of, 233–235
  as saints, 280
indirect employers, 189
individualism, 9, 242, 248
infertility, 122–123
Ingrasci, Zach, 229
injustice
  approaches to, 72–73, 99, 105
  blindness to, 81–82
  definition, 24
  exclusion as, 141
  sources of, 88, 105
  as spiral of violence step, 294
  as violence, 293
inmate training programs, 192
institutional violence, 293, 296–297
interconnection, 264–265, 267, 268–269

interdependence, 69, 90–98, 104, 139, 264–265
International Database of the US Census Bureau, 200
International Journal of Mental Health Systems, 177
International Labour Organization (ILO), 187
International Trade Union Confederation, 175–176
International Union for Conservation of Nature (IUCN), 273
in vitro fertilization, 122
Isaiah, 23, 24, 26, 27
Israelites, 20–22

J

Jeremiah, 23
Jesus
  Christian beliefs in, 25
  as compassion model, 12
  Crucifixion and death of, 33, 153, 291
  ethic of life, 314
  hunger and sharing, 246–247
  inclusion, 151, 152, 161
  justice, 26–27
  Kingdom of God, 27–33, 106
  natures of, 26, 153
  peace, 296, 299–302
  Resurrection, 32, 33–34, 245, 291
  social world of, 30
  solidarity, 186
  trust in God, 251–252
  violence responses, 296, 299–302
  wealth gap parables, 243
  work parables, 178–179
  worldview of, 82–87
Jews
  ancient social structure of, 30–31
  exclusion practices, 152
  peace, 300
  prayers, 21–22
  resource sharing practices, 251
  violence responses, 301–302
job training programs, 100

John Paul II, Pope
common good, 186
consumerism, 241
culture of life vs. death, 114
end-of-life issues, 124
papal encyclicals of, 47
poverty, 204
solidarity, 66, 314
wealth gap, 243
work, 65, 172, 180
John's Gospel, 111–112
John XXIII, Pope, 46, 57–58
joy, 235–236, 238–243, 254–255
judge, as decision-making step, 283, 285
justice
action for, 34, 71–74, 101
as Christian belief, 25
comparative, as just-war criteria, 308
definition, 24
interdependence for, 91–95
for peace, 298, 312–313
prophetic messages of, 23–24
purpose, 24
as response to suffering, 24
restorative, 129
retributive, 129
as salvation plan, 29
works of, 102
Justice, Peace and Integrity of Creation (Carmelites), 67
"Justice in the World" (World Synod of Catholic Bishops), 38
just wages, 43, 64, 174, 177–178, 182
just-war theory, 307–311

K

Kamkwamba, William, 282
Katzeff, Paul, 193–194
Keller, Warren and Tish, 284–285
Kennedy, John F., 64
Khatun, Malekha, 218–219
Kielburger, Craig, 164
Kingdom of God
community, 161
definition, 27
descriptions of, 27–28
equality and inclusion, 106, 152
love reflecting, 28–29, 32, 106
peace, 304
service, 31
social world of, 31, 32–33
work parables on, 178–179
Knights of Columbus, 10–11
Knights of Labor, 41

L

labor. See work; workers' rights
Laudato Sí schools, 67–68
laws
civil rights and inclusion, 159–160
environmental protection, 277
Jewish, 21–22, 251
labor, 44, 64–65, 86, 103, 168
natural, 42
welfare benefits, 177, 215
Lazarus, 243–244
leachate, 281
leatherback sea turtles, 284–285
Lefaucheux, Marie-Hélène, 59
Leo XIII, Pope, 41–45, 46
"Letter Regarding the Jubilee of Mercy" (Francis), 121
Levy, Mark, 239
life
abundance in, 83, 85–86, 140–141
basic requirements for, 199
beginning-of-life issues, 7, 108, 119–123
Catholic beliefs on, 110–113, 119, 128, 130–131
as Catholic social teaching theme, 51, 119
culture of, 117–118, 135
culture of death and view of, 115–117
end-of-life issues, 109, 116, 124–130
ethical scenarios, 108–109
Eucharist as source of, 245–246
inclusion and approach to, 155
as justice foundation, 102
lifestyle choices, 236, 240–243, 254–259, 271
personal responses to, 132
poverty impact on, 200–201
respect for, 105
right to, 112
threats to, 292

Little Rock Nine, 51–53
livelihood, 171, 178. *See also* work; workers' rights
living simply
  benefits of, 254–255
  definition, 236
  as poverty response, 260
  practices for, 257
  societal applications, 257–259
  as solidarity with poor, 255–256
"Living the Gospel of Life" (Francis), 130
living wages, 182, 248
loggerhead sea turtles, 274–275
love
  challenging injustice as, 106
  for community, 141
  of enemies, 33, 105–106, 296
  equality of God's, 138–139
  free will as, 18, 19
  God as, 13, 16
  human dignity and God's, 50–51
  Jesus' teachings on, 27–33
  laws on, 22, 23
  of neighbor, 22, 23, 151, 152–153, 248
  relationships as, 53, 135
  social structure approaches with, 105–106
  as violence response, 291–292, 296, 299–300
  worldviews based on, 82–87
Luke's Gospel
  inclusion, 151, 152–153
  justice, 26–27
  love, 105, 296
  option for poor and vulnerable, 31
  peace, 300
  service, 31
  sharing, 252
  violence responses, 300
  wealth gap, 243

M

machismo, 234
malnutrition, 208, 216, 219, 220
marginalization (the marginalized)
  definition and descriptions, 53, 141
  as poverty consequence, 200
  solidarity and, 191–192
  stereotypes contributing to, 145
  work projects, 236
Martin, James, 286
Martin of Tours, 305
Masih, Iqbal, 6, 164
Maslow, Abraham, 202, 203
materialism, 235, 238–243
Matthew's Gospel
  blindness to injustice, 81
  Jesus' identity in, 26
  love, 22, 28–29, 33, 105–106
  peace, 300, 301
  work parables, 178–179
Maurin, Peter, 31, 37, 247
media, 317
mediation programs, 317
medications, 109, 125, 126
Mehta, Hansa, 59
Menon, Lakshmi, 59
mental health, 100, 146, 177, 207, 216, 217
mercy killing (euthanasia), 116, 124, 125–126
Merton, Thomas, 296
methane, 280–281
Mexico, 233–235
Micah, 23, 24
minimalism, 257
Miriam Theresa, Sister, 249
Mix It Up at Lunch Day, 134–136
monks, 289–290, 291
Moses, 20–21
"Moving Beyond Racism" (Archdiocese of Chicago), 148
Muir, John, 286
multiplication of loaves and fishes, 246–247
murder, 108, 127
Muslims, 145, 147, 289–290

N

National Catholic Board on Full Inclusion (NCBFI), 135
National Conference of Catholic Charities (NCCC), 86
Native Americans, 148, 158, 225, 229, 280
natural disasters, 225
natural law, 42
natural resources
   Catholic social teaching on, 250–251
   Christian views on, 238
   colonial use of, 225–228
   community life and right to, 140–141
   conservation of, 274
   global poverty and extraction of, 227
   living simply for distribution of, 256–257
   materialism and limits of, 242–243
   paper reduction projects, 67–68
   renewable energy, 282
   sustainability of, 265
   wealth gap and, 243
nature. *See* environment; stewardship; sustainability
NCBFI (National Catholic Board on Full Inclusion), 135
NCCC (National Conference of Catholic Charities), 86
nearness of death, 200
neighbors, 22, 23, 151–155, 279
Nelson, Gaylord, 276–277
Nicaragua, 193–194, 227
nonviolence, 296, 297, 301–302, 312, 317
nonviolent noncooperation, 105
Nucleos, 192

O

objective aspect of work, 180
Occupational Safety and Health Administration (OSHA), 167
Ocean Cleanup, 273
Of Gods and Men (film), 290
Old Testament, 301, 314. *See also* Genesis, Book of
"On Capital and Labor" (Leo XIII), 41–45, 46

"On Care for Our Common Home" (Francis)
   care of creation responsibility, 267
   conferences related to, 263
   creation as gift, 271
   environmental degradation, 265, 271
   interconnection of nature, 264–265
   school principles based on, 67–68
   themes in, 266–267
"On Charity in Truth" (Benedict XVI), 47
"On Christianity and Social Progress" (John XXIII), 46
"On Human Work" (John Paul II), 47, 65, 172, 180
"On Reconstruction of the Social Order" (Pius XI), 44, 46
"On Social Concern" (John Paul II), 66, 204, 241
Opeka, Pedro, 222
oppression and the oppressed, 20–21, 96, 114
Optimist, 229
option for the poor and vulnerable
   as Catholic social teaching, 43, 62–63, 202–204, 249
   Jesus' teaching on, 31
   organizations for, 113
   school projects for, 198–199, 203
Origen, 305
Original Sin, 19, 24
Ortega, Maria, 177
OSHA (Occupational Safety and Health Administration), 167
Ozanam, Frédéric, 41, 63

P

pacifism, 306, 310–311
painkillers, 125, 126
Parenting Resource Center, 113
participation
   as Catholic social teaching theme, 53–56
   for community life, 53, 135, 137, 141
   education issues of, 51–53, 157–160
   factors impacting, 145, 200
   global, 160
   as human right, 141, 249
   work as, 168, 178

Pastoral Constitution on the Church in the Modern World (Vatican Council II)
  about, 46
  compassion mission, 37
  human equality and value, 139
  human life and dignity, 110–111
  peace, 290, 298–299
  work as value, 173
Pattillo, Melba, 52–53
Paul (Apostle), 137–138, 246
Paul VI, Pope, 47, 72, 251, 298, 312
peace
  approaches for, 291–292
  as Catholic social teaching theme, 45
  conflict resolution organizations for, 290
  definition, 297
  as gift, 304
  Jewish tradition of, 300
  nonviolence *vs.*, 297
  organizations promoting, 156–157
  papal encyclicals on, 46
  personal promotion of, 317
  practices promoting, 312–315
  requirements for, 298–299, 315–316
  role model for, 299–302
  strategies for, 302–303
Peacemaking (Pax Christi USA), 298
"Peace on Earth" (John XXIII), 46, 57–58
peer pressure, 80, 143
Perkins, Frances, 64
personal sin, 94, 148, 278
Pius XI, Pope, 44, 46
Place at the Table, A (documentary), 190
political rights, 57, 141
politics, 188, 231
poor and vulnerable. *See also* Saint Thomas High School soup kitchen
  exclusion of, 141
  lifestyle choices for solidarity with, 255–256
  preferential option for, 31, 43, 62–63, 113, 202–204
  service and assistance to, 51, 60–61, 71, 74, 75
possessions, 236, 248–249, 254, 260

poverty. *See also* global poverty; homelessness; hunger; poverty in United States
  assistance organizations for, 41, 63, 86, 113, 222, 257–258
  assumptions and myths about, 224–225, 231
  causes of, 71, 89, 93, 94–95, 176–177, 178, 214–217, 225–230
  challenges due to, 206–207
  common characteristics of, 200–202
  consequences of, 207–214, 220–224
  COVID-19-related, 220
  cycle of, 201, 209, 212, 217
  definition and descriptions, 41, 199
  economic development as strategy for, 314
  environmental degradation impact on, 267
  Eucharistic responses to, 245–253
  income statistic comparisons, 220
  as institutional violence, 293
  life ethics and, 112–113
  personal responses to, 231, 260
  public education on, 229
  solidarity programs for, 102–104
  works of mercy movements for, 247
poverty in United States
  causes, 214–217
  homelessness, 209–212
  hunger, 208–209
  statistics, 205
  wealth gap, 237
poverty of being, 240–243
power
  definition, 95
  inclusion and patterns of, 155
  injustice and, 105
  for justice, 98
  personal, 283
  purchasing, 189–190, 196, 205
  sources of, 98
  worldview types of, 95–98
"Power of One, The" (Goodall), 286
power-over worldviews, 95–96
power-with worldviews, 96–98, 105
praxis, 72
prayer, 315
prejudice, 147, 148, 151, 154. *See also* discrimination; racism

prenatal testing, 122–123
principle of discrimination, 309
principle of proportionality, 309
prisoners of war, 49–50
Prison Fellowship, 129
Project Five-Two, 102–104
Project Rachel, 121
Promised Land, 20, 21, 22, 26, 83
property, private, 43, 45, 59, 141, 184, 250
prophets, 22–24
proportionality, 308, 309
purchasing power, 189–190, 205

R

race, 205. *See also* racism
racism
    Church apologies for, 158
    Church's views on, 151, 153
    definition, 148
    in education, 51–53, 150, 157, 213
    employment discrimination, 177
    as exclusion, 142
    experiments in, 149
    as institutional violence, 293
    workplace discrimination, 65, 166
rainforests, 272
reconciliation, 158, 290, 302–303, 314–315
recycling, 273, 278, 287
red-legged fire millipedes, 273–274
Red List, 273–274
refugees, 198, 203, 223, 229
relationship mapping, 90–95
relationships. *See also* community
    with God, 17, 235–236
    importance of, 17, 53, 135
    interdependence of, 69, 90–98, 104
    love, 248
    mapping for social analysis of, 90–95
    materialism impact on, 242
    value of, 235–236, 254–255
Remson, Jane, 67
renewable energy, 282
resources. *See* natural resources
respectfulness, 82–84, 183

responsibilities. *See also* stewardship
    definition, 58
    of employers, 186, 190–194
    with rights, 58–59
    toward work, 171, 174, 181–183
restaurant industry, 190–191
restorative justice, 129
Resurrection, 32, 33–34, 245, 291
resurrection of dead, 124–125
retaliation, 33, 293–294, 299–300
retributive justice, 129
revenge, 132, 293–294
right(s). *See also* civil rights; human rights; workers' rights
    of community life, 140–141
    of education, 185
    to life, 112
    of women, 59
    to work, 141, 174, 182
Rodrigues flying fox, 274
Roman Empire, 305, 306–307
Roosevelt, Eleanor, 59
Roosevelt, Franklin D., 64

S

Sabbath, 32
sacred, defined, 110
Sacred Tradition, 13, 38, 42
Saint Thomas High School soup kitchen
    about, 71, 74
    action opportunity assessments, 99–100, 101
    awareness process, 75, 79, 85–87
    social analysis for, 88–89, 93–95, 98
Salpointe Catholic High School, 67–68
salvation, 29, 124–125, 152
Samaritans, 32, 152
Sanchez, Elisa, 77
sanitation, 218, 221, 272
San Quentin State Prison, 192
Sarem, Ngean, 258
Schneider, Pat, 206–207
Schumacher, Jean-Pierre, 290
science, 120, 267

seamless garment, 111–113
Second Chance Project, 192
Second Vatican Council. See *Pastoral Constitution on The Church in the Modern World*
See, Judge, Act, 283–285
segregation, 51–53, 150
self-acceptance, 154
self-defense, 306
selfishness
    change resistance due to, 259
    environment issues and, 267
    human dignity violations due to, 50
    as opposite of love, 14, 33
    prejudice due to, 147, 151
    service instead of, 31
self-sufficiency, 257–258
Sermon on the Mount, 105
service (charity)
    benefits of, 31
    as compassion, 12
    employment training programs, 193
    homeless student assistance, 198–199
    Jesus' teachings on, 11, 31
    option for poor, 60–61
    soup kitchens, 71, 74–75, 79, 85–89, 93–95, 98–101
    trash pickup, 287
    work camps, 235
    works of, 102
Seuss, Dr., 95–96
sexual harassment, 166
sexuality, 122
Shalam, 156–157
shalom, 300
sharing, 247–251, 252, 256–257, 287
Sharing Catholic Social Teaching (USCCB), 68
Shema, 21–22
Shepherd's Table, 257
sickness, 32, 141
sin, 32, 94–95, 148, 278, 300
sinners, 30, 32, 152
Sisters of the Holy Names, 249
Slat, Boyan, 273

slavery, 6, 21, 81–82, 164
social, defined, 135
social action, 100, 101
social analysis, 73, 88–95, 99
socialism, 39, 42, 45, 248
social justice. *See also* Catholic social teaching
    biblical passages on, 23
    definition, 36
    movements promoting, 36, 37, 247
    newspapers for awareness on, 37
    participation rights of, 137
    prophetic messages on, 22–24
social media, 188, 303–304
social sin, 278
social structures
    action impacting, 101
    of ancient Jews, 30–31
    definition and overview, 93–94
    of injustice and sin, 94–95, 102–105
    as self-sufficiency barrier, 259
    violence due to unjust, 293, 296
Society of Saint Vincent de Paul, 41, 63
solidarity
    acting in, 102–103
    as Catholic social teaching theme, 66–67
    during civil war violence, 289–290
    for community, 139, 141
    and economic globalization, 192–194
    employees and employees, 190–191
    Eucharist as poverty response in, 246
    friendship comparisons, 66–67, 102
    for human power against injustice, 98
    lifestyle choices for, 256
    with marginalized, 191–192
    for peace, 313, 317
    requirements of, 104
    for stewardship, 268, 273, 283
    for workplace justice, 183
    worldviews of, 82–83
Somalia, 200
soup kitchens
    for employment training, 193
    as service projects, 71, 74–75, 79, 85–89, 93–95, 98–101
    volunteering for, 100

South Africa, 148, 314–315
species endangerment, 272, 273–275, 277
spiral of violence, 293–297, 299–300, 312
starvation, 208
stem-cell research, 123
stereotypes, 141–147
stewards, defined, 268
stewardship
    as Catholic social teaching theme, 16, 67–69, 251
    Church land management for, 262–264
    for ecological protection, 269
    endangered species and conservation efforts, 273–275
    global agricultural management for, 194
    as love, 16–17
    papal encyclicals addressing, 67–68, 263, 264–265, 266–267, 271
    paper reduction projects for, 67–68
    personal responses to, 278–285, 287
    quotes on, 286
    responsibility of, 16–17, 268, 275–281
    simple living for, 255
    solidarity for, 268, 273, 283
    worldwide events for awareness of, 276–277
strikes, labor, 64, 97, 176, 183
structures of sin
    approaches to combating, 105
    definition, 94
    social analysis of, 94–95
    solidarity projects to combat, 102–104
subjective aspect of work, 180
subsidiarity, 55–56
substance abuse, 211, 217
sudden wealth syndrome, 239
suffering
    cause of, 13–14, 18–19
    disease and, 109, 125–126
    experiences of, 6–7
    responses to, 7–12, 20, 24
suicide, 109, 116, 124, 126–127
surrogacy, 122–123
survival rights, 56–57
sustainability, 67–68, 263, 265, 267, 269, 282

T

Taylor, Jana, 76, 77, 78, 79
teach-ins, 276–277
Tekakwitha, Kateri, 280
Temple, Chris, 229
Ten Commandments, 21
Thanksgiving Coffee, 193–194
third way, 301–302
Thirteenth Amendment, 81
thrival rights, 57
Tibhirine (Algeria), 289–290
Trinity, 16, 17, 25, 53, 136
"Trócaire Lenten Lecture" (Turkson), 286
trust in God, 251–253, 255
Truth and Reconciliation Commission, 314–315
turbines, 282
Turkson, Cardinal Peter, 286
"turn the other cheek," 301
turtles, 274–275, 284–285

U

unemployment, 172, 176–177
unions
    Catholic social teaching on, 41, 43, 44, 66, 183
    repression of, 175–176
    strikes, 64, 97, 176, 183
United Auto Workers, 64
United Nations, 59, 187
United States. *See also* poverty in United States
    desegregation, 51–53
    materialist culture of, 238
    slavery history of, 81–82
    wealth and purchasing power of, 205
    wealth gap in, 237

United States Conference of Catholic Bishops (USCCB)
  affirmative action programs, 159–160
  care for creation, 68
  community, 135, 137, 161
  conscientious objection, 310–311
  death penalty, 127, 128
  global inclusion, 160
  Indigenous mistreatment apologies, 158
  option for the poor and vulnerable, 63
  peace, 304
  poverty, 200
  racism, 151, 153
  unemployment, 176–177
  war, 305, 308–311
  work, 170
United States Environmental Protection Agency, 277
Universal Declaration of Human Rights, 59
universal destination of goods, 250–251
University of California at Berkeley, 269
Uralova, Evdokia, 59
urban farming, 269
USCCB. *See* United States Conference of Catholic Bishops

V

Vatican Council II. See *Pastoral Constitution on the Church in the Modern World*
"Video Message from Holy Father Francisco on the Occasion of the Fifty-Seventh Colloquium of the IDEA Foundation" (Francis), 172
Vietnam War, 296, 308
violence
  biblical stories on, 314
  Christian responses to, 305–311
  conflict-resolution organizations for reducing, 290
  definition, 292–293
  ethnic cleansing, 223
  housing situations of, 211
  institutional, 293, 296–297
  murder and death penalty, 108, 127–130
  papal encyclicals on, 47
  personal responses to, 317
  poverty fueled by, 229
  responses to, 33, 291–292, 296, 297, 299–304, 312
  solidarity during, 289–290, 291
  spiral of, 293–297, 312
vulnerable species, 274–275

W

wage gap, 59, 149
wages
  gender discrimination, 59, 149
  just, 43, 64, 174, 177–178, 182
  laws on minimum-, 100
  legislation on equal, 64
  living, 182, 248
  theft of, 167
wage theft, 167
Walker, Steve and Lisa, 235
Walsh, Mark, 239
war, 297, 305–311
waste, 272, 273, 280, 281, 287
water issues, 218, 221, 272, 273, 282
Wawasee Cares, 157–158
Wawasee Community Schools, 157–158
wealth, 32, 238–240
wealth gap, 237, 243
Weide, Karsten, 239, 240
welfare benefits, 177, 207, 212, 215
WE (organization), 164
WHO (World Health Organization), 218, 220
Williams, Julie, 233–235
wind turbines, 282
women
  abortions and forgiveness of, 121
  direct assistance programs for, 258
  discrimination of, 59, 148, 149, 166, 177, 229
  as human rights influence, 59
  Jesus' ministry and, 32
  Mexican gender roles, 234
  post-abortion programs for, 121
  workplace sexual harassment, 166
Women's Care Center, 10–11

work. *See also* workers' rights
  barriers to, 177–178, 201, 202, 207
  Catholic social teaching on, 43, 65, 168–169, 178, 185–186, 192
  characteristics of good, 174
  child labor, 6, 164, 165, 175, 185
  definition, 169
  dignity supported by, 183–184
  employers' responsibilities, 186–195
  employment discrimination, 65, 177
  farmworker abuses, 165–166
  gender roles in, 149
  Jesus' teachings on, 178–179
  just wages, 44, 64, 174, 177–178, 182
  papal encyclicals addressing, 41
  perceptions of, 169–170
  personal responses to, 190, 196
  poverty with, 177–178, 205, 207, 225
  right to, 141, 174, 182
  service volunteer camps, 235
  sexual harassment, 166
  solidarity in, 185–186
  subjective *vs.* objective aspects of, 180–181
  unemployment, 176–177
  union organization, 41, 43, 44, 183
  value of, 43, 65–66, 168–173, 183, 195
  wage gap, 59, 149
  workers' responsibilities, 171, 174, 181–183, 190
  working conditions, 165, 174–175
  workplace discrimination, 165, 166
  worst countries for, 175–176
work camps, 235
workers' rights
  archbishop speeches on, 185
  Catholic social teaching on, 64, 66, 182–185
  government protections for, 64–65, 159, 167, 168
  organizations protecting, 167–168
World Day of Peace, 312
World Economic Forum, 157
World Health Organization (WHO), 218, 220

worldviews
  culture of death, 114–117
  culture of life, 117–118
  definition, 77
  factors influencing, 77–81
  friendship characteristics, 82–87
  limitations of, 81
  poverty impacting, 202
  power-over, 95–96
  power-with, 96–98
  work and Christian, 174

Y

Yertle the Turtle (Seuss), 95–96
Yevtushenko, Yevgeny, 48–49
Yosemite, The (Muir), 286

Z

Zorolla, Richard, 217

Acknowledgments

Scripture texts used in this work are taken from the *New American Bible, revised edition* © 2010, 1991, 1986, 1970 Confraternity of Christian Doctrine, Inc., Washington, DC. All Rights Reserved. No part of this work may be reproduced or transmitted in any form or by any means, electronic or mechanical, including photocopying, recording, or by any information storage and retrieval system, without permission in writing from the copyright owner.

All excerpts marked *Catechism of the Catholic Church* or *CCC* are from the English translation of the *Catechism of the Catholic Church* for use in the United States of America, second edition. Copyright © 1994 by the United States Catholic Conference, Inc.—Libreria Editrice Vaticana (LEV). English translation of the Catechism of the Catholic Church: Modifications from the Editio Typica copyright © 1997 by the United States Catholic Conference, Inc.—LEV.

The excerpts on pages 124, 130, and 314 are from "The Gospel of Life" ("Evangelium Vitae"), numbers 64, 21, and 19, at www.vatican.va/content/john-paul-ii/en/encyclicals/documents/hf_jp-ii_enc_25031995_evangelium-vitae.html. Copyright © LEV.

The excerpts on pages 63, 135, 137, 141, 159–160, 160, 161, 176, 200, 249, and 250 are from "Economic Justice for All," by the United States Conference of Catholic Bishops (USCCB) (Washington, DC: USCCB, Inc., 1986), numbers 88; 14; 71; 79, 77, 64; 73; 77; 67; 141; 185, 188; 1, 28; and 34. Copyright © 1986 by the USCCB, Inc. Used with permission. No part of this work may be reproduced or transmitted in any form without permission in writing from the copyright holder.

The excerpt by Pope Francis on page 11 is from "Greeting of the Holy Father," September 24, 2015, at www.vatican.va/content/francesco/en/speeches/2015/september/documents/papa-francesco_20150924_usa-centro-caritativo.html. Copyright © LEV.

The poem on page 31 and page 247 is from *Easy Essays*, by Peter Maurin (New York: Sheed and Ward, 1936), page 72. Copyright © 1936 by Sheed and Ward. Used with permission of Sheed and Ward.

The Catholic social teaching papal documents described in chapter 2 and noted throughout the text can be found at www.vatican.va.

The excerpt on page 38 is from "Justice in the World" ("Justicia in Mundo"), by the World Synod of Catholic Bishops, 1971. To read more, go to www.cctwincities.org/wp-content/uploads/2015/10/Justicia-in-Mundo.pdf.

The excerpt on page 42 is from *The Diary of a Country Priest*, by Georges Bernanos, translated by Pamela Morris (New York: Macmillan Company, 1937), page 57. Copyright © 1937 by the Macmillan Company.

The excerpt on page 42 is from "On Capital and Labor" ("Rerum Novarum"), by Pope Leo XIII, number 2, at www.https://www.vatican.va/content/leo-xiii/en/encyclicals/documents/hf_l-xiii_enc_15051891_rerum-novarum.html.

The excerpt on page 44 is from "On Reconstruction of the Social Order" ("Quadragesimo Anno"), by Pope Pius XI, number 28, at www.vatican.va/content/pius-xi/en/encyclicals/documents/hf_p-xi_enc_19310515_quadragesimo-anno.html. Copyright © LEV.

The excerpt on page pages 48–49 is from *A Precocious Autobiography,* by Yevgeny Yevtushenko, translated by Andrew R. MacAndrew (New York: Dutton Signet, a division of Penguin Books USA), pages 24–25. Translation copyright © 1963 by E. P. Dutton, renewed 1991 by Penguin USA.

The excerpt on pages 52–53 is from *Warriors Don't Cry,* by Melba Pattillo Beals (New York: Pocket Books, 1994), pages 108, 111–112, 121, and 311–312, respectively. Copyright © 1994 by Melba Beals.

The information on pages 51–53 about the Little Rock Nine is from "Melba Pattillo Beals," at usinfo.state.gov/xarchives/display.html?p=washfile-english&y=2007&m=August&x=20070821184213berehellek0.3442957; and "We Shall Overcome: Historic Places of the Civil Rights Movement," at www.nps.gov/history/nr/travel/civilrights/ak1.htm.

The excerpt on page 65, the quotation on page 172, and the excerpt on page 180 are from "On Human Work" ("Laborem Exercens"), by Pope Saint John Paul II, numbers 6, 10, and 6, respectively, at www.vatican.va/content/john-paul-ii/en/encyclicals/documents/hf_jp-ii_enc_14091981_laborem-exercens.html. Copyright © LEV.

The quotation on page 66, the information on page 204, and the excerpt on page 241, are from "On Social Concern" ("Sollicitudo Rei Socialis"), by Pope Saint John Paul II, numbers 38, 27–34, and 28, respectively, at www.vatican.va/content/john-paul-ii/en/encyclicals/documents/hf_jp-ii_enc_30121987_sollicitudo-rei-socialis.html. Copyright © LEV.

The summary of the seven themes of Catholic social teaching in chapter 2 and the quotation on page 68 are from *Sharing Catholic Social Teaching, Challenges and Directions: Reflections of the US Catholic Bishops,* by the USCCB (Washington, DC: USCCB, Inc., 1998), entire document and page 6. Copyright © 1998 by the USCCB, Inc. Used with permission. All rights reserved. No part of this work may be reproduced or transmitted in any form without permission in writing from the copyright holder.

The quotations on page 72 are from "A Call to Action" ("Octogesimo Adveniens"), by Pope Paul VI, number 4, at www.vatican.va/content/paul-vi/en/apost_letters/documents/hf_p-vi_apl_19710514_octogesima-adveniens.html. Copyright © LEV.

The story on pages 76–77 is based on "Poor No More: New Beauty in Child's Pictures," by Daniel B. Wood, in *Christian Science Monitor,* January 5, 1988. Copyright © 1988 by the Christian Science Publishing Society. All rights reserved.

The statistic about hunger on pages 93-94 is from *The Millennium Development Goals Report,* 2006, by the United Nations, Department of Economic and Social Affairs (New York: UN DESA, June 2006), and found at www.devinfo.org/facts_you_decide/1002.htm?IDX=13'.

The summary of the story of Yertle the Turtle on pages 95–96 is from *Yertle the Turtle and Other Stories,* by Theodor Seuss Geisel (Dr. Seuss) (New York: Random House, 1958). Copyright © 1958 by Theodor S. Geisel and Audrey S. Geisel, renewed 1986.

The excerpts on pages 36, 111, 139, 173, 290 and 298–299 are from *Pastoral Constitution on the Church in the Modern World (Gaudium et Spes),* December 7, 1965, by Pope Paul VI, numbers 1, 27, 29, 34, 78, and 78, respectively, at www.vatican.va/archive/hist_councils/ii_vatican_council/documents/vat-ii_cons_19651207_gaudium-et-spes_en.html. Copyright © LEV.

The excerpt on page 113 is from "Cardinal Bernardin's Call for a Consistent Ethic of Life," by Joseph Cardinal Bernardin, in *Origins,* December 29, 1983.

The quotation by Pope Francis on page 116 is from "Address to the Diplomatic Corps accredited to the Holy See," January 11, 2016, at www.vatican.va/content/francesco/en/speeches/2016/january/documents/papa-francesco_20160111_corpo-diplomatico.html. Copyright © LEV.

The excerpt and quotation by Pope Francis on pages 116 and 310 are from "All Brothers" ("Fratelli Tutti"), October 3, 2020, numbers 20 and 22, 258, at www.vatican.va/content/francesco/en/encyclicals/documents/papa-francesco_20201003_enciclica-fratelli-tutti.html. Copyright © LEV.

The excerpt by Pope Francis on page 121 is from "Letter Regarding the Jubilee of Mercy," September 1, 2015, at www.vatican.va/content/francesco/en/letters/2015/documents/papa-francesco_20150901_lettera-indulgenza-giubileo-misericordia.html. Copyright © LEV.

The excerpt on page 127 is from *A Culture of Life and the Penalty of Death,* by the USCCB (Washington, DC: USCCB, Inc., 2005), page 14. Copyright © 2005 by the USCCB, Inc. All rights reserved.

The quotation on page 130 is from *Living the Gospel of Life,* by the USCCB (Washington, DC: USCCB, Inc., 1988), number 21. Copyright © 1998 by the USCCB. All rights reserved.

The statistic on women in Fortune 500 companies on pages 145–146 is from Bureau of Labor Statistics, at www.bls.gov/cps/cpsaat11.htm#:~:text=1%2C669-,29.3,-88.0.

The excerpt on page 148 is from "Moving Beyond Racism: Learning to See with the Eyes of Christ," by the Catholic bishops of Chicago, and is found on the Archdiocese of Chicago website.

The excerpts on pages 151 and 153 are from "Brothers and Sisters to Us: US Bishops' Pastoral Letter on Racism in Our Day," by the USCCB (Washington, DC: USCCB, Inc., 1979), pages 10 and 9. Copyright © 1979 by the USCCB, Inc., Washington, DC 20017. All rights reserved.

The excerpt about Children of Labaneh on page 156 is from "Partners for Peace," by Guy Raz, in *Hope,* Fall 1999.

The story of the Wawasee Community Schools on pages 157–158 is adapted from "Awakenings in Wawasee," by Mary Harrison, in *Teaching Tolerance,* Fall 1999. Used with permission of *Teaching Tolerance* magazine, www.tolerance.org.

The excerpt on page 158 is from "Heritage and Hope: Evangelization in the United States," by the USCCB (Washington, DC: USCCB, Inc., 1991), page 2. Copyright © 1991 by the USCCB, Inc., Washington, DC 20017. All rights reserved.

The excerpt on page 170 is from the pastoral letter "Everyday Christianity: To Hunger and Thirst for Justice," by the USCCB (Washington, DC: USCCB, Inc., 1999). Copyright © 1999 by the USCCB, Inc., Washington, DC 20017. All rights reserved.

The excerpt by Pope Francis on page 172 is adapted from Pope Francis, "Video Message from Holy Father Francisco on the Occasion of the Fifty-Seventh Colloquium of the IDEA Foundation," Buenos Aires, October 13–15, 2021.

Acknowledgments

The excerpt by Pope Francis on page 173 is from "Pope Francis Says Work's Not Just an Occupation, but a Mission," by Hannah Brockhays, Catholic News Agency, as reported in *CRUX,* November 25, 2017, at www.cruxnow.com.

The excerpt by Pope Francis on page 180 is from "Address of Pope Francis to the Manager and Workers of the Terni Steel Mill and the Faithful of the Diocese of Terni-Narni-Amelia, Italy," March 20, 2014, at www.vatican.va/content/francesco/en/speeches/2014/march/documents/papa-francesco_20140320_pellegrinaggio-diocesi-terni.html.

The excerpt on page 185 is from "Archbishop Cupich Addresses Chicago Labor," by Trevor Montgomery. *Arise Chicago,* September 22, 2015, at www.arisechicago.org/.

The excerpt on page 186 and the quotation on page 314 are from *Compendium of the Social Doctrine of the Church,* by Pope Saint John Paul II, numbers 193 and 517, at www.vatican.va/roman_curia/pontifical_councils/justpeace/documents/rc_pc_justpeace_doc_20060526_compendio-dott-soc_en.html. Copyright © LEV.

The quotation and other information on page 187 about the International Labour Organization (ILO) is from "The Mission and Impact of the ILO," at www.ilo.org/public/english/download/glance.pdf.

The statistics about world energy on page 205 are according to the University of Michigan's Center for Sustainable Systems, at css.umich.edu/publications/factsheets/sustainability-indicators/us-environmental-footprint-factsheet#:~:text=With%20less%20than%205%25%20of,for%2015%25%20of%20world%20GDP.

The statistics about US poverty on page 205 and the information in the graphic on page 208 are from the United States Census Bureau, at www.census.gov.

The excerpt on pages 206–207 is from "The Cost of Love: A Journal Entry," by Pat Schneider, in *The Other Side,* March–April 1999.

The statistics about food security in US households on page 209 are from the US Department of Agriculture (USDA), November 2022. Full report available at www.ers.usda.gov/topics/food-nutrition-assistance/food-security-in-the-u-s/key-statistics-graphics/.

The statistics on pages 209–210 and 216 about homeless people are from "Homelessness and Poverty in America," National Law Center on Homelessness and Poverty, at www.nlchp.org/FA_HAPIA/causes.cfm.

The statistic on page 210 about children representing one in five of the homeless population on any given night is from the Children's Defense Fund, at www.childrensdefense.org/state-of-americas-children/soac-2021-housing/.

The excerpts on pages 211–212 and 215 are from *Rachel and Her Children: Homeless Families in America*, by Jonathan Kozol (New York: Crown Publishers, a division of Random House, 1988), pages 2 and 42. Copyright © 1988 by Jonathan Kozol. Used with permission of Crown Publishers, a division of Random House.

The quotation on page 217 is from "Who Are the Poor?" by Peter Davis, in *Hope*, September–October 1996.

The statistic on the world's population struggling to meet basic needs on page 218 is from The World Bank, at www.worldbank.org/en/news/press-release/2018/10/17/nearly-half-the-world-lives-on-less-than-550-a-day.

The statistics from the World Health Organization on page 218 are from www.who.int/news/item/18-06-2019-1-in-3-people-globally-do-not-have-access-to-safe-drinking-water-unicef-who.

The excerpt on pages 218–219 is from "Grameen Bank Borrowers," by Scott A. Leckman, in *Pearls of Bangladesh* (RESULTS Educational Fund, 1993), at the Bread for the World website, at www.bread.org/learn/hunger-basics/faq.html.

The statistic on world hunger on page 220 is from "Hunger Notes," at www.worldhunger.org/alarm-bells-cannot-ignore-world-hunger-rising-first-time-century/.

The statistic about the worldwide food and water supply on page 220 is from the World Health Organization, at www.who.int/news/item/18-06-2019-1-in-3-people-globally-do-not-have-access-to-safe-drinking-water-unicef-who.

The statistic about direct effects of chronic hunger and malnutrition on page 220 is from Action Against Hunger, at www.actionagainsthunger.org/global-poverty-hunger-facts.

The statistics on page 221 about malnutrition and disease are from "Hunger in a World of Plenty," by Church World Service, at www.churchworldservice.org/FactsHaveFaces/hungerfs.htm.

The excerpt on page 222 is from "Friends in Deed," by Magnus MacFarlane, in *U.S. Catholic*, October 1999.

The statistic about refugees on page 223 is from USA for UNHCR, The UN Refugee Agency, at www.unrefugees.org/refugee-facts/statistics/#:~:text=In%20a%20matter%20of%20a,million%20internally%20displaced%20people%3B%20and.

The first statistic on page 224 about the number of youth who don't attend school is from the United Nations Educational, Scientific, and Cultural Organization, at http://uis.unesco.org/sites/default/files/documents/new-methodology-shows-258-million-children-adolescents-and-youth-are-out-school.pdf.

The second statistic on page 224 is from World Bank, at www.worldbank.org/en/news/press-release/2022/06/23/70-of-10-year-olds-now-in-learning-poverty-unable-to-read-and-understand-a-simple-text.

The statistics about hunger on page 223 are from UN News, Global Perspective Human Stories, at news.un.org/en/story/2019/10/1048452#:~:text=Enough%20food%20is%20produced%20today,to%20be%20%E2%80%9Cchronically%20undernourished%E2%80%9D.

The information on pages 225–226 about the legacy of colonialism is from *Justice and Peace: A Christian Primer,* by J. Milburn Thompson (Maryknoll, NY: Orbis Books, 1997). Copyright © 1997 by J. Milburn Thompson.

The excerpt on pages 233–235 is from a letter written by Julie Williams to her former high school teacher Kevin LaNave.

The statistics about the world's wealth and population on page 237 are from the "World Inequality Report 2022," at https://wir2022.wid.world/www-site/uploads/2021/12/Summary_WorldInequalityReport2022_English.pdf.

The statistics about US consumption of the world's goods and services on page 237 are from the Associated Press. Copyright © 2008. https://public.wsu.edu/~mreed/380American%20Consumption.htm.

The statistics about income in the United States on page 237 are from the Economic Policy Institute, at www.epi.org/publication/income-inequality-in-the-us/.

Acknowledgments 349

The excerpts on pages 239–240 are adapted from "The Experience of Being Suddenly Rich," by Laura Fraser, in *The Standard.com*, posted November 29, 1999, at www.thestandard.com.

The excerpt by Dorothy Day on pages 247–248 is from *The Long Loneliness: The Autobiography of Dorothy Day* (New York: Harper and Row, 1952), pages 285–286. Copyright © 1952 by Harper and Row.

The excerpt by Pope Paul VI on page 251 is from "On the Development of Peoples" ("Populorum Progressio"), number 23, at www.vatican.va/content/paul-vi/en/encyclicals/documents/hf_p-vi_enc_26031967_populorum.html. Copyright © LEV.

The excerpt on page 262 is from "How a Young Activist Is Helping Pope Francis Battle Climate Change," by David Owen, *The New Yorker*, February 1, 2021.

The quotation on page 263 is from GoodLands, at https://good-lands.org/services/.

The excerpt on pages 253–264 is from GoodLands, at https://good-lands.org/big-ideas/.

The excerpts by Pope Francis on pages 265, 265 and 271 are from "On Care for Our Common Home" ("Laudato Si'"), numbers 84, 61, and 159, respectively, at www.vatican.va/content/francesco/en/encyclicals/documents/papa-francesco_20150524_enciclica-laudato-si.html. Copyright © LEV.

The statistic on global warming on page 272 is from NASA, "Global Climate Change: Vital Signs of the Planet," at https://climate.nasa.gov/vital-signs/global-temperature/.

The statistics on rainforests on page 272 are from National Geographic, at https://education.nationalgeographic.org/resource/rain-forest.

The statistic on pollution and warming oceans on page 272 is from NASA, Earth Observatory, at https://earthobservatory.nasa.gov/features/Coral.

The statistic on glaciers in Glacier National Park on page 272 is from "The Big Thaw," by Daniel Glick, *National Geographic*, at www.nationalgeographic.com/environment/article/big-thaw.

The statistic on marine biodiversity on page 272 is from "Losing Species," by Boris Worm, *Dal News*, November 3, 2006, at www.dal.ca/news/2006/11/03/oceanstudy.html.

The information and statistics about the Great Pacific Garbage Patch on pages 272 and 273 are from "Great Pacific Garbage Patch," *National Geographic*, at https://education.nationalgeographic.org/resource/great-pacific-garbage-patch.

The information about fossil fuels on page 272 is from Conserve Energy Future, at www.conserve-energy-future.com/various-fossil-fuels-facts.php.

The statistic about plant and animal species on page 273 is from "UN Report: Dangerous Decline 'Unprecedented'; Species Extinction Rates 'Accelerating,'" May 6, 2022, at www.un.org/sustainabledevelopment/blog/2019/05/nature-decline-unprecedented-report/#:~:text=The%20Report%20finds%20that%20around,20%25%2C%20mostly%20since%201900.

The excerpt by Pope Francis on page 276 is from "Homily of Pope Francis," Saint Peter's Square, March 19, 2013, at www.vatican.va/content/francesco/en/homilies/2013/documents/papa-francesco_20130319_omelia-inizio-pontificato.html. Copyright © LEV.

The second quotation by Pope Francis on page 276 is from "Meeting with Authorities and the Diplomatic Corps," November 25, 2015, at www.vatican.va/content/francesco/en/speeches/2015/november/documents/papa-francesco_20151125_kenya-autorita.html.

The excerpt by Gaylord Nelson on page 277 is from his speech on the twentieth anniversary of Earth Day, April 22, 1990, at www.nelsonearthday.net/earth-day/living-tradition.php.

The quotation by Dr. Jane Goodall on page 286 is from "The Power of One," by Dr. Jane Goodall, *Time Magazine*, August 26, 2002.

The quotation by Pope Francis on page 286 is from "Address to the Vincentian Family," Saint Peter's Square, October 14, 2017, at www.vatican.va/content/francesco/en/speeches/2017/october/documents/papa-francesco_20171014_famiglia-vincenziana.html.

The quotation by Fr. James Martin on page 286 is from "Why Is Climate Change a Moral Issue?" *America*, March 29, 2017.

The quotation by John Muir on page 286 is from *The Yosemite*, by John Muir (New York: The Century Company, 1912).

The quotation by Cardinal Peter Turkson on page 286 is from "Trócaire Lenten Lecture," March 5, 2015, at https://ourcommonhome.org/media/docs/cardinal-turkson-lent-lecture-2015.pdf.

The information about Algeria and the quotation by Fr. Jean-Pierre Schumacher on page 290 are from "The Last Monk of Tibhirine: 'God drove that history,'" by Margot Patterson, *National Catholic Reporter*, June 13, 2019. To read more, go to www.ncronline.org/news/people/last-monk-tibhirine-god-drove-history.

The quotation by Thomas Merton on page 296 is from *Faith and Violence: Christian Teaching and Christian Practice*, by Thomas Merton (Notre Dame, IN: University of Notre Dame, 1968). Copyright © 1968 by University of Notre Dame.

The words of Pope Paul VI on page 298 are from Peacemaking, volume 1, by Pax Christi USA (Erie, PA: Pax Christi USA, 1983), page 23. Copyright © 1985 by Pax Christi USA.

The quotation by Pope Francis on page 302 is from "Angelus," September 13, 2020, at www.vatican.va/content/francesco/en/angelus/2020/documents/papa-francesco_angelus_20200913.html

The quotations on pages 304, 305 (second quotation), 308, 310, 311, and 312 from the US Catholic bishops are from the pastoral letter "The Challenge of Peace: God's Promise and Our Response" (Washington, DC: USCCB, Inc., 1983), numbers 68, 114, 85–99, 83, 233, and 78, respectively. Copyright © 1983 by the USCCB, Inc., Washington, DC 20017. All rights reserved. Used with permission. No part of this work may be reproduced or transmitted in any form without permission from the copyright holder.

The first quotation on page 305 is from *Engaging the Powers: Discernment and Resistance in a World of Domination*, by Walter Wink (Minneapolis: Augsburg Fortress, 1992), page 210. Copyright © 1992 by Augsburg Fortress.

The excerpt on page 310 is from, " Pope to Russian Patriarch: 'Church used language of Jesus, not of politics,'" *The Vatican News*, March 16, 2022, at www.vaticannews.va/en/pope/news/2022-03/pope-francis-calls-patriarch-kirill-orthodox-patriarch-ukraine.html. Copyright © LEV.

The quotation by Pope Francis on the back cover is from "Visit at the Homeless Shelter 'Dona Di Maria': Meeting with the Missionaries of Charity," May 21, 2013, number 2, at www.vatican.va/content/francesco/en/speeches/2013/may/documents/papa-francesco_20130521_dono-di-maria.html.

To view copyright terms and conditions for internet materials cited here, log on to the home pages for the referenced websites.

During this book's preparation, all citations, facts, figures, names, addresses, telephone numbers, internet URLs, and other pieces of information cited within were verified for accuracy. The authors and Saint Mary's Press staff have made every attempt to reference current and valid sources, but we cannot guarantee the content of any source, and we are not responsible for any changes that may have occurred since our verification. If you find an error in, or have a question or concern about, any of the information or sources listed within, please contact Saint Mary's Press.

Endnotes Cited in Quotations from Documents Copyrighted by the USCCB

Chapter 5
1. Endnote for "Economic Justice for All," 79: Pope John Paul II, Address at the General Assembly of the United Nations (October 2, 1979), 13, 14.

Chapter 6
1. Endnote for "Economic Justice for All," 141: Richard M. Cohn, *The Consequences of Unemployment on Evaluation of Self*, Doctoral dissertation, Department of Psychology (University of Michigan, 1977); John A. Garraty, *Unemployment in History: Economic Thought and Public Policy* (New York: Harper and Row, 1978); Harry Mauer, *Not Working: An Oral History of the Unemployed* (New York: Holt, Rinehart, and Winston, 1979).

Chapter 8
2. Endnote for "Economic Justice for All," 34: St. Cyprian, "On Works and Almsgiving," 25, trans. R. J. Deferrari, *St. Cyprian: Treatises*, 36 (New York: Fathers of the Church, 1958), 251. Original text in Migne, *Patrologia Latina*, volume 4, 620. On the Patristic teaching, see C. Avila, *Ownership: Early Christian Teaching* (Maryknoll, NY: Orbis Books, 1983). Collection of original texts and translations.

Chapter 10
1. Sulpicius Severus, *The Life of Martin*, 4.3.

Endnotes Cited in Quotations from the *Catechism of the Catholic Church*, Second Edition

Chapter 4
1. Francis, "Address to Participants in the Meeting Organized by the Pontifical Council of the Promotion of the New Evangelization," 11 October 2017: *L'Osservatore Romano*, 13 October 2017, 5.

Chapter 8
1. *Lumen Gentium,* 3; St. Ignatius of Antioch, *Ad. Eph.* 20, 2: *Sources Chrétiennes* (Paris: 1942–), 10, 76.